Sociology

Sociology

Basic Concepts

H.K. Rawat

RAWAT PUBLICATIONS
Jaipur • New Delhi • Bangalore • Gawahati • Kolkata

ISBN 978-81-316-0054-2 (HB)
ISBN 978-81-316-0055-9 (PB)

Reprinted, 2026

Published by
Prem Rawat for **Rawat Publications**
Satyam Apts, Sector 3, Jawahar Nagar, Jaipur 302 004 (India)
Phone: 0141 265 1748 / 7006
E-mail: info@rawatbooks.com
Website: www.rawatbooks.com

New Delhi Office
4858/24, Ansari Road, Daryaganj, New Delhi 110 002
Phone: 011 2326 3290

Printed and bound in India

Contents

Preface

Sociology is fast developing in India but it is felt that there is not a suitable introductory book on this subject in English barring a few books written by foreign authors which do not serve much purpose of Indian students. Looking to this problem, I have attempted this book with a particular aim of writing a text book (not a scholarly work) to provide a systematic introduction to the students of sociology, especially graduate and postgraduate students. But I believe that it will also help the layman—a general reader who wants to have a glimpse of this subject or to know sociology in the nutshell. I also feel that the candidates appearing in various competitive examinations offering this subject as an elective option, will find this book much illuminating and indispensable in their studies.

As it is a book on principles of sociology, it has become bit abstract at certain places, yet I have tried to make it more and more interesting and useful by citing examples, similies and metaphors to clarify the principles or the point in question. To make my point clear, understandable and authentic, I have drawn long references freely from many scholar by works and recent text books of renowned authors. As it is a text book, as said above, I have not followed any perspective—Marxism, functionalism, symbolic interactionism or any other blindly or dogmatically. I have structured the contents according to the need of a text book (quoting definitions, forms, functions, typologies etc.) keeping in mind the questions asked in examinations at various levels.

In the preparation of this book, I have ventured to explore and consult many classical and standard works along with the books of the modern scholars and sociologists and tried to include their views, definitions and analogies at appropriate places. Not only this, the book takes full account of theoretical and empirical developments in the subject and incorporated substantial coverage of the latest issues of post-modernization, globalization and liberalization.

For writing this book, the credit goes to my niece Rashi Gupta who in reality actuated me to write a book in English on sociology while she was preparing for her degree course and found not a suitable book in English on the subject in the market. My younger brother Shri Kailash Rawat, who is also the publisher of this book, endorsed the idea and offered unwavering support and encouragement. Without his unstained help, and interest this book might not have seen the light of the day.

As said above, I have drawn freely from many sources and as such I recognize my earnest duty to express my sense of gratitude and indebtedness to host of writers in the field of sociology and allied subjects. In view of the nature of the book, I have not felt it necessary or indeed appropriate to attempt to acknowledge the indebtedness in detail. Not to make the book bulky and cumbersome, I have avoided giving frequent footnotes but was conscious to mention the names of the writer, with the year of publication wherever I found it necessary.

The ritual of giving thanks to the persons who have helped or encouraged me directly or indirectly in writing this book is a most difficult task. Let me first thank my wife Smt. Saroj Rawat and other family members who have supported my efforts unostentatiously during writing this book. I would like to thank a number of people including Shri K.S. Yadav and Shri Sanjay Pande who always made themselves available in offering constructive suggestions. A special word of thanks is due to Dr. S.L. Jain my erstwhile student and colleague for going through some of the computerised chapters of this book.

Suggestions, comments and criticism are needed and earnestly solicited. Only by such co-operation a text book can be significantly improved.

H.K. Rawat

Chapter 1

Sociology: Scope, Subject Matter, Origin and Modern Trends

Key features

What is Sociology?

What is sociology? It is a very tricking question. To answer this question in a precise way on which there can be unanimity is very difficult even for a professional sociologist. This is why, at the time of the Ninth World Congress of Sociology (1976), the Mayoress of Uppsala (Sweden) while welcoming the delegates commented on the printed programme that "sociology is everything and everything is sociology". Common man understands sociology right in this way.

Generally and in a very simple manner, sociology is defined as the study of society (more specifically, human society or societies or human behaviour in societies). But, this definition does not tell us much about sociology. It leaves unanswered a description or definition of the term 'society'. We learn about man and society or about human behaviour in psychology, anthropology, economics, political science and many other disciplines. Then, why we study sociology? We study sociology because the perspective of all social sciences that study society is different from one another. For instance, poverty, a problem of society, is a cultural, political, economic, psychological, historical as well as a sociological problem. Or, in other words, this is a common problem. But, all social sciences view it differently and try to solve it in their own way. Of all the social sciences, it is sociology that most closely scrutinises such problems and tries to synthesise different particularistic viewpoints in an attempt to discover universal principles of social behaviour. Thus, sociology may claim to have a broader perspective of social problems or society than all other social sciences.

Sociology and Commonsense

Many times, sociology is charged with what it studies we have at least a bit of knowledge about it or we have experienced it sometimes in our own lives or we know it through our popular wisdom. This knowledge, while sometimes accurate, is not always reliable, because it rests on commonly held beliefs rather than systematic analysis of facts. It was once considered 'commonsense' to accept that the earth was flat. This question was questioned by Pythagoras and Aristotle. Such notions still remain with us today. For thousands of years people's commonsense told them that big objects fall faster than small ones, that stone and iron were perfectly solid materials, that colds are caused by chills and wet feet, that the desire for children is instinctive in women, that with the spread of education, the institutions of caste and dowry will automatically wither away, yet today we know that none of these statements is true. These commonsense statements based on popular wisdom illustrate our point that commonsense knowledge is not always true. Some popular observations may be true but many others are not supported by empirical data. Many commonsense conclusions are based on guesses, hunches, ignorance, prejudices, mistaken interpretation and haphazard trial and error learnings. Commonsense can lead us astray when we are studying other societies and also when we are studying our own society.

Like other scientists, sociologists do not accept something as a fact because "everyone knows it". Instead, each piece of information must be tested and recorded, then analysed in relationship to other data. Sociology relies on facts gathered scientifically in order to describe, understand and predict about any social phenomenon.

Linguistic Origin of the Word 'Sociology'

Etymologically, the word 'sociology' has a hybrid origin of two languages—Latin and Greek. The word 'socius' is a Latin term meaning friend, companion or associate. The Greek 'logos' or 'ology' means study of. It also means doctrine, discourse or theory. By combining the words, it can be illustrated in the following form:

socius+logos=sociology (study of human association)

Thus, literally, sociology is the study of companionship, meaning social interaction and its resultant relationship that exists between companions or groups of human beings.

How Dictionaries Define Sociology?

One of the earliest dictionaries of sociology, edited by H.P. Fairchild (1955), defined sociology as "the study of the relationships between man and his human environment".

The Concise Oxford Dictionary of Sociology (1994) is quite silent about the definition of the word 'sociology'. It has explained the origin of the word and then thrown light on its historical moorings.

According to the *Penguin Dictionary of Sociology* (1994), "sociology is the analysis of the structure of social relationships as constituted by social interaction".

The Blackwell Dictionary of Sociology (1995) defines it as: "Sociology is the study of social life and behaviour, especially in relation to social systems, how they work, how they change, the consequences they produce and their complex relation to people's lives."

Since the time of Auguste Comte (1798-1857), who coined the word 'sociology' and Herbert Spencer (1820-1903) who developed it, sociology has been defined variously by various writers. Indeed, there are as many definitions as there are sociologists. Sociology has been called the study of society, of human societies and their cultures, of human behaviours, of social interactions and relationships, of men in groups, of groups of people, of man's social life, of the social bond, of social institutions, of social actions, of social structure and social systems, and in various other ways. Sometimes, the word 'scientific' is also used before the words "study of". This clearly means that sociologists have discarded metaphysical speculation and moral judgement in favour of scientific inquiry. The diversity of points of view about its subject matter as reflected from the textbooks used in the universities of English-speaking countries (especially in America and Britain) is so large that it is not possible to quote and analyse all definitions.

For our convenience, we classify some important definitions into the following five groupings:

1. Sociology as the study of society.
2. Sociology as the study of social groups.
3. Sociology as the study of social actions, interactions or social relationships.
4. Sociology as the study of social institutions.
5. Sociology as the study of social bonds, social processes, social system, social structure, social life, social phenomena and so on.

1. Sociology as the study of society

The writers, who advocated this view, emphasised that sociology need not be the study of any one part, it should be the study of the whole. Its purpose would be to discover how the different institutions (economic, political, religious etc.), which make up a society, are related to one another in different social systems. Giddings, Ward, Odum, Lundberg, Davis, Horton and Hunt and many others have defined sociology as the study of society. Their language may little bit differ but their overall emphasis remains on the study of society. For example:

> "Sociology is a science of society."
>
> — G.A. Lundberg (1939)

> "Sociology is the science which studies society."
>
> — H.W. Odum (1947)

> "Sociology attempts to study society scientifically."
>
> — Horton and Hunt (1964)

> "Sociology is an understanding of society."
>
> — Stewart and Glynn (1991)

2. Sociology as the study of social groups

A small number of writers like H.M. Johnson, Kimball Young and others have followed this pattern and defined it as under:

> "Sociology is the science that deals with social groups, their internal forms or modes of organisation, the processes that tend to maintain or change these forms of organisation and relation between groups."
>
> — H.M. Johnson (1960)

> "Sociology deals with the behaviour of man in groups."
>
> — Kimball Young (1942)

3. Sociology as the study of social actions, interactions or social relationships

Early German thinkers like Max Weber, Leopold Von Wieste and Georg Simmel advocated that sociology should exclusively devote itself to the study of social actions, social interactions or social relationships. Among contemporary sociologists, Talcott Parsons (1951) has also followed this line. Some definitions in this category are:

> "Sociology is the science which attempts the interpretive understanding of social action."
>
> — Max Weber (1949)

> "Sociology is about 'social relationships', the network of relationships; the network of relationships, we call society."
>
> — MacIver and Page (1949)

> "Sociology may be said to be the study of interactions arising from the association of living beings."
>
> — Gillin and Gillin (1948)

> "Sociology is the synthesising and generalising science of man in all his social relationships."
>
> — A.W. Green (1952)

> "Sociology is the science of human relationships."
>
> — Merrill and Eldrige (1952)

> "The study of social interaction is central to sociologists"
>
> — Gouldner and Gouldner (1963)

> "Sociology is the study of systems of action and of their interrelations."
>
> — Alex Inkeles (1964)

4. Sociology as the study of social institutions

Some of the writers or thinkers have opined that the distinctive unit of sociological study is not whole society, but specifically the relations between the institutions (family, church, school or political party etc.) which compose it. They said that society as a whole is already the unit of analysis in the fields of history and anthrcpology, as such sociology should limit itself with the study of relations of the institutions only. Main champion of this view is Durkheim, who as long ago as 1901, said that sociology "can be defined as the science of institutions" (*The Rules of Sociological Method*, 1895).

5. Sociology as the study of social bonds, social processes, social system, social structure, social life, social phenomena and so on

Some writers defined sociology in a very wide perspective using different terminologies such as:

> "Sociology is concerned with the study of the social life of man."
>
> — Ogburn and Nimkoff (1964)

> "Sociology is the study of social processes."
>
> — Reuter and Hart (1933)

> "Sociology is the study of human beings within their social contexts."
>
> — Smith and Preston (1977)

> "Sociology is the study of the basic structure of society."
>
> — Weinberg and Shabat (1956)

> "Sociology is the science of social phenomena."
>
> — E.A. Ross (1901)

> "Sociology is the science of the structure and functions of social life".
>
> — Bennet and Tumin (1946)

"Sociology is the study of human beings with their social contexts."

— R.W. Smith and F.W. Preston (1977)

"Sociology is a generalising science of socio-cultural phenomena viewed in their generic forms, types, and manifold interconnections."

— P.A. Sorokin (1947)

How Modern Popular Textbooks Define Sociology?

According to Anthony Giddens (*Sociology*, 1977), "sociology is the study of human social life, groups and societies".

Mike O'Donnell (*Sociology*, 1977) defines it as: "Sociology is the systematic study of societies (tribal and modern both) . . . . sociology studies interaction between the self (or individual) and groups, and interaction between groups."

To conclude, it can be said that a concise definition of sociology that can be agreed upon, at least by most of sociologists, if not by all, has yet to be formulated. Short definitions do not really define it, whereas long definitions are usually cumbersome. Yet, a definition of some sort is needed. The common idea underlying all above definitions is that in a broad sense, sociology is concerned with society, and social life. It encompasses all aspects of knowledge about society—economic, political, psychological and social, their effects and mechanisms of action—but most importantly those that are relevant to effective building of social relationships.

Man behaves differently from other animals. Man has unique forms of group life, pursues customs, develops institutions, and creates values. Sociology studies these phenomena in the search of valid and reliable knowledge and for this it applies scientific methods as well as the informal *Verstehen method* (introspective and interpretive understanding). Generally, sociology concentrates itself upon man's group life and products of group life. The basis of social or group life and social behaviour is the unit social actions and interactions in group situation. These actions and interactions help in building the network of social relationships, which eventually form a structure of society. Thus, sociology, in all its ramifications, is a long discourse about human society, which is based on the edifice of social actions, interactions and the web of interrelationships. Society is rooted in interaction and interaction is based on social action and reciprocal action. Action and interaction are the building blocks of social relationships, which is the core to the formation of society. This conceptualisation may be illustrated in the following way:

Proposed Model of Sociology

Social actions → Social interactions → Network of social relationships → Social groups and social institutions → Society

In the above proposed model of sociology an attempt has been made to combine all the different viewpoints of various sociologists:

1. Study of social actions—Max Weber
2. Study of interactions—Gillin and Gillin, Gouldner and Gouldner
3. Study of social relationships—MacIver and Page, A.W. Green
4. Study of social groups and social institutions—H.M. Johnson, Durkheim etc.
5. Study of society—Giddings, Ward, Odum etc.

Scope of Sociology

To understand sociology, we need to know something about its scope and subject matter. Anthony Giddens has written, "the scope of sociological study is extremely wide, ranging from the analysis of passing encounters between individuals in the street to the investigation of global social processes". As with other disciplines the delineation of fields changes over time. The older terrains of synthetic sociology (Comte and Durkheim) and formal sociology (Simmel, Tonnies, Von Wiese etc.) have now been transformed and broadened into various fields and sub-fields. Whether the nature of sociology is synthetic (generalistic) or formalistic (specialistic), this controversy does not exist in contemporary sociology. We even do not find any reference about this controversy in the modern standard textbooks of sociology. What was that controversy? We shall mention here in brief in the following lines.

Almost all earlier sociologists agreed on this view that the proper subject matter and scope of sociology is the study of social interactions and social relationships. But their approach of study has led them to form into groups. They have distinguished two major approaches of sociology to study society, viz., (1) formal or specialist sociology, (2) synthetic or general sociology.

1. Formal or specialistic sociology

There is a group of German sociologists who have distinguished the forms and content of social relationships. They insist that sociologists should delimit their study of the forms of social relationships (competition, assimilation, conflict, cooperation etc.). The contents of relationships should be left to be studied by other social sciences. For example, competition may be viewed as a relationship with distinct formal characteristics, no matter what the setting—whether occurs in the market place, on the sports field, or in the political arena.

Basically, it is a process having many expressions as the struggle between plants for space and food and light, animals for food and shelter, businessmen for customers, athletes for a place on the team, politicians for votes, and so on. Sociologists study only the formal characteristics of competition. Its different manifestations, i.e., competition in the market place (field of economics), in the political arena (field of political science) etc., is left to be studied by other sciences. As such, sociology would be a specialistic science dealing only about the forms of social relationships.

To illustrate the difference between form and content a simile can be given. A glass or plastic bottle can be seen from two angles—form and content. The shape of the bottle—round, square, triangular or octangular—is its form and the water, wine, fruit juice or anything else can be its content that is filled in the bottle. If we fill round shaped bottle with water, it will not turn into wine, nor the water will change the shape of the bottle. The contents of the bottle do not change the form of the bottle. Form and content of the bottle remain unaffected by each other. Similarly, the forms of relationships (cooperation, conflict, adjustment or accommodation etc.) do not affect the types (content) of relationships (politics, family, education, religion, industry etc.). Forms of social relationships do not change with the change in the content of social relationships. For example, the study of co-operation (of conflict)—a form of social relationship—will not make any difference whether we study it in the field of religion or politics or economics. Sociology has been compared with geometry which only studies about the forms of physical things—triangular, rectangular, square or circular. Thus, according to formalistic school, sociology studies one specific aspect of social relationships, i.e., their forms in their abstract nature and not in any concrete situation.

Georg Simmel is known to be the main champion of formal sociology. Formal sociology is an attempt to determine the basic forms of social interaction that underlie more complex forms and contexts of social behaviour. Simmel suggested that one could isolate the form of interactions from the content, so that apparently very different interactions (with different contents) could be shown to have the same form. For instance, the relationship between the aristocrat and writer in the eighteenth century England and the relationship between a peasant and his landlord in the twentieth century India are apparently different reactions. However, they do have the same form, in that they are both examples of patronage relationships. Other followers of this view are F. Tonnies, Von Wiese, Vierkandt and Max Weber. Some American writers like Robert Park, Albion Small and E.A. Ross have also favoured this view.

2. Synthetic or general sociology

As against the views of formal sociologists, who wanted to shape sociology as a specialistic science like economics, political science, psychology etc., the other school of thought, which is known as synthetic sociology, wants that sociology should study both the forms and content of relationships. Not only this, sociology should also study such issues and subjects, which do not come under the purview of any other discipline. The followers of this school of thought are Comte, Durkheim, Sorokin, Hobhouse, Ginsberg etc. In their view, sociology is a generalising and synthesising science. Comte, the pioneer of sociology, proposed a synthetic view that could unite all knowledge about human activity and society. Like Comte, Durkheim, attempted to establish sociology as a distinctive science of social facts. It is a distinctive discipline in the sense that it integrates the findings of economics, political science and psychology, since the 'social' is not an autonomous datum but is constituted by the intersection of economics, politics, geography, history and psychology.

To conclude this discussion about the formalistic and synthetic nature of sociology, it can be said that sociology is a special and general science both. To be clear enough, it is a specialistic science not in the sense of economics, political science or psychology, which studies only the partial reality of society. It is a special science in the sense that its holistic, synthesising or generalising view of looking at the society is quite different from all other social sciences. This point of view can be termed as 'sociological perspective' which distinguishes it from all other social sciences. Huntington Carins aptly remarked, "sociology deals with social phenomena that are in part dealt with other social sciences, but no social science except sociology studies all of them, and no other social science approaches any of them solely from the point of view of a sociologist".

Subject Matter of Sociology

Auguste Comte (1798-1857)

Auguste Comte who invented the word *sociology,* did not specify in detail the sub-fields of sociology, but he did propose to divide the sociology into two major groupings:

1. *Social Statics*: Study of social structure, functions, social system, social relationships etc.

2. *Social Dynamics*: Study of social change, development, transformation and revolutions etc.

This basic sub-division in the subject matter of sociology still persists in some or the other forms and guises in the history of its field. Comte believed that this new science could produce knowledge of society based on scientific evidence. He argued that sociology should contribute to the welfare of the humanity by using science to understand and to control human behaviour.

Emile Durkheim (1858-1917)

Another pioneer French sociologist, Emile Durkheim grouped the subject matter of sociology as under:

1. *Social Morphology*: Study of social forms and structures.
2. *Social Physiology*: Study of social processes.
3. *General Sociology*: Study of social problems etc.

Durkheim has had a more lasting impact on modern sociology than those of Comte. For Durkheim, sociology must study social facts, aspects of social life that shape our actions as individuals.

Georg Simmel (1858-1918)

A contemporary of Durkheim and the champion of *formal sociology*, German sociologist Georg Simmel proposed three major areas of sociological study:

1. *General Sociology*, which studies the whole of historically developed life in so far as it is formed societally. This area includes the study of rhythms, stages and patterns of development, particularly processes of growth and decline.
2. *Formal Sociology*, which studies societal forms or forms of interaction such as competition, conflict, subordination and superordination etc.
3. *Philosophical Sociology*, which he defines as the epistemology of the social sciences.

In his later works, Simmel has given much attention to the analysis of conflict especially positive functions of conflict, e.g., in relieving tensions, in providing a motivation to action or in leading to a reaffirmation of group solidarity.

Max Weber (1864-1920)

Another architect of sociology, Max Weber's conceptualisation of the subject matter of sociology revolves round the study of social action—the primary unit of social relationships which makes the social structure of society. According to Weber, the proper object of social science (sociology) is social action: action directed towards significant others to which we attach meaning. Sociology attempts an interpretative account of such action using an ideal-type methodology.

According to a last mid-20th century text (*What is Sociology*, 1965), written by Alex Inkeles, sociology may be seen as a collection of sub-disciplines dealing with institutions and social processes not claimed by more specialised disciplines. He argued that societies, institutions, social relationships and social processes such as differentiation, cooperation, evaluation and competition are the main foci of sociological studies. Inkeles has divided the subject matter into *four* major areas:

1. *Sociological Analysis*: Study of human culture and society.
2. *Primary Units of Social Life*: Study of social acts and social relationships, individual personality, social groups, communities, associations and populations.
3. *Basic Social Institutions*: Study of family and kinship; economic, political, legal, religious, educational and scientific institutions; recreational, welfare, aesthetic and expressive activities.
4. *Fundamental Social Processes:* Study of differentiation and stratification, cooperation, accommodation, assimilation, social conflict, socialisation and indoctrination, communication; social values, social control and deviation; social integration and social change.

What should be the proper subject matter of sociology? Answering this question, *The Concise Oxford Dictionary of Sociology* (1994) tried to synthesise the views of classical and modern thinkers. It states the proper objects of sociological interest are:

1. *Study of Social Structure*: It is studied in the sense of patterns of relationships, which have an independent existence over and above the individuals or groups. There are two versions of this approach: (i) Marxism, which conceptualises the structures of modes of production, and (ii) Parsonian structural–functionalism, which identifies systems, sub-systems and role-structures.
2. *Study of Durkheim's Perspective of Collective Representations*: It includes meanings and ways of cognitively organising the world which have a continued existence over and above individuals who are socialised into them. Much modern structuralist and post-modernist work can be seen as part of this tradition.
3. *Study of Meaningful Social Action*: This is Weberian approach of studying sociology. For Weber, the proper object of sociology is social action. The implicit or explicit assumption behind this approach is that there is no such thing as society: merely individuals and groups entering into social relationships with each other. There are widely differing ways in which such interaction can be studied: (i) Weber's perspective of studying rational, traditional and affective action; (ii) symbolic interaction perspective of studying production, maintenance, and transformation of meanings in face-to-fact interaction; and (iii) ethnomethodological perspective which places emphasis on the study of construction of social reality through linguistic practices.

Since Second World War, the subject matter of sociology has become highly diversified. It is now no more limited to a few subjects—social morphology, social physiology, collective representations, social dynamics, and so on. These subjects were used to be discussed at the time of its inception. Not only this, the perspective, methodologies and the images of sociology have also undergone sea change, but the fundamental questions, such as, what is the structure of society, how it operates or functions and how and why it changes, have not much changed. Even classical sociologists, like Weber, Durkheim and Marx, have also anticipated and were seeking to explain the transition from traditional to modern. Recently, one of the leading Indian sociologist Andre Beteille in his article 'Sociology and Current Affairs' (Sociological Bulletin, 2006) also suggested, "sociologists main task is to explain how the society or an institution works, what is its impact on the people. His main concern is to enhance the critical understanding about the phenomenon he studies".

The main agenda of modern sociology is understanding the impact of modernity and globalisation on society. This has changed the boundaries of 'society'. Nineteenth century issues, when sociology originated, are now no more much relevant. If sociology is to be created anew, which can keep pace with the time, the issues like family and gender, cultural dimensions of class, ethnicity, community and the emergence, maintenance of a legitimate nation-state and so on shall have to be investigated in a new context—a *global* context.

Changing Sociological Agendas (Subject Matter)

How subjects of study changed from time to time and what is the contemporary concern of sociology is well exemplified in a recent textbook *Introductory Sociology*, written by Tony Bilton, Adrew Webster and others (1996), as under:

Some key concerns of classical sociology

- The growth and impact of industrialisation.
- The development of capitalism and class conflict.
- The emergence and legitimacy of the nation-state.
- The growing complexity and differentiation of social institutions.
- The congruence between 'society' and 'nation'.
- The importance of class-based sources of protest and change.

Some key concerns of contemporary sociology

- The emergence of global industrialisation.
- Capitalism as a world economy.
- The growth of transnational economic and political structures.

- The compression of time and space.
- The legitimacy and role of nation-bound political institutions.
- The origins and impact of (non-class) social movements.

Origin and Development of Sociology

Sociology is the newest of the social sciences to establish itself in the western universities of the English-speaking world (in 1876 Yale University, United States, in 1889 France and in 1907 England). In Asia, the formal teaching of sociology began in 1893 in Tokyo University and in India in 1919 in Bombay University. Men have always reflected upon the societies in which they lived, yet sociology as a modern science developed only in 19th century, largely out of concern about the changes wrought by the industrial revolution. Historically, the word *sociology* was invented by Auguste Comte, although a concern with the nature of society can be found throughout the Western (Plato and Aristotle's Greek philosophy and the works of European and Scottish Enlightenment thinkers) and Eastern (Hindu societal writings of Manu and Kautilya and Islamic jurisprudence of Ibn Khaldun) thought. However, it was not until the middle of the 19th century, in the aftermath of industrial revolution and the consequent upheavals, that we find a concern with society and thus the need for a "science of society" was recognised. These conditions gave impetus to French philosopher Saint Simon and his secretary-colleague Comte to think about human society on scientific lines. They believed that positivism can provide a scientific basis for the study of society. The new science—sociology—would discover the laws of the social world equivalent to our knowledge of the laws of nature. We could then determine the general laws of social change similar to those found in Newtonian physics or Darwinian biology. These optimistic beliefs of these early thinkers were overly ambitions.

In his most celebrated work, *The Structure of Social Action* (1937), Talcott Parsons has written that in the late 19th and early 20th centuries, sociology broke free of its earlier ideological shackles and establish itself as a science proper, especially in the works of Max Weber and Emile Durkheim. However, the subject was also deeply influenced by Karl Marx in his analysis of social structure, class and social change. Although these three thinkers have much influence over modern sociology, yet the philosophical and political inheritance of sociology is complex and no single tradition can be regarded as entirely dominant and also responsible for the development of the subject in its present form.

What the Founding Fathers Say?

In this section, we will briefly examine the views and main contributions of founding fathers of sociology—Comte, Spencer, Durkheim, Marx and Weber, who had a major and lasting impact (especially the last three thinkers) on the discipline of sociology. An understanding of the origins of sociology helps us to grasp of what the discipline is today.

Auguste Comte (1798-1857)

As written earlier, the term 'sociology' is usually credited to 19th century social philosopher Auguste Comte. He is considered as the father of sociology. He originally used the phrase 'social physics' for his new science of society but he had to drop this after sometime because his intellectual rival the Belgian statistician Adolphe Quetelet used this as the title of his book in 1835. Comte wanted to distinguish his own views from early thinkers of society, so he coined the word 'sociology' in 1838 to describe the subject he wished to establish. He regarded sociology as the last science to develop in the chain of sciences—Mathematics, Astronomy, Physics, Chemistry, Biology and Sociology—but as the most significant and complex of all the sciences.

For Comte, *sociology is the study of the fundamental laws of social phenomena in accordance with the methods of the positive sciences*. He believed that this new science could produce knowledge of society based on scientific laws. Sociology, he argued, should contribute to the welfare of the community by using the canons of science to understand, predict and control of human behaviour. He also propounded a new religion of humanity based on scientific knowledge. As stated earlier, although Comte did not specify in detail the sub-fields of sociology, he did propose to divide sociology into two main parts: *social statics* and *social dynamics*. The former is concerned with the anatomy of society and the latter is related with natural progress of mankind towards scientific rationality. Comte saw society in organismic terms, as an entity made up of interdependent parts, which are in balance with each other and create an integrated whole.

Against the trend of intellectual differentiation prevailing in his time, Comte wanted sociology to be a synthetic science, which attempts to integrate political, economic and social phenomena.

Herbert Spencer (1820-1903)

Another early great social theorist of society Herbert Spencer accepted the word 'sociology' without any hesitation in 1877 and titled one of his books as *Principles of Sociology*. He defined this new science as a science of societies. He was much more precise than Comte in specifying the topics or special fields of sociology. The subject matter of sociology, according to Spencer includes family, politics, religion, social control and industry or work. In addition, Spencer also included study of associations, communities, the division of labour, social differentiation or social stratification and many other topics in the domain of sociology. He clearly mentioned that sociology should accept the whole society as its unit of analysis.

Spencer is also known for introducing Darwin's theory of scientific evolution in sociology. Another significant contribution that Spencer made is the so-called *organic analogy* in which society is compared with human organism, but did not describe society as an organism.

Emile Durkheim (1858-1917)

The first French academic sociologist Emile Durkheim, who is widely known as a 'founding father' of modern sociology, has attempted to define its subject matter and establish sociology as a separate discipline studying society. He had a more lasting impact on modern sociology than those of Comte. Vine (1954) has made an interesting observation about him: "*While Comte laid the foundation of sociology, it is Durkheim who cemented it*." He is long acknowledged as the founding figure of *functionalism*, a perspective which permeates through almost all social sciences but more recently hailed by leading authorities on structuralism, socio-linguistics and post-modernism. He adopted collectivist perspective throughout his sociological analysis.

To Durkheim, sociology is the study of social facts (aspects of social life) that have distinctive social characteristics and determinants. They shape our actions as individuals. He defined social facts as "every way of acting, fixed or not, capable of exercising on the individual an external constraint". They include such things as folkways, customs, laws, and the general rules of behaviour that people accept without question. In this connection, he said that social facts should be studied as things. By this he meant that social life can be analysed as rigorously as objects or events in nature. Social facts are exterior to individuals and cannot be reduced to psychological data. They are characterised by their potentiality for constraint or coercion relative to individual. They can be tested empirically. The outstanding example of this approach in Durkheim's work is his study of suicide.

Durkheim was of the view that sociology should concern itself with a wide range of institutions—their development and functioning and social processes as its subject matter. Like Spencer, Durkheim also spoke of sociology as the "science of societies", and repeatedly emphasised the importance of studying different types of society comparatively. This must be done by analysing institutions in different types of society at comparable stages of evolution.

Durkheim's main contributions are:

1. Durkheim attempted to establish sociology as an autonomous and distinctive science of social phenomena.
2. For Durkheim, the main domain of sociology is the study of social facts and not individuals. He believed both that societies had their own realities which could not simply be reduced to the actions and motives of individuals and that individuals were moulded and constrained by their social environments. The reality of society for Durkheim lay in its values, ideas and beliefs.
3. The central theme of Durkheim's sociology is the idea of moral comparison and normative constraint.
4. He saw social norms as regulating people's behaviour by means of institutionalised values which the individual internalised rather than society simply acting as an external constraint.
5. Durkheim has explained the universal function of religious systems for the continuity of society as such.
6. He argued for guild socialism as a means of rebuilding cohesive and solidary social communities.
7. He developed concepts of collective conscience, collective representation, organic and mechanical solidarity and many others in various contexts.
8. In spite of empirical orientation, Durkheim was very much concerned with the problem of making value judgements and believed that sociologists should be able to say what ought to be or to make diagnosis of social ills. For Durkheim, the *raison d'etre* of science was to help men live a more satisfying life. In this connection, he argued that criminality as a general characteristic is normal to all societies and as such its presence is not a

sign of pathology. Durkheim wished to apply sociological knowledge to social intervention by the state in order to recreate social harmony.

Max Weber (1864-1920)

After Durkheim, in the galaxy of sociologists, the German social scientist Max Weber is the second prominent and most dominant figure who influenced the course of sociology. His influence still persists in various special fields of sociology. Ritzer wrote, "Weber was a prolific writer and a complicated thinker.... His work is provocative and rich in insight". Sociology, according to Weber, "*is a science which attempts the interpretive understanding of social action in order thereby to arrive at a causal explanation of its course and effects*" (1947). In other words, it is the search for the causes of social action Action is behaviour to which the individual attaches meaning and social action is meaningful in that it takes into account the behaviour of others. Weber believed that sociologists must study not just social facts and social structures, but also social actions, the external objective behaviours as well as the internalised values, motives and subjective meanings that individuals attach to their behaviours and to the behaviour of others. This view clearly suggests that Weber regarded the 'social act' or the 'social relationship' as the particular subject matter of sociology. He distinguished four types of social action: (1) *Traditional*, (2) *Affectual*, (3) *Zweckrational* (instrumental action), and (4) (value rationality).

Weber contended that social actions should be studied through qualitative (subjective methods) as well as objective and quantitative techniques. In this respect, he developed a sociological perspective that balanced two views. On the one hand, he advocated that social scientists should study the subjective values and meanings that individuals attach to their own behaviour and that of others. At the same time, he believed that social scientists should study these values and meanings of actions objectively, remaining morally neutral or value-free. The goal, Weber believed, was to achieve a "sympathetic understanding" of the minds of others. He called this approach *verstehen*, i.e., understanding human action by examining the subjective meaning that people attach to their behaviour and to the behaviours of others.

His approach to sociology, however, has probably been as influential as his ideas. His predecessors considered societies in terms of their large structures, social divisions and social movements. Spencer based his studies on the belief that societies evolved like organisms, Marx considered society in terms of class conflicts, and Durkheim was concerned with the institutional arrangements that maintain the cohesion of social structures. These theorists assumed that society, although composed of individuals, existed apart from them.

The main contributions of Max Weber may be summarised as under:

1. For Weber, sociology should concern itself with the meaning of social action and the uniqueness of historical events. He developed a coherent philosophy of social science (sociology), which aimed at the understanding of the meaning of action.
2. Weber denied that sociology could (a) discover universal laws of human behaviour comparable with those of natural science; (b) confirm any evolutionary progress in human societies; and (c) provide any evaluation of, or moral justification for, any existing or future state of affairs.
3. Weber attempted to explain the basic characteristics of a modern, industrial civilisation (bureaucracy).
4. He emphasised on value neutrality in the subjective interpretation of action. The findings of sociologists should be open to academic scrutiny and criticism.
5. Weber rejected as unwarranted the claims of positivism. He did not believe that sociology could be a natural science, as positivists claim. Instead, he devoted his efforts to historical analysis.

6. Weber implicitly presented rationalisation as the master trend of Western capitalist society. He regarded capitalist society as having a logic which operated independently of the subjective attitudes of social actors.
7. Weber also contributed to the sociology of comparative religion and through his study of "The Protestant Ethic and the Sprit of Capitalism" tried to establish that economic phenomena themselves are governed by cultural ethos, particularly religion.
8. Weber constructed a typology of social action—rational, traditional, affective and evaluative.
9. Weber analysed authority, which has stimulated a great deal of empirical research, particularly in the field of bureaucracy. His typology of authority is (1) rational, (2) legal, (3) traditional, and (4) charismatic.

Karl Marx (1818-1883)

Along with Emile Durkheim and Max Weber, Karl Marx is generally regarded as one of the key figures in the development of sociological thinking. Like Comte and Durkheim, he sought to explain the changes in society that took place at the time of the industrial revolution. It is said that Marx was not a sociologist (he never claimed himself to be a sociologist), but there is sociology in his all writings. His writings covered a diversity of areas. Much of his writings revolve round economic issues. His views about the relationship between economic life and social institutions attracted sociologists to study him deeply. He regarded all sciences, including sociology, as emancipatory. Marx has been a major influence on the development of sociology, as often a subject of criticism as of inspiration.

Marx's main contributions are:

1. The whole ideas of Marx are founded on what he called the *materialistic conception of history.* According to this view, it is not the ideas or values human beings hold that are the main

sources of social change. Rather, social change is prompted primarily by economic influences. Marx sees the structure of economic relations as the most basic and important element in society as a whole.

2. Marx is best known for his views on the relationship between economic life and other social institutions. On the basis of his ideas, it is often said that he was an economic determinist, believing that the nature of a society is determined by the manner in which economy is owned and organised.
3. In his early work Marx was interested in the concept of *alienation*—a theme that was to run through all his subsequent contributions. He used this concept in the sense of alienated labour—the work which is imposed on the labour. Marx's basic analytic concern was with the structures of capitalism that cause this alienation.
4. Marx analysed societies on the basis of social classes, which are organised in relation of production in the economic system. For him, those who own and control the means of production from one class—capitalist (bourgeoise) and those depend on their own labour constitute another class—industrial labour (proletariat).
5. Marx believed that there has always been a conflict or contradictions between the classes. This conflict is inevitable because of their different relationship to the means of production. There has always a dominant and a subordinate class. For example, capitalists within a capitalist society effectively exploit workers by appropriating the product of their labour. He argued that history could be understood in dialectical terms as record of the inevitable conflicts between economic classes. In Marx's words, *all human history thus far is the history of class struggles*.
6. Marx argued that this class conflict or class struggle is the 'motor of history'. It provides the motivation for historical development which suggests a theory of social change. He believed that change does not follow automatically from changes in the economic structure; class struggle as the active intervention of human beings is necessary.

7. Marx was pre-eminently a theorist of capitalist society. He developed the economic mechanism of capitalist society, labour theory of value, the theory of capital accumulation, the concepts of historical materialism, commodity fetishism and predicted the possibility of the collapse of capitalist society—ushered by a classless socialistic society.
8. For Marx, the key to understanding a particular society is its predominant *mode of production* which consists of the tools and techniques (*forces of production*) and the compatible *relations of production* (class relations).

Modern Trends in Sociology

Sociology, as we know it today, draws upon the firm foundation developed by Emile Durkheim, Max Weber and Karl Marx. The trio has been seen by some sociologists as epitomising modern sociology. However, the discipline has not remained stagnant over the last century. Sociologists have gained new insights which have helped them to better understand the workings of society. Contemporary sociology reflects the diverse contributions of earlier theorists like G.H. Mead (1863-1931), C.H. Cooley (1864-1929), Talcott Parsons (1902-1979), Robert Merton (1910-2003) and many others speaking through the pages of current research. Sociologists expect the 21st century to be perhaps the most exciting and critical period in the history of the discipline because of a growing recognition that social problems must be addressed in the near future.

The far going long description and analysis about the nature, perspective, scope, and subject matter will be incomplete if we do not reflect on the modern trends in sociology. It is a fact that during the last quarter of the 20th century, many new thinkers who were (most of them) not trained as sociologist, have entered into the arena of sociology, notable among them are Michel Foucault (1926-1984), Jurgen Habermas (1929-), Pierre Bourdieu (1930-2002), Jacques Derrida (1930-) and Anthony Giddens (1938-). They have in some way or the other amply influenced the course of sociology, especially the methods of investigation. This new generation of sociologists has invented or used many concepts as tools of sociological research such as *Habitus* (Bourdieu), *Deconstruction* (Derrida), *Structuration* (Giddens), etc. With their efforts new perspectives have developed such as post-industrialism, post-structuralism, post-modernism, neo-functionalism, neo-Marxism, etc.

The types of questions the classical thinkers—Comte, Durkheim, Marx and Weber sought to answer—what is human nature? why is society so structured? why and how do societies change? what directions will change take in the future?—are the same questions modern thinkers try to answer today but their approaches are different. Our modern world is radically different from the past and this has an impact on the development of sociology also. Now, it is the task of sociology to help us understand the rapidly changing world in which we live and reflect about the nature of the future world.

What the Modern Thinkers Say?

Pierre Bourdieu (1930-)

For Bourdieu, the objective of sociology is to unveil the hidden culture of the society. For achieving this objective, sociologists should study cultural practices of the masses rather than classes. As such, sociology should take up cultural analysis as their primary concern to uncover the political uses of science, the authority of science—physical or economic science, not to mention the biology or sociology, of the advanced forms of racism. Being a neo-Marxist, he emphasised on the culture of the proletariat to which he calls 'counter-culture' (a culture which is against the established culture).

What should be the shape of sociology? Answering this question, Bourdieu in his later works, *The Logic of Practice, (1990) and Craft of Sociology* (1991) observed that the subjective and objective aspects of social life are inescapably bound together, as such there is no fun in the dualism of macro versus micro and structure versus agency. Instead, he calls for a constructivist approach to sociology, transcending both essentialism and all ideas taken for granted in everyday life.

Jurgen Habermas (1929-)

Jurgen Habermas is perhaps the most influential social thinker today with an explicit allegiance to Marxist thought. He is known as a best spokesman of the Frankfurt School of Critical Theory. Habermas has severely criticised positivism. In his opinion, it has limited our understanding of natural and the social world. He focussed particularly on three major contributions which have become prominent in the 1960s: (1) the phenomenological sociology, (2) anthropological extension of Wittgenstein's notion of language games, and (3) Hans-Georg Gadamer's philosophical hermeneutics.

He has been a severe critique of capitalist societies in which, according to him, change is ever present, tend to destroy the moral order on which they in fact depend. We live in a social order where economic growth tends to take precedence over all else but this situation creates a back of meaning in everyday life.

Jacques Derrida (1930-)

French philosopher and post-modernist, who himself decried to be called as sociologist, but who has definitely made imprint on the modern sociology is Jacques Derrida. His ideas are developed primarily from linguistics. Through his most popular concept—*deconstruction*, he has pleaded for the deconstruction of sociological texts (texts of founding fathers—Comte, Durkheim, Weber, Marx and modern sociologists—Parsons, Merton etc.). In his opinion, these texts demystified the social reality. They do not always unveil the truth of society. By deconstruction, Derrida means that the textual reading is not always correct, it does not lead us to know the reality of society. Deconstruction brings out what the texts exclude by showing what it includes. It highlights what remains indecidable and what operates as an indecidable in the texts itself. It is the task of sociology to deconstruct the narratives of the texts through the explicit and implicit analyses.

Some Other Renowned Theorists of Twentieth Century

French sociologist Alain Touraine (1929-), who specialised in the study of social movements, proposed that sociology of society be replaced with the sociology of actors (*The Return of the Actor*, 1988). His purpose has been to overcome what he sees as a false division in sociology between objective and subjective or system and action approaches. Touraine's method of intervention not only treats social movements as one of the most fundamental forms of citizen action, but also requires that sociologists join the action not just to study but to encourage it.

Recently, Jeffrey Alexander (1947-) in his four-volume study *Theoretical Logic in Sociology* (1984) argues for multidimensional sociology, bringing together the metaphysical and empirical, individual volition and collective domination, and normative and instrumental action. He opined that grand theorist Talcott Parsons tried to achieve this synthesis than did any other sociological theorist.

Inventor of the theory of 'structuration', Anthony Giddens (1938-) argues that sociology emerged in an attempt to make sense of the profound social transformation between traditional and modern societies, and as that change continues and gathers pace so the attempt to understand it becomes more important. The changes involved are not just large-scale ones. Major shifts have also occurred in the most intimate and personal characteristics of people's lives. Take as an example the transformations taking place affecting marriage, sexuality and the family.

Fields of Sociology in the Twenty-First Century

Contemporary sociology has been divided and sub-divided into a wide range of specialised fields of research and theory. The prominent fields of research now-a-days are:

- Interpersonal relations
- Rural and urban life
- Marriage and family
- Social differentiation, stratification and inequality
- Caste (especially in India)

- Gender
- Population and demography
- Subaltern people (Dalits)
- Economic sociology
- Political sociology
- Educational sociology
- Formal sociology
- Race and ethnicity
- Formal organisations
- Linguistics
- Criminology
- Gerontology
- Social change, modernity and post-modernity
- Globalisation and world system
- Other important branches are: Sociologies of Religion, Knowledge, Law Science, Work and Occupation, Professions, Industry, Architecture, Art, Music, Literature, Health, Illness and Medicine, Development and Welfare, Leisure, Sports and Tourism, Popular Culture, Militarism, Sexuality, Body, Deviance and many other subjects along with sociology of sociology and sociological methodology.

In a recent edition (Fifth edition) of a popular textbook written by Haralambos and Holborn (*Sociology*, 2000) the following subject matter of sociology has been suggested:

1. Culture and society
2. Socialization
3. Norms and Values
4. Feminism
5. Interactionism (concept of self and construction of meaning)
6. Postmodernism
7. Positivism
8. Social Action Perspective
9. Phenomenology

Chapter 2

Nature of Sociology

Key features

Since the time of Auguste Comte (1842), the founder of sociology, it is debated that can there be a "natural science of society?" In what ways and to what extent sociology is a science? It is a long-standing controversy in sociology. It is the basic issue over which sociologists even today find themselves in disagreement. Many early sociologists were quite optimistic about this new discipline as science. They believed that sociology seeks to apply the methods of science to the study of man and society. Sociology modelled itself after the natural sciences since its inception in the nineteenth century, collecting data through observation and experiment (wherever possible) and devising and testing hypothesis. This procedure is known as *scientific method*. Many sociologists, often called positivists, believe that since sociology uses this method/procedure for arriving at the empirical truth, it has every right to be called a science. Even Comte believed that "a science of sociology should be based on systematic observation and classification, not on authority and speculation".

Modern sociologists are of the view that sociology is a science (as claimed by positivists) and art (as believed by interpretative sociologists) both. Science and art are two major forms of knowledge. Science deals in facts, while art in precepts. As science, its language is "This is" or "This is not", "This does or does not happen". The language of art is "Do this" or "Avoid this". If we apply these canons of science and art on sociology, then sociology is a science and not an art. Sociology, like all other sciences, chiefly deals with the questions: what it is? how it is? and why it is? The questions like what should be? or what should exist? do not come under the purview of sociology. Any knowledge which does not pertain to observable events or empirical world, such knowledge is either religious or ideological or a formal system of logic such as mathematics. To peep into the factual knowledge, we require understanding which is a form of art. The distinction between knowledge and understanding is a major difference between sociology as a science and sociology as an art.

A sociologist, as an artist, tries to understand things by "taking the role of other", i.e., by perceiving the world from the point of view of the subject of investigation. 'Understanding' refers to what might be called 'deep level acquaintance'. Early sociologists Max Weber and C.H. Cooley used and laid emphasis on the method of understanding in the study of social relationships. Their methods are known as *Verstehen* and *sympathetic introspection* respectively. For full comprehension of the social world, perspectives of art (taking the role of other) and science (a natural observer) both are required. This viewpoint is emphasised by great humanist C.W. Mills and eminent sociologist Robert A. Nisbet. Nisbet observes that we must never forget that sociology is both an art as well as a science, otherwise we run the risk of losing the science findings ourselves with a sandheap of empiricism or methodological narrcism. Mills argues that sociology is better practised with imagination and flexibility than with rigid adherence to the models of natural science. Most of the sociologists who see sociology as an art are staunch humanists.

What is Science?

In the popular imagination, science is sometimes associated with a particular content, such as protons, neutrons, cells, skeletons, skulls or stars. For a common student, it is only physics, biology or chemistry are sciences, which have big laboratories fitted with jars, balances, test tubes and many other instruments and equipments. This identification of science with particular kinds of content or with laboratorial experiments is not correct. Today, it is generally agreed that science is not a body of content but a method of approach to any content. Long back, philosopher of science, Karl Pearson (*Grammar of Science*) said that "the unity of all sciences lies only in their method and not in the material they study. The classification of facts, the recognition of their sequence and relative significance is the function of science".

Science has been defined in many ways. For our purpose two definitions will suffice. According to Churchman and Akoff (1950), "science is a systematic method of getting knowledge". A.W. Green (1952) wrote, "science is a way of investigation". In modern times, science is seen chiefly in two distinct though related ways as systematic knowledge and as method of study.

1. Science as systematic knowledge

As systematic knowledge, science is an accumulation of organised and verified knowledge, based on reliable observation and organised into a system of general propositions and laws.

2. Science as method of study

Science is a method of approach to the entire empirical world. It is an approach by which systematic, accurate and verified knowledge is acquired. This method of getting knowledge is opposed to the intuition, speculation, revelations, traditions or authorities. 'Method of approach' is a mode of analysis that permits the scientists to state proposition in the form of 'if and then'.

Science, both as knowledge (goal) and as method (means), incorporates two essential elements—*rationality* and *empiricism*. As substantive knowledge, science is made up of logical related propositions that must also be supported by empirical evidence. As method, it places emphasis on reliable and objective observation and logical analysis. Neither of these elements alone constitutes science.

Characteristics of Science/Scientific Method

The following are the main characteristics of science and scientific method:

1. Objectivity

Scientific knowledge is objective. Objectivity simple means the ability to see and accept facts as they are, not as one might wish them to be. To be objective, one has to guard against his own biases, beliefs, wishes, values and preferences. Objectivity demands that one must set aside all sorts of the subjective considerations and prejudices.

2. Verifiability

Science rests upon sense data, i.e., data gathered through our senses—eye, ear, nose, tongue and touch. Scientific knowledge is based on verifiable evidence (concrete factual observations) so that other observers can observe, weigh or measure the same phenomena and check out observation for accuracy.

Is there a God? Is 'varna' system ethical or questions pertaining to the existence of soul, heaven or hell are not scientific questions because they cannot be treated factually. The evidence regarding their existence cannot be gathered through our senses. Science does not have answers for everything. It deals with only those questions about which verifiable evidence can be found.

3. Ethical neutrality

Science is ethically neutral. It only seeks knowledge. How this knowledge is to be used, is determined by societal values. Knowledge can be put to differing uses. Knowledge about atomic energy can be used to cure diseases or to wage atomic warfare. Ethical neutrality does not mean that the scientist has no values. It here only means that he must not allow his values to distort the design and conduct of his research. Thus, scientific knowledge is value-neutral or value-free.

4. *Systematic exploration*

A scientific research adopts a certain sequential procedure, an organised plan or design of research for collecting and analysis of facts about the problem under study. Generally, this plan includes a few scientific steps—formulation of hypothesis, collection of facts, analysis of facts (classification, coding and tabulation) and scientific generalisation and predication.

5. *Reliability*

Scientific knowledge must occur under the prescribed circumstances not once but repeatedly. It is reproducible under the circumstances stated anywhere and anytime. Conclusions based on casual recollections are not very reliable.

6. *Precision*

Scientific knowledge is precise. It is not vague like some literary writing. Tennyson wrote, "every moment dies a man; every moment one is born", is good literature but not science. To be a good science, it should be written as: "In India, according to the 2001 census, every 10th second, on the average, dies a man; every 4th second, on the average, an infant is born." Precision requires giving exact number or measurement. Instead of saying "most of the people are against love marriages," a scientific researcher says, "Ninety per cent people are against love marriages".

7. *Accuracy*

Scientific knowledge is accurate. A physician, like a common man, will not say that the patient has slight temperature or having very high temperature but after measuring with the help of thermometer, he will pronounce that the patient is having 101.2 F temperature.

Accuracy simply means truth or correctness of a statement or describing things in exact words as they are without jumping to unwarranted conclusions.

8. Abstractness

Science proceeds on a plane of abstraction. A general scientific principle is highly abstract. It is not interested in giving a realistic picture.

9. Predictability

Scientists do not merely describe the phenomena being studied, but also attempt to explain and predict as well. It is typical of social sciences that they have a far lower predictability compared to natural sciences. The most obvious reasons are the complexity of the subject matter and inadequacy at control etc.

Basic Principles (Phases) of Scientific Procedure

There is a little bit disagreement among social scientists about the number of steps in a scientific research. Some scientists, like Roy G. Fransis (1954), have enumerated as many as twelve steps while others have condensed them into four or five steps. The important phases of research process are as follows:

1. Formulation of working hypothesis

A working hypothesis is a penetrating hunch, guess or the provisional explanation of the problem under study. This is found on the basis of preliminary observations of the facts related to the problem. In brief, the problem is stated in the form of a proposition, i.e., 'if' and 'then'. Hypothesis serves as tentative explanation which can be tested empirically. It guides the researcher in the selection of pertinent facts needed to explain the problem at hand. Here, one thing is to be noted that hypothesis is not needed in all researches. Some researches develop hypotheses as the end results of a preliminary inquiry for further testing.

2. Preparation of research design

A research design is a detailed plan or a strategy of conducting research. It answers the questions—what, how, when/where, and why about the facts to be collected for the study. It is a process of making decisions with respect to: (a) types of data required; (b) sources of data and field of study; (c) method of data collection and preparation of tools (Questionnaire, Interview Schedule etc); and (d) sample design. Designing the research ensures against its failure.

3. Collection of data

Actual gathering of data and information begins in accordance with the research design. By collecting the data, the researcher tests the hypotheses which he may ultimately accept, change, or abandon.

4. Analysis of data

After the data are collected, they must be assembled, organised and classified in such a way that the hypothesis can be tested. It is said that *mere collection of facts is no science.* Facts become meaningful when they are logically connected with other facts and sorted according to their nature. Broadly, this step of scientific research includes coding, classification and tabulation of gathered data. These days, much of this work is done by computers. The computer gives the desired computations and comparisons including data for statistical tests.

5. Drawing conclusions in the form of theoretical formulations and generalisations

Scientists are not concerned with isolated phenomena or events. They aim to discover under the surface layer of diversity of these events, a thread of uniformity. On the basis of this uniformity they try to formulate generalisations or a scientific theory. A generalisation is a statement about a number of events rather than about a unique event. Thus, the original hypothesis, if formulated in the beginning of the research, is either confirmed or rejected.

The basic procedure, as outlined above, is the same for all scientific researches or inquiries. Only the tools and techniques may vary according to the problem under study. Researchers may make changes and adjust to unforeseen difficulties once the study is under way.

Is Sociology a Science?

The term 'science' refers to the body of knowledge obtained by methods based upon systematic observation. As a systematic observation, sociology fulfils all the requirements of a science. It is objective, empirical, logical, value-neutral, and parsimonious. It has other characteristics of science also such as verifiability, reliability, precision, accuracy, predictability and the power of generalisation. All allegations levelled against its scientific nature are partially true.

According to Anthony Giddens (2000), "Science is the use of *systematic methods of empirical investigation the analyses of data, theoretical thinking and the logical assessment of arguments* to develop a body of knowledge about a particular subject matter. According to this definition, sociology is a scientific endeavour". Robert Bierstedt (*The Social Order*, 1957) has discussed the following distinguishing features of sociology as a science:

Sociology is	**Sociology is not**
Social	Natural
Generalising	Particularising
Abstract	Concrete
Categorical	Normative
Pure	Applied
General	Special

1. *Sociology is a social science*

Sciences are commonly divided into natural and social sciences. Natural science studies natural phenomena (animate and inanimate both). Astronomy, biology, chemistry, physics and geology are all natural sciences. Social science is the study of various aspects of human society. The social sciences include sociology, anthropology, economics, political science etc. Sociology broadly studies human behaviour, man in society, social life of human beings and the structure of society. It is neither philosophy nor socialism as is sometimes thought but a social science.

2. *Sociology is generalising science*

This is an important feature of sociology which distinguishes it from history which is particularising (idiographic). For instance, sociology is not interested in a particular war (e.g., war of Mahabharat) but in war or revolution as a recurrent social phenomenon. Sociology seeks general laws or principles about human behaviour and association. It is interested in formulating generalisations of general validity.

3. *Sociology is an abstract science*

The concerns of sociology are relatively abstract not concrete. As a science, it proceeds on a plane of abstraction. For example, sociology is interested not in particular families but in the family as a social institution that exists in all societies—modern or preliterate.

4. *Sociology is categorical science*

Sociology is concerned with the questions of what, when, how or why and where about man and society and not what ought to be. It gives categorical judgements rather than normative ones. It is this feature of sociology that distinguishes it from ethics or moral and political philosophy.

5. *Sociology is a pure science*

Sociology is engaged in the acquisition of knowledge and not in its application. This distinction is like chemistry and pharmacy, physics and engineering or biology and science of medicine.

6. Sociology is both rational and empirical science

As an empiricist, a sociologist collects facts and as a rationalist, he coordinates and arranges them.

7. Sociology is a generalistic science

The nature of sociology is synthesising and generalising. It is not a specialistic science like economics or political science. The focus of sociology may be special one, as is the focus of every other science, but its area of study is general. P.A. Sorokin has given the following paradigm and explanation about its synthesising character:

Subject	Subject Matter of Study					
Economics	a	b	c	d	e	f
Political Science	a	b	c	g	h	i
Psychology	a	b	c	j	k	l
Ethics	a	b	c	m	n	o

In all above phenomena, whether economics or political science or ethics, a, b, c occur. These are the social factors that they all have in common. It is on this level that sociology operates and it does not, of course, investigate the special factors like d, e, f, g, h, i, etc., which are the subject matter of study of specialised sciences like economics, ethics or political science etc. The focus of sociology may be special one, as is the focus of every other discipline but its area of inquiry (subject matter) is general.

Objections Against Sociology as a Science

Not everyone regard sociology as a science because sociology does not possess all the dimensions of science as it is defined. Most of these objections are of two kinds. First, it has been argued that human beings cannot be treated in the same way as objects in the natural world because, among other things, they have the capacity to reason and to make active sense of their world. The second objection to the positivists' view of sociology is that, unlike natural sciences, sociology cannot be separated from value judgements about social behaviour. While the first argument is related with the subject matter of sociology, i.e., human being and their social behaviour, the second argument pertains to the method of study, which is pursued in sociology. These arguments run as under:

(1) Subject matter of sociology, i.e., human behaviour and social life is too complex, which cannot be studied scientifically. It is full of vested interests.
(2) Sociology is too young a discipline to have developed the kinds of laws and principles found in the natural sciences.
(3) Sociology lacks scientific objectivity.
(4) Sociology has no laboratories to conduct controlled experiments to verify facts.
(5) Sociology is incapable of measuring its subject matter.
(6) Sociology has no predictability.
(7) Sociology is not an exact science.
(8) Sociology is incapable of maintaining detachment of the researcher from his subject matter of study.

Defences in Favour of Sociology as a Science

The above objections against the nature of sociology as a science have not much weight. All these are not even tenable. To say that sociologists cannot study their subject matter objectively, is not fully correct. We can agree on this point that absolute objectivity is not possible in social research because of the special character of its subject matter. It is argued that human beings cannot be totally objective. Sociologists studying communal relations have found that a journalistic account of an event by a Muslim writer differs from an account of the same event by a Hindu writer. But, there are many procedures for minimising the level of this subjectivity. Sociologists apply those procedures and techniques to make their study more and more objective.

Another objection is that sociology has no laboratory. No doubt, sociology has no such laboratory which is hedged in a small room, fitted with some test tubes, balances and other gadgets of science to study and measure their subject matter. The laboratory of sociology is whole world wherever human beings are found. Even in the physical sciences, there are certain phenomena which cannot be subject to controlled laboratory experiments, still they are considered as science. Newton, Archimedes and Marconi and many other scientists had no laboratories in the modern sense of the term; their laboratories were whole physical world. But still they were successful in formulating scientific laws.

It is often said that the subject matter of sociology is too complex and there is a presence of vested interests in the material of sociology. Any subject may seem complex to an untrained observer, however, the people have been 'doing' sociology for thousands of years. The real difficulties in studying sociology scientifically involve the issues of 'free will' and autonomy of human beings and also the closeness of the subject matter of sociology to the observer; sociologists are part of societies they are studying, which makes it extremely difficult to detach themselves sufficiently from their subject matter. Although it may be impossible to predict exactly how an individual will behave in a particular situation, defenders of sociology as a science argue that certain groups tend to behave in a predictable ways in similar situations. In response to the second criticism that due to their closeness to the subject matter, it is difficult to prevent bias from affecting their perceptions, it can be argued that sociologists can be objective by separating themselves from the subject, by repeating studies using multiple observers, and by making cross-cultural and historical comparisons.

To conclude this futile debate about the nature of sociology as a science, it can be said that sociology in all respects is a scientific discipline like all other sciences because it uses scientific method to arrive at the generalisation. All allegations levelled against its scientific nature do not hold true in the broader framework of science. The goals of all sciences, including sociology, is the formulation of scientific laws or principles. "But it cannot be modelled directly on the natural sciences, because studying human behaviour is in fundamental ways different from studying the world of nature" (Giddens, 1997). Now, there has been diminishing controversy about whether sociology be called a science or not.

Chapter 3

The Sociological Perspective

Key features

Perspective simply means the way how we look at the things. Every person has got his own angle to see or view things. Broadly, every man sees the world differently. This difference in the point of view is called 'perspective' in the scientific parlance. A point of view is a position from which reality is observed and interpreted. To better illustrate the meaning of the word 'perspective', we take an example of a very old legend from Jain religious books:

Six blind men were asked what is an elephant? Every blind man described the elephant differently depending on whether they felt its trunk, ear, tail, body or leg. Each person gave his own interpretation of the elephant.

This legend is an analogy to the way each of us sees the world. Our different interests and occupations limit our interpretation of events and activities. Many more such examples can be given to explain the meaning of perspective. A school building may be viewed as a place of work by a teacher, as a place of study by a student, as a particular structural design by an architect or a builder, as a tax liability by the building owner, as a fire hazard by a fire brigade and so on. This example also shows how a particular thing or a phenomenon can be viewed from different angles. *Thus, perspective defines the boundary, periphery and the subject matter of a subject of study.*

What is Sociological Perspective?

"The perspective of sociology involves seeing through the outside appearances of people's actions and organisations" (Peter Berger, *Invitation to Sociology*, 1963). It is the way of looking at the society and the social behaviour—the subject matter of sociology. It goes beyond identifying patterns of social behaviour. It also attempts to provide explanations for such patterns. Thus, the broad societal forces become a central consideration of sociology. Sociologists are not interested in individual personalities, such as Mahatma Gandhi, Martin Luther King, Nelson Mandela or Ravi Shanker, rather they try to identify the shared traits and behaviour and the underlying patterns in those traits and behaviour of millions of human beings. One major goal of sociological perspective is to identify and interpret patterns underlying the recurrent regular aspects of social life and also to investigate the influences on social behaviour.

Now, we will attempt to highlight the main focus of sociological perspective in brief as under:

1. *Sociology is a scientific endeavour with a strong humanistic bent.* The old notion that whether sociology is scientific or humanistic has been replaced by the modern view that it is scientific and humanistic both. As a scientific discipline, it aims at value-free and objective causal analysis of social phenomena. It tries to generate general laws and make predictions. Humanistic perspective, on the other hand, tries to emphasise on *Verstehen* (understanding) through reflexivity the humanistic ethos and cultural creativity of all forms of social existence rather than on

predictions. Such an image of sociology comes close to what Peter Berger (1963) calls "sociology as a form of consciousness".

2. *Sociology views society or social relations as structured, constituting a reality that transcends individuals.* Like psychology, sociology is not interested in behaviour of an individual (suicide by a single person) but in the patterns of behaviour (suicide patterns) or the behaviour of group of persons. Sociology is concerned with how the structure of society is created, maintained and changed.
3. *Sociology tries to investigate the processes through which society shapes the individual and in turn individuals create the structure of society.* In the words of Giddings, "it investigates the connections between what society makes of us and what we make of ourselves".
4. *Sociology studies social phenomena from holistic and relational points of view both.* This perspective enables sociologists to identify underlying recurrent patterns of and influences on social behaviour.
5. *Sociology studies human behaviour in group context.* For a sociologist, a man/woman and his/her particular act or activity is not important but his/her status and role in which the activity is performed is important.
6. *Sociological perspective is neither utopian* (what is desirable), *nor fatalistic* (inevitability of existing state of affairs), *but scientific* (what it is, how it is and why it is). But at times, it sometimes goes beyond the questions of what, how, why and where and assumes the role of an applied science. Thus, sociological perspective is neutralistic (pure scientific) and interventionistic (applied or social engineering) both. Early sociologists were positivists, emphasised its neutralistic character, but modern sociologists (humanists) argue that sociologists should adopt the role of an interventionist (wherever is necessary) along with his traditional role of a scientist. In the interventionist conception of sociology, the discipline is treated as a problem solving craft. Recently, this approach was much emphasised by Alain Touraine (*The Return of the Actor*, 1988).

7. *Sociological perspective involves the investigation of the problem on micro and macro levels both.* At micro level, sociology studies how individuals behave in social situations—at work, at play, at home, or in school, or in small and large groups. It deals with people's everyday interactions (social interactionist, ethnomethodological and phenomenological approaches of study). At macro level, sociology focuses on patterns of behaviour and forms of organisation that characterise entire societies (classical and grand theorists approaches). At this level, sociology deals with large-scale structures (such as bureaucracy), broad social categories, institutions, social systems, and social problems such as war, unemployment, poverty, corruption, and solutions to these problems are sought at the structural or organisational level. In their studies, sociologists utilise both approaches of study, i.e., qualitative (introspective-participant method) and quantitative (statistical, interview and survey techniques).

Major Perspectives in Sociology (Methodological View)

Sociologists are by no means in total accord regarding the objectives, the mode of analysis or even all the basic assumptions of their discipline. As stated above, a fundamental question is sometimes asked as to whether it is scientific or humanistic discipline. There are sociologists who consider it to be both. They say that sociology is and must be a scientific endeavour with a strong humanistic bent. For them, the two worlds of science and humanities are not mutually exclusive. Yet there is a difference between these two major perspectives in sociology. We shall deal these differences in brief in the following paragraphs:

Empiricist or scientific perspective

Sociology seeks to apply to the study of man and society the methods of science. It rests upon the assumption common to all the social sciences that the scientific method can make a significant contribution to our understanding of human behaviour. The objectives of science is the gaining of empirically verified knowledge. The empiricists or the positivists, as they are sometimes called, believe that there is no difference in the methods used to study physical or natural world and those used to study social world. Sociologists of this tradition emphasise that sociology is a "pure" science, i.e., the pursuit of knowledge in a value-free scientific manner. For them, "knowledge for knowledge sake" should be the main goal of sociology. The objective of science is the gaining of empirical knowledge about the world without regard for the possible uses of such knowledge.

Many of the founding fathers, including Auguste Comte (1798-1857), argued that it would be possible to establish a 'positive science of society' on the same principles and procedures (methodology) as the natural sciences such as physics, chemistry and biology. Comte stated that the purpose of sociology is "to understand, in order to predict, in order to control society". Positivist sociology is largely based on this assumption that behaviour in the social and natural worlds is governed by the same principles of cause and effect, then natural science methodology (observation and experimentation) is appropriate for the human society also. It argues that both man and matter are part of the natural universe and the behaviour is governed by natural laws. Sociology's main aim is also to establish universal social laws. Just as matter reacts to external stimuli, so man reacts to forces external to his being. Social and natural behaviour is therefore determined and can be explained in terms of cause and effect relationship. The same procedures are possible in the observation of human behaviour as used in natural sciences. Just as natural science involves the construction of theories based on observable data, so sociology can also develop theories based on direct observation of human behaviour. Thus, natural science methodology is applicable to the study of man and human society.

The main adherents of this tradition were Emile Durkheim, Lundberg, Talcott Parsons, K. Davis, R.K. Merton and Paul Lazarsfeld. Contemporary sociologists are more cautious about claims for the scientific status of their discipline. Indeed many reject the view that natural science methodology is appropriate for the study of human behaviour; for instance, C.W. Mills (*The Sociological Imagination*,

1959) wrote: "Some sociologists become so committed to being scientific that they loss sight of the practical value of sociology. The major defect of empiricist is that they do not accept the fundamental difference between natural and social data that affect the way in which the broader principles are applied."

Humanistic perspective

Sociologists, who believe in humanistic perspective, are interested in and concerned about human welfare, values and conduct. They want to improve the lot of man. An ultimate goal for the humanist is self-realisation and full development of the cultivated man. The main advocates of this school of thought are C.W. Mills, Alfred McClung Lee, Peter Berger, Robert Nisbet and so many modern sociologists.

Humanists hold that human social world is different from the natural world. As a result, the methods and assumptions of the natural sciences are inappropriate to the study of man and society. The natural sciences deal with matter. It has no meanings, feelings and purposes which affects its behaviour. Matter simply reacts 'unconsciously' to external stimuli. But quite different from matter, man has consciousness—thoughts, feelings, meanings, intentions and an awareness of being. His actions are, therefore, meaningful. As a result, he does not merely react to external stimuli like physical matter but he acts. He attaches a range of meanings to it and these meanings direct his actions. He actively constructs his own reality. Meanings do not have an independent existence—a reality of their own, which is somehow separate from social actors. It follows that sociologists must discover those meanings in order to understand social actions. This approach is quite different from the positivists who believe that facts like meanings, feelings and purposes are not directly observable, as such they are not much important in the study of man. But, this claim of the positivists, when applied to human behaviour, is not tenable. This can obscure the real cause or intention of their behaviour. To treat social reality as anything other than a construction of meanings is to distort it. It is constructed and reconstructed by actors in the course of social interaction.

Humanist sociology is a philosophical orientation and sense of responsibility for the welfare of mankind as well as an academic school of thought. The proponents of this perspective tend to emphasise an existential view of society. They believe that society and institutions should be analysed in terms of the shared realities and actions of individuals as they understand them. Existentialists believe man as an individual rather than a group animal. Thus, where Durkheim believed that individual cannot, without contradicting his very nature, liberate himself from the limits imposed upon him by his participation in the social world, the existentialist argues that man cannot be 'authentic' if he says, "I am as you want me".

This newly developed perspective in sociology has altered the oft-repeated very important question of Prof. R. Lynd from "knowledge for what?" to "knowledge for whom?" This thought demands that the benefits of social scientific research and study should not be limited to a particular class of people but these are to be used for the welfare of humanity as a whole, specially for the downtrodden, exploited, oppressed and deprived class. This perspective encourages such enquires, which help in bringing changes in social life so that human dignity, freedom, creativity and on the whole human life can be saved. For the investigation of this type of knowledge, humanistic sociology gives more importance to the methods of historical introspection, intuition, empathy and interpretative understanding. These sociologists do not believe in the differentiation of morality of what is said and what is done. Sociologists of this tradition attempt to provide a social analysis in the service of humanity. They act as critics, demystifiers, reporters and clarifiers.

In contrast to the traditional positivist or scientific perspective of sociology, these days, we find a growing interest in the application of humanist values to the sociological enterprise. John R. Strande (*Humanistic Society: Today's Challenge to Sociology*) has attempted to indicate the various orientations that make up the humanistic approach. These include: *ethnomethodology* (Harold Garfinkel), *phenomenology* (Alfred Schuz), *existential sociology* (Tiryakin), *the sociology of knowledge* (Peter Berger and Luckman), *neo-symbolic interactionism* (Erving Goffman), *the sociology of the absurd* (Scott and Lyman), and *the sociology of everyday life* (Marcello Truzzi). It is not possible here to discuss each of these orientations at length. They have in common an attitude that sociology should study "man in society" or that it should place the interaction between individuals in the centre of social life. This perspective (interactionism of various brands) places emphasis on the interaction of self with others. All the approaches (as mentioned above) committed to humanism in some way or the other are known today as 'Interpretative Sociology' from methodological view.

All these approaches have a common background in the ideas of Max Weber and Alfred Schutz. Weber emphasised that sociology should base its explanations of society in the intuitive understanding of people's actions and motivations (*Verstehen method*), which direct the actions of the actor. Schutz combined Weber's inductive methods with the phenomenology of Edmund Husseral, which emphasises that the social world is a world of meaning. There is no objective reality which lies behind that meaning. To treat this aspect of 'social facts' as things (as Durkheim said), is to distort and misrepresent social reality. The responsibility of sociology, according to Schutz, is to first understand the meaning that individuals give to their experiences and then construct more abstract explanations of those experiences and their meaning in a societal context. For understanding meaning phenomenological perspective emphasises direct observation of everyday activity as against interview, questionnaire and social surveys employed by mainstream sociologists.

Thus, it is clear that positivist and humanistic perspectives employ very different research methodologies because of their diametrically opposed assumptions about the nature of social reality. This leads on the one hand to an acceptance of the logic and methods of the natural sciences as appropriate for the study of man and society and, on the other, to an outright rejection of this research strategy. To many sociologists, an objective science of society remains the goal of sociology. For such sociologists, "*objectivity* means that the conclusions arrived at as the result of inquiry and investigation are independent of the race, colour, creed, occupation, nationality, religion, moral preference and political predispositions of the investigator. If his research is truly objective, it is independent of any subjective elements, any personal desires, that he may have" (Bierstedt, *Social Order*, 1963). The implications of this view are serious. An increasing number of sociologists now argue that the pursuit of an objective, value-free sociology is the pursuit of an illusion. In this connection, Derek Phillips (1971, 1973) words seems worth quoting, "An investigator's values influence not only the problems he selects for study but also his methods for studying them and the sources of data he uses".

Recently (after 1967), one more approach has developed as an offshoot of humanistic sociology, which is popularly known as 'radical sociology'. There is a small group of sociologists, whose number seem to be increasing, who believe that they have a responsibility to work towards a new form of socialism. Intellectually, they are neo-Marxists and prefer to call themselves 'conflict theorists'. They are the most vocal critics of the traditional functional sociology or so-called positivistic sociology. They have a value commitment to provide the intellectual groundwork for a restructuring of the field of sociology to make it more equalitarian and responsible to democratic norms.

Humanistic and scientific combined perspective

Sociology is, on the one hand, a humanitarian discipline and on the other plane it is a positive science. Martindale writes: "Humanism is a system of values describing what ought to be and modes of conduct designed to secure them; science is the value-free pursuit of knowledge, 'of what is', renouncing all concern with what ought to be. Scientist is more interested in 'means'—gaining knowledge; the humanist, in the ends—improving the lot of man." Despite these varying positions, it is reasonable to say that modern sociologists are attempting to direct their energies towards humanistic goals. The disagreement seems to be over the means to attain them. Perhaps, this agreement is a sign of the vitality of this discipline.

Most sociologists operate with a combination of scientific and humanistic viewpoints. Peter Berger (*Invitation to Sociology*, 1963) puts this view when he argues that sociology must be used for humanity's sake: "Social science, like other sciences, can be and sometimes is dehumanising and even inhuman. It should not be. When sociologists pursue their task with insight, sensitivity, empathy, humility and a desire to understand the human condition rather than with a cold and humourless scientism, then indeed, the sociological perspective helps illuminate man's social existence."

Sociology and Other Social Sciences

The perspective of sociology is closely related to the subject of relation of sociology with other social sciences. This relation will indirectly clarify the attitudinal distinction between sociology and other social sciences.

Sociology, in the broadest sense of the term, is usually defined as the science of society or a science which studies social life, or behaviour of human beings. This is a very comprehensive outlook indeed to view society. Sociology deals with social world, of course, but the sociologist is only one among a number of social scientists studying social world. We know that the social world is made up of many aspects—economic, religious, political, familial, educational, and others—all of which can be defined independently of one another, but all of which influence one another in practice. Corresponding to these aspects are various branches of the social sciences, such as psychology, anthropology, economics, political science, history including sociology and many other disciplines. But, the focus of none of these other sciences is identical with that of sociology, and it is always the focus of interest (perspective or point of view), which distinguishes one social science from another. It would not be exaggerating to say that no other discipline focuses attention on human behaviour or on human relationships *per se*. It is here that sociology differs from all other social sciences. Sociology does not study the unique and particular aspects of human relationships; they are to be studied by other social sciences which have a special interest in such phenomena. Sociological approach of studying social relationship is holistic. It studies any social phenomenon in its totality and in relation to other social phenomenon.

Every science is a study of one aspect of reality or the other. All emerge from the common spring of man's eternal quest for knowledge. From this point of view all sciences are related to one another. In spite of this common relationship, sciences differ in their approach of study, in their perspective of looking at things. In this connection, Gillin and Gillin (*Cultural Sociology,* 1948) aptly remarked: "It is true that in each sciences a general class of objects tend to receive more attention than other classes of objects, but it is also true that different sciences may study the same objects but with different points of view". For example, consider man as the object of study. The physicist might be interested in the system of stresses in his skeleton; the chemist in the elements and compounds in his body; the anatomist in the relationship of mussels, bones and organs; the psychologist in his reactions to stimuli; and the sociologist in his behaviour in relation to other human beings.

Social sciences have been defined as the study of the behaviour of people in human society. All social sciences thus share in common the task of exploring the reality of society, i.e., social behaviour of human beings. Each social science (major social sciences are psychology, anthropology, economics, political science and sociology) focuses attention on one particular dimension of social reality. Each social science studies man from their own particular angle. Their approach of study or perspective is different from one another. *Anthropology* modestly designates itself as "the study of man (especially primitive man) and his works". *Psychology* is often defined as "the science of mind or the mental processes". It is primarily concerned with individual human behaviour. It tries to analyse behaviour of a person in terms of its relationship to personality structure. *Economics* studies "the ways by which man makes a living". It concerns with how goods, services and wealth are produced, consumed and distributed within societies. *Political Science* investigates the ways in which people govern themselves. Its main focus of study is power, government and political processes. *History* claims to study the significant past (chronological records of distant past events). It is treated either a social science or one of the humanities. *Sociology* tries systematically and objectively to understand social life and predicts how various influences will affect it. It claims to study those aspects of social life, which are present in all social sciences. It also tries to bring together and extend the knowledge and insights of all the other fellow disciplines. The real basis of differentiation is not of a difference in their concrete subject matter but it is rather a difference in their point of view or focus of attention that creates boundaries between different social sciences. These boundaries are not neat but hazy and overlap each other.

We can illustrate this point of difference of perspectives from the most popular example. Eating a slice of buttered toast can be analysed in terms of the nutritive value of the food consumed, the eating habits of the individuals, the economics of the bread, dairy, and home appliance industries, a conventional or customary dietary pattern. Not only this, the toast can be seen from social relations point of view. It can be a possible source of social friction between husband and wife because the wife does not make the toast dark enough to shift the taste of her husband or because the toast was bit burnt in the course of its preparation.

We may take another familiar example of social pattern of gift-giving. Gift-giving is something that we all engage in, in one way or another, hardly giving a thought to its importance. The interests of sociologists, while analysing the phenomenon of gift-giving, differ markedly from the interests of psychologists, political scientists, economists, historians and anthropologists. Each discipline tends to raise different kinds of questions about human behaviour. For example, the economist might note that gift-giving customs are commercialised in our society. It increases business activity during certain times of the year, for instance, during marriage season in India. A political scientist might undertake studies of the gifts that how individuals give to the campaign chests of political parties. A psychologist might be interested in the attitudes people have about giving and receiving gifts, emphasising different motives for gift-giving. Historians might examine some specific event or notable occasion of gift-giving such as the gifts that ambassadors brought to various monarchs, for example, gifts given by the officers of the East India Company or by Christian missionaries to Muslim rulers in medieval India. A sociologist, on the other hand, would examine rules of giving, accepting and reciprocity of this specific social custom as we find in the classical study by Marcel Mauss (1954). Sociologist would say that one of the important things that perpetuates gift-giving is that it initiates and reinforces friendly and familial feelings and relations. He can also examine the consequences of the rules of reciprocity. This example is sufficient to state that social sciences do not differ in what they study (i.e., society) but rather, in their approach to human behaviour.

Likewise, any social problem can be viewed from different angles. For example, in analysing alcoholism, whereas a physicist will be concerned with its effects on its body, a psychiatrist will be concerned with its effects on attitudes and behaviour, an economist will see its effects on state revenue, a sociologist will be concerned with its effects on social relations and roles and with neighbours and friends as well as its effects on work, efficiency, status and so on. As far as the sociologist's perspective is concerned, he views social problems as problems which arise out of the functioning of systems and structures in society or which are the result of group influences. He is concerned with social relationships which emerge and are sustained because of social problems. Thus, the above discussion about the perspective of sociology clearly highlights that whereas other disciplines dealing with society and human behaviour are usually one-dimensional, sociology can reasonably claim to be multi-dimensional.

Chapter 4

Basic Sociological Concepts

Key features

All sciences have their technical terminologies, their own sets of concepts and professional words. Such terminologies are indispensable, for they reduce the vagueness, the ambiguity and the confusion. Without a technical language, scientific communication becomes cumbersome and inefficient. Sociologists, like other scientists, have technical vocabulary. Most of the sociological vocabulary is taken from ordinary English words and has given them a technical meaning. 'Culture', for example, does not mean refinement in artistic or literary taste or good manner, when it is used in sociology or anthropology. Each term is a technical term and has a set of connotations different than its everyday usage. Sociological concepts are different from the ideas of commonsense.

In everyday conversation we use such words as 'society', 'community', 'institution', 'culture', 'custom' and the like. These words or concepts are also basic to an understanding of sociology. Stuart Chase (1941) termed them as 'big words'. As such, it is important at the outset that these 'big words' of sociology be clarified and rendered precise. Definitions are elusive because these words as said above are part of everyday speech and this creates confusion in the minds of social scientists.

It must be admitted that, at the present time, the technical vocabulary of sociology is not fully 'settled' or so finely established as the technical vocabularies of some of the natural sciences. Sociologists themselves do not always use the same words in the same technical senses. Within sociology one may come across several usages and numerous definitions of a single term. Sociologists are often criticised for the use of jargon and giving new and often strange meanings to old and familiar terms. This makes the position of the subject somewhat ridiculous in the eyes of layman and even the scientists of other disciplines.

Concepts of sociology are numerous but here we shall deal only the following basic concepts in brief:

(a) Society
(b) Community
(c) Association
(d) Institution
(e) Social Structure
(f) Culture

Society

Wallerstein, in his *World Systems Analysis* (1974) writes: "No concept is more pervasive in modern social science than society, and no concept is used more automatically and unreflectively than society, despite the countless pages devoted to its definition." In popular speech the word 'society' has several meanings. Scores of definitions of the word 'society' exist and the word has a range of meanings extending far beyond sociology, including history, economics and political science. In everyday life this term is used for various kinds of social units or social aggregates as if it exists 'out there' and beyond the individual subject such as Indian Society, French Society, American Society, Capitalist Society, etc. At many times, we associate this term for secondary associations—Indian Sociological Society, The Theosophical Society, Society for the Prevention of Cruelty to Animals or to Children. Likewise, in everyday speech, there is probably little distinction being made between society and nation, whereas in sociology such distinction would be significant. Not only this, the word 'society' is interchangeably used for the community also. Such a usage has its problems. Because of these problems Wallerstein argued that the concept of 'society' should be dropped from social analysis. Some symbolic interactionists say that there is no such thing as society. It is a useful covering term for things we do not know about or understand properly. Others, such as Emile Durkheim, treat society as a reality in its own right.

How sociologists view society?

As against its commonsense usage, sociologists use this term in a specific sense and in a precise way. In social sciences since nineteenth century there is a long debate about the use of the concept 'society'. It was taken to mean as tissues of manners and customs that hold a group of people together. In some sense, 'society' represented something more enduring and deeper than the 'state', less manipulative and certainly more elusive.

Sociologists have defined society with two angles:

1. In *abstract terms,* as a network of relationships between people or between groups.
2. In *concrete terms,* as a collection of people or an organisation of persons.

An earlier social scientist, L.T. Hobhouse (1908) defined society as "tissues of relationships". R.M. MacIver (1937) also defined it in more or less the same terms as "web of social relations which is always changing". Refining this definition, MacIver, along with his co-writer Charles Page, later on defined it in his new book *Society: An Introductory Analysis* (1949) thus: "It (society) is a system of usages and procedures, of authority and mutual aid, of many groupings and divisions, of controls of human behaviour and of liberties. This ever changing, complex system we call society." For MacIver and Page, society is an abstract entity as they write, "we may see the people but cannot see society or social structure but only its external aspects ... society is distinct from physical reality".

Talcott Parsons (*Encyclopaedia of the Social Sciences*, 1934) wrote: "Society—may be regarded as the most general term referring to the whole complex of relations of man to his fellows."

Characteristics

1. *Society is abstract:* If society is viewed as web of social relationships, it is distinct from physical entity which we can see and perceive through senses. As written earlier, MacIver argued, "we may see the people but cannot see society or social structure, but only its only external aspects". Social relationships are invisible and abstract. We can just realise them but cannot see or touch them. Therefore, society is abstract. Reuter wrote: "Just as life is not a thing but a process of living, so society is not a thing but a process of associating".
2. *Likeness and difference in society:* Society involves both likeness and difference. If people are all exactly alike, merely alike, their relationships would be limited. There would be little give-and-take and little reciprocity. If all men thought alike, felt alike, and acted alike, if they had the same standards and same interests, if they all accepted the same customs and echoed the same opinions without questioning and without variation, civilisation could never have advanced and culture would have remained rudimentary. Thus, society needs difference also for its existence and continuance. We can illustrate this point through the most familiar example of family. The family rests upon the biological differences between the sexes. There are natural differences of aptitude, of capacity, of interest. For they all involve relationships in which differences complement one another, in which exchange take place.

Likeness and difference are logical opposites but for understanding likeness, comprehension of its relation to the other is necessary. Society exists among those who have some degree of likeness in mind and in body. F.H. Giddings called this quality of society as "consciousness of kind" (a sense of likeness). Though likeness and difference both are necessary for the society to exist, but difference is always subordinated to likeness in society. Likeness has a predominant share in the constitution of society.

3. *Cooperation and conflict in society*: Cooperation and conflict are universal elements in human life. Society is based on cooperation but because of internal differences, there is conflict also among its members. This is why, MacIver and Page observed that "society is cooperation crossed by conflict". We know from our own experience that a person would be handicapped, showed down, and feels frustrated if he is expected to do everything alone, without the aid of others. "Cooperation is most elementary process of social life without which society is impossible" (Gisbert, 1957). Though cooperation is essential for the constitution of society but modern conflict theorists (such as Marx) have highlighted the role of conflict in society. If there is no conflict, even in small measure, society may become stagnant and people may become inert and inactive. However, the expression of disagreement in the form of conflict must always be held within tolerable bounds.
4. *Society is a process and not a product*: "Society exists only as a time sequence. It is becoming, not a being; a process and not a product" (MacIver and Page, 1956). In other words, as soon as the process ceases, the product disappears. The product of a machine endures after the machine has been scrapped. To some extent the same is true not only of material relics of man's past culture but even of his immaterial cultural achievements.
5. *Society as a system of stratification*: Society provides a system of stratification of statuses and classes that each individual has a relatively stable and recognisable position in the social structure.

Society in concrete terms: "a society"

When society is viewed from the point of view of persons who constitute it, it takes the shape of 'a society' instead of 'society' in general terms. A society is the largest number of human beings who interact to satisfy their social needs and who share a common culture. "A society may be defined as a network of interconnected major groups viewed as a unit and sharing a common culture" (J.H. Ficther, *Sociology*, 1957). A similar definition of society is offered by Ian Robertson (*Sociology*, 1977): "A society is a group of interacting individuals sharing the same territory and participating in a culture." This definition of 'a society' is quite rearer to the definition of 'community' explained in the following pages. Thus, a society is different from society in general; 'a society' is any organisation that enables people to carry on a common life. It is concrete, having physical reality and is an aggregate of persons while society is abstract and is something more than an aggregate of individuals and the sum of individuals. It refers to the whole constellation of associations that characterise a people. When we talk about Indian society, French society, or American society, we generally have the idea of 'a society' in our mind.

Defining society Mike O'Donnell (1997) writes: "A society consists of individuals belonging to groups which may vary in size." Anthony Giddens (2000) states: "A society is a group of people who live in a particular territory, are subject to a common system of political authority, and are aware of having a distinct identity from other groups around them." This definition is a mixture of characteristics of a community and a nation-state. From this view, some societies, like those of hunters and gatherers are very small, others are very large involving millions of people such as modern Indian society.

Community

Like the concept of society, the concept of community is ill-defined and loosely used in social sciences. It is a term having numerous meanings both sociological and non-sociological. It is used in an omnibus way to refer to a wide variety of specific social units. In common parlance, the word 'community' is used for a collection of people who do related kinds of work, such as the "teachers community" or the "doctors community". It is also used to denote a collection of people who share something in common as the "Hindu community", the "Parsi community", or the "Christian community" without necessarily living in a particular area. Sometimes, it is used to describe a supposedly coherent group, such as 'international community'. Such loose use of the word 'community' is always misleading and indicate just to amorphous mass.

The term has been used in the sociological literature to refer directly to types of population settlements, such as rural community or urban community, to supposedly ideal-typical ways of life in such places; and to social networks whose members share common characteristics apart from or in addition to common location. It has also been used to focus primarily cultural differences as traditional communities and modern communities. A nineteenth century sociologist, F. Tonnies, who has been described as the founder of the theory of community, defined 'community' in his book *Geminschaft and Gesallschaft* (*Community and Society*) "as an organic, 'natural' kind of social collectivity whose members are bound together by a sense of belonging, created out of everyday contacts covering the whole range of human activities". Tonnies contrasted this type of collectivity with another, called an *association*, which is consciously organised for specific purposes and whose members are bound together by common regulations or interests. In nineteenth century thought this form of social association was characterised by a high degree of personal intimacy, emotional depth, moral commitment, social cohesion, and continuity in time. It was feared that these were precisely the features which were disappearing in the transition from a rural-based to urban industrial society.

Definitions

There have been many attempts to define the concept community. These have taken two distinct directions—the 'organic' conception and the 'ecological' conception of community. Scholars (such as F. Tonnies and Max Weber), who have persued the organic conception, placed emphasis primarily on belongingness, close personal contacts and identity of interests as the chief characteristics of community, while the followers of second conception, i.e., ecological, have highlighted its geographical or territorial character. For them, it is a collectivity the members of which share a common territorial base of operations for daily activities. As R.E. Park (1921) writes: "Community, in the broadest sense of the term, has a spatial and a geographical connotation." This geographical conception of community involves the idea of a definite and permanent occupation of a given territory. But community is not a mere geographical expression. The relations among the people resident within an area must be such as to constitute those people a community. There must be some degree of mutuality, organisation and consensus, some interaction and communication.

By 'community', Weber meant that members "known each other" and have a degree of common consciousness and identity and exclude those unlike themselves. MacIver and Page write (1949): "Wherever the members of any group—small or large—live together in such a way that they share, not this or that particular interest, but the basic conditions of life, we call that group a community." At other place, they have defined it as "a strongly knit group occupying a single geographical area and living a common life".

Sociologically, the idea of community often includes some commitment, identity and a feeling of common living and shared fate. Thus, close-knit neighbourhood or religious groups are communities. In this sense, Weber regarded status groups, like Indian castes, as communities. But MacIver and Page here differed with Weber who have not regarded castes as communities. They have stated, "a social caste has social coherence but it lacks the community's territorial basis". Many sociologists (past and present) have attached much importance to the territorial character of the community as we see in the following definitions.

According to Bogardus (*Sociology*, 1952), "a community is a social group with some degree of *we-feeling* and living in a given area". Similarly, Eshleman and Cashion (*Sociology*, 1983) defined it as "a collection of people within a geographic area among whom there is some degree of mutual identification, interdependence or organisation of activities". For Dotson (1991), "a community is a spatial or territorial unit of social organisation in which people have a sense of identity and a feeling of belonging".

A recent textbook of sociology (Mike O'Donnel, 1997) has analysed the various definitions of community and grouped them in three main categories:

1. The term 'community' is employed to describe *a fixed locality* (a given geographic area) as a basis of social organisation. Thus, from this point of view, a traditional rural village is a community where people are born, live and die.
2. Community is used to refer to a local *social system* or set of relationships that centre upon a given locality. From sociological point of view, it is the concentration of relationships, rather than the geographical factor that matters.
3. The term 'community' is also used to describe a *quality of relationship* which produces a strong sense of shared identity. This usage does not give any importance to the spatial or geographical aspect of the community. It does not depend on physical whereabouts or even on people having met each other.

For the last few years, this third sense of community is gaining ground and has been widely used. The old territorial character of the community (closed boundary) has relatively little to do and more or less given up in favour of quality of relationships (a sense of belonging and shared identity). As such, hamlets, towns, cities and under modern conditions, the whole world with all its differences of race, of culture, and of interests are communities. Not only this, youth sub-cultures, especially the hippies, or adherents of Osho's thought are thought of as lifestyle communities. The commune movement (Kibbutzim) attempted to give territorial reality to 'search for community'.

Summarising the ideas of different writers, the characteristics of community may be stated as under:

(1) A grouping of people.

(2) A delimited geographical area or locality (not much applicable to modern communities).

(3) A common culture and a social system which organises their activities.

(4) Consciousness among the members about their unity and a sense of belongingness (we-feeling).

(5) Act collectively in an organised manner.

(6) A division of labour into specialised and interdependent functions.

Bases

MacIver and Page (1949) have listed two important bases of community:

(1) *Locality*: A community always occupies a territorial area. Almost all sociologists (e.g., A. Green, K. Davis, Lundberg, Bogardus etc.) have mentioned it as a basic condition in their definitions of community. The strong bond of solidarity that we find in the members of a community is derived from the conditions of locality—living in a definite geographical area. This bond is weakening today due to the development of modern means of communications. But, the extension of communication has in some other way helped in territorial bond. Now, the territorial area of the modern communities is expanding far and wide. Common place of residence does not automatically yield a community. "A community of like-minded men" and "the world-wide community of scholars" are such expressions which deny sharing a specific and delimited area of residence.

(2) *Community sentiment:* Locality, though a necessary condition, is not enough to create a community. There must be the common living with its awareness of sharing a common way of life. Local areas, which lack the social coherence, cannot be termed as community. Such areas lack 'community sentiment', an utmost necessary condition for the existence of a community. Community sentiment involves sufficient contacts and common

interests to instil conscious identification with the area along with 'we-feeling', i.e., a feeling of belonging together. It is a sense of what they have in common—memories, traditions, customs and institutions.

According to Alex Inkeles (*What is Sociology*, 1965), the following three elements are relevant as a basis of a community. A community exists (1) when a set of households is relatively concentrated in delimited geographical area; (2) their residents exhibit a substantial degree of integrated social interaction; and (3) they have a sense of common membership, of belonging together, which is not based exclusively on ties of consanguinity.

Thus, the *essence* of community is a sense of common bond, the sharing of an identity, membership in a group, holding some things physical or spiritual, in common esteem, coupled with the acknowledgement of rights and obligations with reference to all others so identified (Alex Inkeles). The natural small community of permanent residents such as a village, a town, or a neighbourhood combines all these elements. F. Tonnies (1887), L. Wirth (1938) and many other sociologists contend that as community grows in size, the nature of relationships between its members changes accordingly. Wirth noted that the size of the community prevents residents from getting to know most of the people in the community. It also facilitates spatial (or physical) separation, based on race, ethnicity, social class and lifestyles. *Physical proximity, though an important element of community, does not itself make a community*. Direct face-to-face interaction can be replaced to some degree by symbolic interaction fostered by the media of communication.

Communities may be large as much as a vast nation or they may be very small like a primitive tribe, a horde, a nomadic group, or neighbourhood. A village, a town or a metropolis are other examples of a community. Community exists within greater communities—the town within a state, the state within a nation and the nation within the world community. There are certain human groupings for which there is no clear-cut answer about their community character. Such groups may be termed as borderline cases such as a monastery, a convent, an immigrant group or a prison. MacIver and Page have accepted these groups as a community.

Changing concept of community

The stable, solidary and intimate primary group type of 'perfect community' is fast disappearing as a result of industrialisation, urbanisation, modern means of communication and information technology. The local unit is increasingly absorbed into the larger economic and political society. Individuals no longer live wholly or even largely within the primary group but are oriented with reference to the larger social world outside. Individual interests, transcending the locality, are integrated on a national or international level. As contacts have become more varied and extensive, they have also become more formal and external. The person is fractionalised, participating in each of his several or many groupings with only a limited aspect of his total self. As a concrete, total personality, he is commanded by no one group, not even by his family. *Intimacy has given way to acquaintanceship or to anonymity* on the basis of above ideas, some sociologists have put forth a thesis known as "loss of community".

Old characteristics of community, i.e., locality and community sentiment or 'we-feeling' are being eroded by the forces of modernity. These forces have fractured the myth of 'homogeneous community'. The 'Muslim community', the 'Hindu community', the 'Black community' or the 'women's community' are now fractured into feminists versus conservatives or liberals versus conservatives or various other strands (leftist versus rightest) of opinions. At many times, it is seen that women do not necessarily side with women just because they are women or belong to women community. In the end, we may conclude that the concept of community has become uncommonly elastic when we hear about the newly developed concepts like 'global village' or 'global community. Thus, this concept is now no more limited to a single or limited geographical area.

Association

The most characteristic feature of modern complex societies is the associations, which are organised to promote specific interests. We become members by virtue of particular attributes or qualifications corresponding to the particular purposes for which it is organised. We profess a faith or cultivate an art or pursue some kind of knowledge or run some kind of business or have an interest in social service of any kind and in so doing find it desirable or advantageous to join with others. Practically, all associations arise in this way. College or trade unions, schools, social and sports clubs, political parties, professional societies, business firms, religious organisations and NGOs are some of the examples of such associations.

There are three ways in which men may pursue their ends or interests: (1) *Independently,* each following his own way without thought of his fellows and their actions. But this is an unsocial way wherever one live together. Moreover, some interests cannot be achieved independently. (2) They may seek them through *conflict* with one another. But this is opposed to the very existence of society. (3) They may pursue their ends in company, on some cooperative basis, so that each is in some degree and manner contributing to the ends of his fellows. This last method, *cooperative pursuit,* may be spontaneous, such as offering a helping hand to a stranger or an old man/woman in fulfilling their some need. It may be casual or by way of some custom of a community, or in an organised way by forming an organisation. When individuals come together for realising some specific end(s), they are said to have formed an association. Associations develop as means or modes of our common interests. MacIver and Page write: "An association is likely to be formed wherever people recognise a like, complementary, or common interests sufficiently enduring and sufficiently distinct to be capable of more effective promotion through collective action." Like interests are individualised whereas common interests are necessarily shared.

Definitions

"An organisation deliberately formed for the collective pursuit of some interest which the members of it share is termed as an association" (Eubank, 1932). It is an organised group of persons pursuing a common purpose through some cooperative action. Defining an association, MacIver and Page (1953) stated: "An association is a group organised for the pursuit of an interest or group of interests in common." In reality, associations are agencies whose major task is to promote awareness and solidarity among members of a collectivity to achieve some goal.

Characteristics

Associations are groups in which membership is in no sense obligatory, generally it is *voluntary*. So these units are often called 'voluntary associations'. They may be *closely or loosely structured* with formal role systems, offices, operating rules, procedures and goals. Business corporations are normally closely structured while religious organisations are generally loosely structured. At many times they have a *constitution*—methods of procedure, rules and regulations for running the organisation and *formal organisation*—division of labour but may and may not have paid officials. The life of members of an association is an organised kind of life. Associations do not spring up spontaneously like community but are *consciously and deliberately formed* to fulfil certain purpose or purposes. As soon as the purpose is achieved, they may be dismantled. As such associations have *temporary character*.

Association and community

From the above discussion, it is clear that an association is not a community, but an organisation, a group within a community. An association is deliberately created to pursue some specific interests whereas in community all types of interests are taken into consideration. We belong to associations only by virtue of some specific interests that we have. For example, we belong to a cricket club for purpose of physical recreation or game. Thus, an individual may belong to many associations for pursuing his different interests. Associations normally do not have that type of 'we-feeling' as we find in community. The membership of an association is voluntary while community's membership is almost decided by birth and not by choice. One's whole life is lived within one or the other community. An association is run on the basis of certain written rules and regulations (laws) whereas the community is generally guided by customs and traditions. There are certain social organisations which lie on the borderline between associations and communities such as the family and the state.

Association and institution

Often, in general parlance, association and institution are confused with each other and used interchangebly as synonymous concepts but scientifically such uses are not correct. Associations refer to the group—the interaction system—while institutions constitute the formalised and regularised procedures through which the group interacts and functions. An institution is basically a set of norms and ideas, together with the necessary rules and procedures, while an association is basically a group of people who have organised to pursue a particular activity or objective. Associations are deliberately formed groups such as political parties and trade unions, while institutions are system of norms, such as education or religion. When we consider something as an organised group, it is an association, but when we consider it as a form of procedure or a system of behaviour, it is an institution. Association denotes membership, whereas institution denotes a mode or means of service. This is why, MacIver and Page observed, "we belong to associations but not to institutions." How can we belong to institutions which constitute rules, regulations or procedures of working, but we do belong to associations which are groups of people like families, clubs, unions etc. Institutions are an abstraction, while associations have the concrete form in the shape of groups.

While institution and association are separate concepts, they are not entirely detached from each other. If we create associations, we have to create rules and procedures also to run those associations. These rules and procedures are distinctively institution. Family though an association but to regularise mating relationship, it has marriage as an institution. Some associations are attached to an institution, helping it to pursue one or a few of its purposes. An institution is a set of relationships and a system of behaviour and this requires people and these people organised themselves into groups, forming associations. Thus, each institution has many satellite associations, which carry out institutional behaviour. Thus, institutions and associations are very much interrelated yet the concepts are distinct. For instance, a college is an institution and association both. As an institution of learning, it comprises of the admission procedure, registration, lecture system, examination etc. But, when we look at the college from the point of view of organised group of teachers, or students or clerical staff, it represents different associations. As the institution of education, it guides and organises the total associational activity and gives to these extremely complex groups (teachers, students and staff) an order and symmetry, which makes their goals and functions possible. Similarly, a hospital can be viewed from both the angles. When we speak of a hospital established to meet certain needs or to guide the interaction between persons, it becomes an institution, but when we think of it as a body of doctors, nurses, compounders and other attendants, it becomes an association.

Institution

When associations are formed, they evolve certain rules, regulations and laws and also certain ways of behaviour, which keep them together. Associations viewed in this way are called institutions. "Institutions are the ways in which the value patterns of the common culture of a social system are integrated in the concrete action of its units in their interaction with each other through the definition of role expectations and the organisation of motivation" (Parsons and Smelser, 1956). Social institutions are generally patterns of norms that define behaviour in social relationship. They define how people ought to behave and legitimate the sanctions applied to behaviour. They define the broad rather than the detailed conditions of balancing of performances and sanctions. They set limits within which sanctions are permitted to operate. According to H.E. Barnes (1938), "social institutions are the machinery through which society organises, directs and executes the multifarious activities required to satisfy human needs".

Definitions

The term 'institution' is sometimes used to refer to organisations or associations and sometimes to designate a normal principle that defines clusters of important behaviour, such as marriage or property. Organisations and institutions are not the same thing as discussed above. An organisation is a group formed to meet a specific goal, e.g., a college or a hospital. An institution, however, in not an actual group or association. It is a system of beliefs, norms, values, positions, and activities that develop around a basic societal need. The concept institution is abstract and is used to refer to a fundamental form of social organisation that meets a broad social goal.

Long back, W.G. Sumner (*Folkways*, 1906) defined it as: "An institution consists of a concept (idea, notion, doctrine, and interest) and a structure (a framework or apparatus)." According to Horton and Hunt (*Sociology*, 1964), "an institution is an organised system of social relationships which embodies certain common values and procedures and meets certain basic needs of the society". In this definition, 'common values' refer to shared ideas and goals, the 'common procedures' are the standardised behaviour patterns the group follow, and the 'system of relationship' is the network of roles and statuses through which this behaviour is carried out. One of the most inclusive and descriptive definitions is that of Joyce O. Hertzler (*Social Institutions*, 1946), which is as follows: "Social institution are purposive, regulatory, and consequently primary cultural configurations, formed unconsciously and/or deliberately, to satisfy individual wants and social needs bound up with the efficient operation of any plurality of persons. They consist of codes, rules and ideologies . . . . and essential symbolic organisational and material implementations." In this definition, Hertzler has explained the purpose, function, mechanism and structure—all the four important elements of an institution.

Emphasising social control as the main function of social institution, Talcott Parsons observes (*Essays in Sociological Theory*, 1954): "Institutions are normative patterns which define what are felt to be, in the given society, proper, legitimate, or expected modes of action or of social relationships".

Thus, almost all above definitions of institutions imply both a set of behaviour norms and a system of social relations through which these norms are practised.

Types

According to W.G. Sumner (*Folkways*, 1906), institutions are of two types: (1) *Crescive:* Institutions that take shape in the mores are known as crescive institutions. Property, marriage, religion are all crescive institutions. (2) *Enacted:* Institutions that are productions of rational invention and intention such as schools, colleges, corporations, banks etc. Every major social institution is the product of a long period of trial and error, none was developed in a rational way. It is the product of social process. In its developed form, an institution has a definite structure (machinery) that grows up to control the practices and administer the rules.

E.W. Burgess has offered four-fold classification:

1. *Cultural institutions* for transmitting social heritage like family, school, church (religious institutions).
2. *Economic institutions* for organising of services of utility like bank, labour union, commercial and industrial enterprises.
3. *Recreational institutions* for satisfying human desire of entertainment, amusement and play etc.
4. *Social control institutions* for solving social problems of society and personality.

Functions

Institutions develop out of certain human needs or interests. It is an organised way of doing something. They are the standardised solutions to collective problems. Every institution performs some functions—manifest and latent both. Manifest functions are those which are easy to recognise as part of the institution and latent functions which are unintended and may be unrecognised or if recognised, regarded as by-product (Merton, 1957). Manifest functions are of two types: (1) the pursuit of its objectives, and (2) the preservation of its own internal cohesion so that it may survive. The manifest function of mass public education is to enable all to share the knowledge and skills. Some of the latent functions of this activity would be weakening of the control of parents, altering the class system and keeping the youth off the labour market till he finishes the education.

The most fundamental function of institutions, according to Talcott Parsons, is to regulate social relations (social control). There are two main aspects of these regulations: (1) the maintenance of relative conformity with the normative requirements of the value pattern; and (2) the maintenance of relative consistency of the system of institutionalised patterns themselves, both in terms of generality of application and in terms of the different 'fields' or ranges of application. In both these senses institutions contribute to, indeed constitute, the primary focus of the integration of any social systems.

Institutions form the foundation of society and supply the basic prerequisites of group life: the reproduction and the socialisation of children (family); the affirmation of values and an approach to non-empirical questions (religion), the transmission of cultural heritage, knowledge, and skills from one generation to the next (education); the production and distribution of goods and services (economy); and social leadership and the protection of individuals from one another and from forces outside the society (politics). Besides these there are also many other important institutions, which perform various functions needed for the maintenance of society.

Social Structure

The concept of 'social structure' is widely used but is also most elusive concept in the social sciences. There is little agreement on a precise definition and general meaning of this concept. It can be conceived of in a variety of ways. However, the enduring, orderly and patterned relationships between elements (groups, institutions etc.) of a society are usually described as social structure. It directs attention to their internal configurations (such as the status and role relations), to the interrelations of component parts to a designated whole and external relations (such as whether in horizontal or vertical order, degree of interconnectedness and stability).

What is structure ?

In simple terms, the formal arrangement or ordering of elements, parts, events or facts is known as structure. It is the way in which the things we are analysing are put together, or the relationship of its parts to one another. A botanist will describe the structure of a leaf the way it is put together. A chemist is concerned with the structure of a compound, or the relationship of the elements in the compound to one another. A biologist refers to the structure of an organism, meaning a relatively stable arrangement of tissues and organs and the relationships between the different cells and interstitial fluids. When a builder speaks of the structure of a building, he is talking about the materials (sand, bricks, lime, cement, stone, timber, etc.) of which it is composed, the relationships between the parts (walls, rooms, stairs, passages, open space and their arrangement) and the building as a unit as a whole. Thus, structure generally refers to a set of relatively stable patterns of relationship between interdependent elements or parts of any given unit (biological, physical or social). An important term closely related with the concept of structure is 'function', which refers to those consequences of any activity that make for the adaptation or adjustment of a given structure or its parts. In other words, 'structure' refers to a system with relatively enduring patterns, and 'function' refers to the dynamic process within the structure. Thus, the main characteristics of a structure are:

(1) Constituent elements.

(2) Parts and sub-parts.

(3) Interrelation between parts.

(4) Arrangement of parts in a particular order.

(5) Parts are relatively stable and permanent.

(6) Changing character.

Definitions

Social life does not happen in a random fashion. Most of our activities are structured. They are organised in a regular and repetitive way. Interaction tends to develop certain uniformities over time, some of which tend to persist. As they are *orderly* and *systematic*, they can be recognised as 'social system'. Because the social system is composed of identifiable and interdependent parts, it is said to possess 'social structure'.

In the beginning of this chapter, social structure has been defined in myriad ways. Early social anthropologist A.R. Radcliffe-Brown (1950) viewed social structure as a mesh of mutual positions and interrelations, with interdependence of the component parts. He said, "components of social structure are human beings, the structure itself being an arrangement of persons in relationship institutionally defined and regulated". Some writers have defined it in terms of roles performed by people and the statuses occupied by them. It has also been seen in terms of process.

According to Talcott Parsons (1951), "social structure is a term applied to the particular arrangement of interrelated institutions, agencies and social patterns as well as status and roles which each person assumes in the group".

Oxford Dictionary of Sociology (1994) defines it as "a term loosely applied to any recurring pattern of social behaviour, or more specifically, to the ordered interrelationships between the different elements of a social system or society". Thus, for example, the different kinship, religious, economic, political and other institutions of a society may be said to comprise its structure as might such components as its norms, values, and social roles. According to Anthony Giddens (2000), "patterns of interaction between individuals or groups are known as social structure".

On the basis of above definitions, the following characteristics of social structure may be delineated:

(1) Social structure is not monolithic whole but made up of parts and sub-parts. It is not mere sum of its parts but there is a definite arrangement between parts. These parts cannot be explained outside the structure.

(2) It is an abstract and intangible phenomenon.

(3) As individuals are units of associations and institutions, so these institutions and associations (groups) are the units of social structure.

(4) These institutions and associations are interrelated in a particular arrangement and this arrangement creates the pattern of social structure.

(5) It refers to the external aspect of society which is relatively stable as compared to the internal (functional) aspect of society.

(6) It is not static but dynamic yet there is not much change in its basic form. It is relatively permanent through time.

(7) There is a systematic and orderly relationship between parts which gives a special shape to its outer form.

(8) Statuses and roles along with norms and values that govern social roles form the main constituents in the formation of social structure.

(9) There is a functional unity among the units of structure.

Elements

There is some disagreement as what would count as an 'element' of social structure. Main elements that constitute the social structure may be grouped as under:

1. Normative system – norms and values.
2. Position system – status and roles of individuals.
3. Sanction system – system of rules.
4. Action system – goal or object of society.
5. Anticipated response system – desires, aspirations and expectations.

Culture

The term 'culture' means different things to different people. Like most sociological concepts, culture is a term with both a popular as well as a sociological meaning. In common parlance, when we speak of 'culture', many of us think in terms of 'cultured' or 'refined' individuals. It is also used to convey social charm and intellectual excellence. To social scientists culture is not limited to refinement or social charm. Sociologists do not judge culture on the basis of the taste or refinement of society it is a part of. They do not use it in any such sense which connotes the evaluation in any form, i.e., what is good or what is bad. Their use is quite objective having the quality of ethical neutrality.

The Sanskrit term for culture is *sanskriti*. Both 'Sanskrit' and 'Sanskriti' are derived from *samaskar*, meaning ritual performance, which is a process of refinement. Man is born of as a social being, he attains sociality and becomes a cultured man by going through the *samaskars*.

In general (widest sense) terms, a culture can be said to include all the human phenomena in a society that are not the products of biological inheritance. The ways in which we adapt to our environment are called collectively as culture. The classic definition of culture, given by Sir Edward Tylor (1871), reads as follows: "Culture is that complex whole which includes knowledge, belief, art, morals, law, custom, and any other capabilities and habits acquired by man as a member of society." To put it in simple terms, culture is everything which is socially learned and shared by the members of a society. It clearly means that human behaviour is largely culturally and not genetically determined. For M.J. Herskovits (1948), culture is a way of life of a people (or members of a society). According to Horton and Hunt (1964), "it is the set of rules and procedures, together with a supporting set of ideas and values."

No society is devoid of culture. To put it in other words, all societies (preliterate or literate) have culture in some or the other form. But it differs from societies to societies or communities to communities. As a repository of social heritage, it helps in maintaining social order, control the behaviour of people, and establish uniformity in the behaviour of people. Clark Wissler (1923) pointed out nine cultural facts found in all societies:

(1) *Speech* including language and writing systems.

(2) *Material traits* such as food habits, shelter, tools, utensils, dress etc.

(3) *Mythology* and scientific knowledge.

(4) *Art* including carving, paintings, drawings, music and dance etc.

(5) *Religious beliefs and practices* including ritualistic forms, treatment of the sick and treatment of the dead.
(6) *Family and the social system*—marriage forms, inheritance, social control, sports and games.
(7) *Property*—real and personal property, trade and exchange.
(8) *Government*—political forms, judicial and legal procedure.
(9) War.

Characteristics

Most of the definitions that have been offered and studied, emphasise certain features of culture:

(1) it is *shared* by the members of a society;
(2) it is *learned and acquired*, not inborn or instinctive;
(3) its elements are *interrelated,* constituting a complex whole;
(4) it is *transmitted* from generation to generation or historically derived;
(5) it is *made or created*;
(6) it is *material and non-material* both, whether it is something concrete like a chair, a fan or a car or abstract like a belief or superstition;
(7) it has *adaptability*;
(8) it is both *super-individual* and *super-organic* (its formation and continuity do not depend on any one individual); and
(9) it is composed of *ethos* (formal appearance of culture) and *eidos* (cognitive process of culture).

Culture and Civilisation

In the Anglo-French tradition, the concept of 'culture' was often used synonymously with 'civilisation'. Even in our day-to-day talks and discussions, we use the two terms interchangeably. The earlier idea that culture and civilisation refer to the same state of development of humanity has now been abandoned. As long as people thought of primitive (or preliterate) societies as consisting of persons living in a state of nature, they could contrast 'civilisation' to this state. However, anthropological studies showed that preliterate people created rules, religions, beliefs and tools, developed agriculture and made other changes in the natural order of things, which are the characteristics of culture, in the modern sense of the term.

The concept of civilisation was also equated with highly valued things, respect of people for one another, the sanctity of life, and a high regard for the good, the ethical and the beautiful. In this sense, those who were not civilised were barbaric or barbarians. According to MacIver and Page (1961) "By civilisation we mean the whole mechanism and organisation which man has devised in his endeavour to control the conditions of life."

Sociologists do not use the term 'civilisation' in both the above senses. For Robert Merton (1936), civilisation is impersonal, accumulative and objective. MacIver and Page (1961) note four differences between civilisation and culture: (1) civilisation has a precise standard of measurement; (2) it is always advancing; (3) it is passed on without effort; and (4) it is borrowed with change or loss. None of these attributes is true of culture.

Some definitions of civilisation simply stress technology, and for some people technology has been synonymous with progress. Bierstedt (1974) emphasises sophistication, self-criticism and other-awareness as the essence of civilisation. William F. Ogburn (1950), in his theory of social change, described two aspects of culture, viz., material and non-material. For him, material aspect of culture represents civilisation. In brief, culture represents what we are, whereas civilisation is what we have and will accumulate. The distinction between culture and civilisation is that of end and the means. Culture represents the end (values and goals) and civilisation, on the other hand, represents the tools and techniques that help in achieving the end.

Culture and Society

These two terms are also used synonymously at many times. Sociologists use the term 'society' to mean a group of interacting people living in a specific geographical area, organised in a cooperative manner, and sharing a common culture. It refers to the whole complex of relations of man to his fellows. Robert MacIver defined society as “the web of social relationships, which is always changing”. A society is made of people who are interacting on the basis of shared beliefs, customs, values and activities, whereas common patterns which govern their interaction make up a culture of the society.

Sociologists use the term ‘culture’ to mean all the components of a society including all learned behaviour as well as material and non-material aspects such as symbols, language, ideas, beliefs, knowledge, values, norms and technology. Culture exists because people are able to share creations, pass knowledge from one generation to the next, and thereby change the very conditions for existence. A culture is a system of behaviour shared by the members of a society.

A society is a social group; a culture is a society’s system of common heritage. Each of us has a culture, because we are all raised in society. We express our culture continuously in our dress, food, work, language, and other activities. We learn our culture from our forebearers and contemporaries and then we pass it on to future generations. There cannot be a culture apart from society, and no society exists without a culture. As Gillin and Gillin (1948) state, “culture is the cement binding together into a society its component individuals . . . human society is interacting; culture is the patterning of their behaviour.” In nutshell, society refers to people and culture to patterns of behaviour.

Chapter 5

Social Norms and Values

Key features

Social Norms

In general parlance, the term 'norm' refers to that which is most common, or that which is 'normal'. For sociologists, norm means any shared standard of behaviour which in turn entails certain expectations of behaviour in a given situation. As such, that which is normal (most common) is not necessarily normative (a shared expectation). According to *Oxford Dictionary of Sociology* (1994), "a norm is a shared expectation of behaviour that connotes what is considered culturally desirable and appropriate". M. Haralambos (2000) defines it as "a norm is a specific guide to action acceptable and appropriate behaviour in particular situation".

In simple terms, norms are guidelines which direct our conduct in particular situation. They are similar to rules and regulations in being prescriptive, although they lack the formal status of rules.

These rules or social expectations (norms) specify how people should and should not behave in various situations. They are both *prescriptive*—they tell us what they should do and *proscriptive*—they tell people what they should not do. Laws, dress codes, rules of sports and games—all express social norms. For instance, norms of dress provide guidelines for what to wear on particular occasions—at funeral, at dinner party, at dance, in the bank, in the hospital and so on. Norms of dress vary from society to society. In terms of laws governing dress, the nude bather on a public beach is subject to official punishment.

Norms are established standard of behaviour maintained in a society. "Thou shalt not kill" is a norm found almost in every culture. We typically expect that people will be quite in the theatre hall while the film is shown. This is an example of a most general social norm expectation. Norms are relative. In different societies, there can be different norms for some particular behaviour. Even in one society, the norms may differ from community to community. They are not static, but change from time to time and society to society.

Types

Norms can be classified in many ways but the most important distinction, as stated earlier, is between prescriptive and proscriptive norms. A *prescriptive* norm is positive in form and spells out forms of behaviour which role-players are expected to follow. A *proscriptive* norm is one which directs a role-player to avoid or abstain from certain type of activity. The later tend to be more inflexible in that behaviour is defined as either compliant or deviant, whereas prescriptive norms involve behavioural degrees of conformity. Some sociologists see norms as either formal or informal. *Formal* norms have generally be written down and involve strict rules for punishment of violators. Laws are an example of formal norm. *Informal* norms are generally understood but are not precisely recorded. Standard of proper dress is a common example of informal norm.

Norms are also classified by their relative importance to society. When classified in this way, they are known as mores, folkways and customs. Some writers have also included law in the category of norms. This typology is distinguished by the intensity of feelings they arouse and the consequences that flow from violations of them. Kingsley Davis (1960) has given an exhaustive list of social norms as under:

1. Folkways
2. Mores
3. Laws (customary and enacted laws)
4. Institutions
5. Custom, morality and religion
6. Conventions and etiquette
7. Fashion and fad

Functions

Social norms, in the sense of shared standards, have great power to motivate behaviour. Societies exist because through the internalisation of norms, human agents monitor their behaviour in anticipation of sanctions, i.e., reward and punishment from other social actors. Social norms perform the following main functions:

1. They direct, regulate and control human behaviour. The process by which norms and other behavioural regulators are transformed into personality elements is called *socialisation*.
2. They help in satisfying our social needs.
3. They help in establishing social order by mitigating tensions and conflicts in society.
4. They act as measuring scale to evaluate social behaviour.
5. They act as ideals and objectives in certain situations.
6. They help in predicting behaviour.

Social Sanctions

All social norms are accompanied by social sanctions. Any system of social control depends on sanctions. The sanctions which enforce norms are a major part of the mechanism of social control. A sanction is any reaction from others to the behaviour of an individual or group. According to *Oxford Dictionary of Sociology* (1994), any means by which conformity to socially approved standards is enforced, is called *social sanction.* Sanctions may also be defined as the deprivations which accompany or follow behaviour which is disapproved. The concept has played an important part in the explanation of social order.

Types

Sanctions may be both *positive* and *negative*. In folk wisdom, it is known as the "carrot and the stick principle". When our actions meet normative expectations or conform to wider expectations, we are generally rewarded (or subject to a positive sanction); failure to meet such expectations leads to punishment (punishing the various forms of deviance) known as negative sanction. Not all norms carry the same sanctions because not all norms are of equal importance in a culture. Rewards are explicit and definite expressions of group approval. The thing given as reward may be wholly immaterial. Penalties (punishments) are always coercive. They may vary in severity from death or violence against the person, imprisonment, deprivation of some sort, the infliction of pain, or mutilation, loss of liberty or civil privileges, social disapproval like avoidance, ostracism, jeering, or the use of unfriendly nicknames. There is a considerable variation in different societies in who is supposed to apply the sanctions. The list of possible sanctions in social interaction is huge, as is the range of their severity.

Sanctions can be *informal,* such as approving or disapproving glance or verbal abuse and *formal*, such as a fine or reward given by an official body or some kind of legal restraint. Sanctions serve to reinforce both formal and informal social norms. Sanctions may also be divided into external and internal. *External* sanctions are those which are applied by others to the actor of whose acts they disapprove, whereas *internal* sanctions are applied by the actor to himself. A person who has done wrong in other's eyes has also done wrong in his own, and experiences accordingly unpleasant feeling of guilt, shame, remorse, or self-accusation. Social control depends more on internal sanctions than external ones. To rely entirely on external sanctions would be wasteful of time and effort both.

Social sanctions are used by society to motivate people to act in ways considered right. Sanctions do not have to be activated to be effective; often, the anticipation of reward or punishment is sufficient to ensure conformity. C.W. Mills (1951) wrote: "the mere anticipation of probable sanctions (ranging from embarrassment to imprisonment) is often sufficient to restrain the behaviour in question".

Folkways

Noted early American sociologist, William G. Sumner (1840-1910) identified two types of norms in his book *Folkways* (1906), which he labelled as 'folkways' and 'mores'. They represent modes of procedure in a society or in a group. They present to us the most frequent or most accepted or most standardised ways of doing this or that. Folkways are distinguished from mores not by their content but by the degree to which group members are compelled to conform to them, by the degree of importance, by the severity of punishment if they are violated, or by the intensity of feelings associated with adherence to them.

What are folkways?

According to Reuter and Hart (1933), "The folkways are simple habits of action common to the members of the group; they are the ways of the folks that are somewhat standardised and have some degree of traditional sanction for their persistence". MacIver and Page (1949) defined it as: "The folkways are the recognised or accepted ways of behaving in the society."

In simple terms, folkways are the customary, normal and habitual ways of the group to meet certain needs or solving day-to-day problems. The time of meals, the number of meals per day, the manner of taking meals—lunch or dinner, the kind of food used, the manner of its preparations, the manner of speech and dress, forms of etiquette and the numerous other facts of daily life are some of the examples of customary practices to which individuals conform in their personal habits. Any routine activity in itself is a habit from the point of view of the individual person but when it becomes general among the communicating folk, it is known as folkway, i.e., a habit of a group. Out of habits develop the uniformities in habit to which sociologists term as *folkways* or *customs*. Not all (group) habits become general. They differ from individual to individual and place to place.

Habits are repetitive actions of a person. They are learned in the process of socialisation. They become the second nature of the individual. When habits are socially approved and followed by a number of persons in a society, they become folkways, for example, habits of exchanging greetings and courtesies. The wearing of a cap, hat or turban and many other matters of dress are habits of individuals but they are folkways from the point of view of the group. Shaking hands, eating with forks and knives, driving on the left or right hand side of the street, attending classes in paints and skirts rather than gowns or bathing suits or writing as 'Dear Sir', Gentleman in the letter are a few of many western or American folkways.

Similarly, wearing turban and *sherwani* (long embroidered coat) and riding the female horse by the bridegroom at the time of marriage procession, wearing a *Mangal Sutra* (a gold chain with beads) by a married Hindu woman, bidding 'Namaste' with joined palms or cleaning of hands before taking food are some of the examples of Indian folkways. Folkways cover a good proportion of our daily habits from the rules of simple etiquette to the technical way of handling problems.

Characteristics

W.G. Sumner (1906) wrote: "The folkways are unconscious, spontaneous, uncoordinated adjustment of man to his environment, the product of the frequent repetition of petty acts, often by great numerous acting in concern or at least acting in the same way when face to face with the same need." The major characteristics of folkways are as under:

(1) Folkways arise spontaneously out of the fundamental fact that man must act in order to live. They generally arise

unconsciously in a group such as shaking hands, tipping the hat, calling on strangers and without planned or rational thought.

(2) Folkways develop out of group experience. They are passed down from generation to generation through interaction.

(3) They change as culture changes or when we enter different situations.

(4) Folkways are the weakest norms, which are most often violated but least likely to carry any severe punishment. Violations of folkways bring only mild censure in the form of some smiles, glances, or occasional comments from others.

(5) Folkways are not looked on by most people as moral matters. They are deemed the 'right' way and 'normal'. People accept most of them unquestionably.

(6) Folkways differ from mores in that they are less severely sanctioned and are not abstract principles.

(7) Folkways (customs) may and sometimes do become burdensome. They sometimes exact more energy than they conserve.

(8) Every society have some/many folkways. Even the most primitive society will have a few hundred folkways. In modern industrial societies they become even more numerous and involved.

Importance

Folkways are the basis of culture. They give us better understanding about a particular culture. They are regulative and exert pressure upon the individual and the group to conform to the norms. They are most powerful and control the behaviour of individuals in society even more than the state action. Folkways are as indispensable to social life as language, and they serve much the same purpose.

Customs

Customs stand in between folkways and mores. They carry with them less intense feelings than mores, and violations of them are likely to meet less severe condemnation. It you witness the violation of a custom, you may feel revolted, but you would not be morally incensed as you would be if mores were violated. Customs are often rigid, tyrannical, burdensome and difficult to escape. They often enforce conformity irrespective of the benefits or advantages derived. Both savage and civilised men, particularly the latter, invent ingenious explanations and justifications for customary modes of behaviour.

According to *Oxford Dictionary of Sociology* (1994), "customs are established ways of thinking and acting in societies". Alex Inkeles (1965) defined it as "Custom is any standardised and more or less specialised set of actions, which is routinely carried out according to a generally accepted pattern in a group life". In brief, it denotes established patterns of behaviour. It refers both to the routines of daily life and to the distinctive features which mark off one culture from another.

Characteristics

Unlike mores, customs are not evaluative. For instance, generally, Indians (Hindus) expect youngsters to bow and touch the feets of their parents, teachers and elders, but this expectation is typically not one of 'ought'. The point is that although individuals expect particular types of conduct in some situations, they may not condemn those who act contrarily. So customs are not norms, if norms are defined only in terms of evaluation of conduct, that is, to the exclusion of expectations. Evaluations and expectations may and may not diverge. Customs breed monotony and deprive life of freshness and spontaneity.

Customs play a less important role in modern society than in the communities of any earlier day. A number of factors have weakened their effectiveness. Development of science, rational attitudes towards events and persons have helped in weakening the old customs. People have become less bound by customs; they are now more individualistic, more direct. Society has become more complex, democratic, competitive and information-oriented. Moreover, the general increase in literacy and extension of communication means have provided better ways for understanding human behaviour.

Mores

Mores are the strongest of the social norms, which relate to the basic moral judgements of a society. They tell us to do certain things, such as pay proper respect to our parents and teachers. They can also tell us not to do certain things, such as not to kill other human beings or do not indulge into adultery or homosexuality. They are considered more important than folkways or customs, and reactions to their violations are more serious. They are more closely associated with values a society consider important. According to Giddings and Halt (1906), "a practical distinction between folkways and mores is that violation of a folkway is generally met with laughter and though this is often punished, it is much severe than the social ostracism (extermination from the group) which may penalise the transgressor of the mores". A man who eats six meals a day instead of the conventional two or three is just a source of amusement or irritation to his colleagues, while a nudist who carries his practice into a public situation may become a social outcast. Similarly, a man should walk on the left side is a folkway, whereas a man should marry the woman he has seduced is a mos (singular of mores).

In all modern societies, the mores centre around sex, property rights and getting ahead in the world. They include such prohibitions as "thou shalt not kill", 'No parking' for motorists, do not steal anything, positive injections as protecting children, caring for the aged parents, duty to one's country, property rights and sexual fidelity.

What are mores?

W.G. Sumner (1906) holds that the folkways become mores when philosophical and ethical generalisations pertaining to societal welfare were added. MacIver and Page (1949) write: "When the folkways have added to them conceptions of group welfare, standards of right and wrong, they are converted into mores." Similarly, Dawson and Gettys (1948) state: "Mores are folkways which have added to them, through some reflections, the judgement that group welfare is particularly dependent upon them."

Modern writers such as Alex Inkeles (*What is Sociology*, 1965) have defined mores as "such customs which are not routinely followed, but are in addition, surrounded by sentiments or values such that failure to follow the expected pattern would produce strong sanctions from one's group". According to P.B. Horton and C.L. Hunt (*Sociology*, 1968), "By the mores ('mos' in the singular) we mean those strong ideas of right and wrong which require certain acts and forbid others . . . Mores are beliefs in the rightness or wrongness of acts."

All above views can be illustrated in the following algebraic formula:

folkways (customs) + judgement of right and wrong +the element of group welfare = mores.

Thus, folkways or customs become mores when the ideas of right and wrong along with the doctrine of group welfare are added to them.

Characteristics

Mores are not deliberately invented or thought of or worked out by some people in the society. They emerge gradually out of the customary practices of the people, largely without conscious choice or intention. In the long run, the origin of such group ways or customary practices is forgotten and the conviction arises that they are useful and necessary to the welfare of the group and contrary ways of acting are inimical to the welfare.

Like folkways, mores are also learned either consciously or unconsciously. They are taught to the young as a set of sacred things or verse (mantra). They are nearly synonymous with morals. Wherever the mores are firmly established, obedience is automatic. Violations of mores inspire intense reactions, and some type of punishment inevitably follows. The punishment may involve expulsion from the group, harsh imprisonment, or in some cases even death. In Hindus, marriage within one's caste (endogamy) is a rule. It has become a 'mos' for the people (Hindus) of India. Any person transgress this rule and contracts intercaste marriage is either expelled from the caste or fined heavily. Similarly, masturbation in public or doing sexual intercourse in public or to become naked in the public or breaking modesty taboos which forbid exposure of certain parts (like breast) of the body, and betraying country for money are some other mores of Indian society.

Not all violations of group standards excite moral indignation at all places and in all times. They differ from time to time and place to place. Though mores are stable but change also usually slowly, and sometimes dramatically. The social rules (folkways, customs or mores) are always relative. There is the widest possible divergence from group to group. The practice approved at one time may be disapproved by the same people at another time. A form of marriage—polygyny or polyandry—is right in one group and wrong in another. It may have moral sanction in a group sometime back but may be forbidden later on. Infanticide, slavery, child labour have been within the mores of most people and for most of the history of the world, are forbidden by many of the modern peoples. In brief, since folkways and mores are elements of culture, they vary from one society or sub-culture to another.

Values

Generally, value has been taken to mean moral ideas, general conceptions or orientations towards the world or sometimes simply interests, attitudes, preferences, needs, sentiments and dispositions. But sociologists use this term in a more precise sense to mean "the generalised end which has the connotations of rightness, goodness or inherent desirability". These ends are regarded legitimate and binding by society. They define what is important worthwhile and worth striving for. Sometimes, values have been interpreted to mean "such standards by means of which the ends of action are selected". Thus, values are collective conceptions of what is considered good, desirable, and proper or bad, undesirable, and improper in a culture.

According to M. Haralambos (2000), "a value is a belief that something is good and desirable". For R.K. Mukerjee (1949) (a pioneer Indian sociologist who initiated the study of social values),

"values are socially approved desires and goals that are internalised through the process of conditioning, learning or socialisation and that become subjective preferences, standards and aspirations". A value is a shared idea about how something is ranked in terms of desirability, worth or goodness. Familiar examples of values are wealth, loyalty, independence, equality, justice, fraternity and friendliness. These are generalised ends consciously pursued by or held up to individuals as being worthwhile in themselves. It is not easy to clarify the fundamental values of a given society because of their sheer breadth.

Characteristics

Values may be *specific*, such as honouring one's parents or owning a home or they may be more *general*, such as health, love and democracy. "Truth prevails", "love thy neighbour as yourself", "learning is good as an end itself" are a few examples of general values. Individual achievement, individual happiness and materialism are major values of modern industrial society.

Value systems can be different from culture to culture. One may value aggressiveness and deplores passivity, another the reverse, and a third gives little attention to this dimension altogether, emphasising instead the virtue of sobriety over emotionality, which may be quite unimportant in either of the other cultures. This point has very aptly been explored and explained by Florence Kluchkhon (1949) in her studies of five small communities (tribes) of the American south-west. One society may value individual achievement (as in USA), another may emphasise family unity and kin support (as in India). The values of hard work and individual achievement are often associated with industrial capitalist societies.

The values of a culture may change, but most remain stable during one person's lifetime. Socially shared, intensely felt values are a fundamental part of our lives. Values are often emotionally charged because they stand for things we believe to be worth defending. Often, this characteristic of values brings conflict between different communities or societies or sometimes between different persons.

Most of our basic values are learnt early in life from family, friends, neighbourhood, school, the mass print and visual media and other sources within society. These values become part of our personalities. They are generally shared and reinforced by those with whom we interact.

Types

Values can be classified into two broad categories:

(1) Individual values

These are the values which are related with the development of human personality or individual norms of recognition and protection of the human personality such as honesty, loyalty, veracity and honour.

(2) Collective values

Values connected with the solidarity of the community or collective norms of equality, justice, solidarity and sociableness are known as collective values.

Values can also be categorised from the point of view their hierarchical arrangement:

(1) Intrinsic values

These are the values which are related with goals of life. They are sometimes known as ultimate and transcendent values. They determine the schemata of human rights and duties and of human virtues. In the hierarchy of values, they occupy the highest place and superior to all other values of life.

(2) Instrumental values

These values come after the intrinsic values in the scheme of gradation of values. These values are means to achieve goals (intrinsic values) of life. They are also known as incidental or proximate values.

Importance and functions of values

Values are general principles to regulate our day-to-day behaviour. They not only give direction to our behaviour but are also ideals and objectives in themselves. Values deal not so much with what is, but with what ought to be; in other words, they express moral imperatives. They are the expression of the ultimate ends, goals or purposes of social action. Our values are the basis of our judgements about what is desirable, beautiful, proper, correct, important, worthwhile and good as well as what is undesirable, ugly, incorrect, improper and bad. Pioneer sociologist Durkheim emphasised the importance of values (though he used the term 'morals') in controlling disruptive individual passions. He also stressed that values enable individuals to feel that they are part of something bigger than themselves. Modern sociologist E. Shils (1972) also makes the same point and calls 'the central value system' (the main values of society) are seen as essential in creating conformity and order. Indian sociologist R.K. Mukerjee (1949) writes: "By their nature, all human relations and behaviour are imbedded in values."

The main functions of values are as follows:

1. Values play an important role in the integration and fulfilment of man's basic impulses and desires in a stable and consistent manner appropriate for his living.
2. They are generic experiences in social action made up of both individual and social responses and attitudes.
3. They build up societies, integrate social relations.
4. They mould the ideal dimensions of personality and range and depth of culture.
5. They influence people's behaviour and serve as criteria for evaluating the actions of others.
6. They have a great role to play in the conduct of social life.
7. They help in creating norms to guide day-to-day behaviour.

Norms and Values

Both terms—norms and values—are at many times used interchangeably in our day-to-day discourse. But social scientists use them in a specific sense. Social norms are standards, rules, guides and expectations for actual behaviour, whereas values are abstract conceptions of what is important and worthwhile. Honesty is a general value; the expectation that students will not cheat or use such material forbidden by the codes in the examinations is a norm. Values are general guidelines, while norms are specific guidelines. Values are general standards, which decide what is good and what is bad. Norms are rules and expectations that specify how people should and should not behave in various social situations. To conform to a particular value of a society, there can be many norms. Norms link values with actual norms. In brief, values are ends while norms are means to achieve these ends. Sometimes, the values and norms of a society conflict with each other. The change in one element of material culture (mechanisation of agriculture) may sometimes conflict with the associated aspect of non-material culture (system of joint family or collective living).

Though there is a difference between norms and values, still, there is often a direct relationship between values, norms, and sanctions of a society. For example, if a society highly values the institution of marriage, it may have norms and strict sanctions which prohibit the act of adultery and allow divorce only in hard cases. If a society views private property as a basic value, it will probably have stern laws against theft and vandalism. The most cherished values (right of life) of a society will receive the heaviest sanctions (capital punishment), whereas matters regarded as less critical will carry light and informal sanctions.

Chapter 6

Social Groups

Key features

All human life is group life. Group life is not even limited with man. It is also found in animals. Solitary life is the exception in animal world. Men everywhere live in close association with their fellow men. This is even evident from the lives of primitive peoples. Even pre-human ancestors (chimpanzees, gorilla, utang etc.) of man lived an associated life. Group life is so universal among man that it has been usual to speak of man as a gregarious animal. The origin and ultimate basis of group life lie in human needs of food, sex and protection and these needs cannot be met by individuals struggling alone. The complete dependence of human child for care, protection and upbringing proves the necessity of group life.

What is Group?

It is frequently stated that sociology is the study of 'groups' (Johnson, *Sociology*, 1960), yet it is difficult to define this word in exact terms. The term 'group' presents definitional difficulties. Sometimes it is related to a specific pattern of common action. Again, it is used to include every conceivable form of human activity. It has been used to describe such diverse things as families, nations, crowds, sects, clubs and even a whole society. In the elementary sense, a group is a number of units of anything in close proximity to one another such as group of trees in a forest, or group of airplanes in an airport. Thus, the term 'group' is used generally to state the fact of association. It implies nothing as to the size, form, function, permanence or cohesive principle.

Definitions of social group

In common parlance or generally, a social group is regarded as a collection of some people at a certain place. But, from sociological point of view, mere collection of people at a certain place does not constitute a group unless there is a common interest which holds its members and the social interaction through which they influence one another. The essence of the social group is not physical closeness (as we find in physical objects) but a consciousness of joint interaction for certain purpose. This may develop at any place and at any time. Thus, a social group comes into existence, "whenever two or more persons interact, whether in the intimacy of a family picnic or in the roar of a bargain sale, they are groups". Social group is a mental phenomenon, rather than a physical entity. It requires three things for its formation: (1) reciprocal stimulus, (2) response, and (3) mutual awareness, that is, the consciousness of interaction.

According to MacIver and Page (1949), "by group, we mean any collection of human beings, who are brought into social relationships with one another". Bogardus (1949) writes: "A social group may be thought of as a number of persons, two or more, who have some common objects of attention, who are stimulating to each other, who have a common loyalty and participate in similar activities." This definition, though exhaustive, applies only to small groups, the members of which come to know each other. Similarly, Ogburn and Nimkoff (1955) stated, "whenever two or more individuals come together and influence one another, they may be said to constitute a social group".

The criterion of pattern of interaction is important which distinguishes social groups from the terms like *category* and *aggregates* which are at many times used synonymously as we find in the definition of Horton and Hunt (1964) which states, "groups are aggregates or categories of people who have a consciousness of membership and of interaction". Let us explain what is category and aggregate. A *category* is any number of items (or people), which have some characteristics in common, for example, males, senior managers, graduates etc. An *aggregate* or aggregation is any number of individuals who are clustered together in space. The population of Rajasthan or Assam or passengers on a train may be considered an aggregate. *All groups are categories and most are aggregates but not all categories or aggregates constitute groups*.

We may, thus, define social group as a number of individuals, defined by formal or informal criteria of membership, who share a feeling of unity, having similar norms, values and expectations and who are bound together in relatively stable pattern of interaction. To distinguish social groups from aggregates, sociologists generally use the criterion of feeling of unity or stable pattern of interaction as their basis of distinction.

Characteristics

On the basis of above definitions, the following main characteristics of social groups may be discerned:

1. Two and more than two persons.
2. Some kind of regular and conscious interaction through direct or indirect communication.
3. Some degree of reciprocity (common interstimulation and meaningful response).
4. Some common interest or some common object of attention.

5. A feeling of unity (similar norms, values and expectations).
6. Some measure of mutual awareness.
7. Common understanding.
8. Collective behaviour.

A social group is not static but dynamic, changing in activity and in form. It may seem standstill but change gradually. It has some kind of temporary or permanent structure and organisation (rules, procedures and conventions etc).

Types

Groups vary tremendously in size, purpose and degree of intimacy among its members. It ranges from a pair, a couple, or a dyad, a triad, a tetrad, to a national group of millions of people. Thus, groups can be classified in a wide variety of ways. The bases of classification of groups are many and varied. Different criteria have been used by different writers, but a common classification is made on the basis of kinds of activities or functions. Other main bases of classification of groups are size, quality of social interaction that operates within groups, open or closed, voluntary or involuntary, informal or formal and temporal persistence etc. We here discuss only those types which are most often referred in sociology, viz., in-groups and out-groups, primary and secondary groups, quasi groups, reference groups and gemeinshaft and gesellschaft.

In-groups and Out-groups

One of the key characteristics of a human group is the member's sense of belongingness. Those who belong think of one another as forming a social unit. This unit has boundaries that separate 'us' from 'them', that differentiate those who are 'in' from those who are 'out'. This type of differentiation was made by W.G. Sumner in his classic study of *Folkways* (1906). He observed that people tend to like their own group, to which he termed *in-group*, over other competing or opposing group—the *out-group*.

An in-group is a social category to which persons feel they belong and share a consciousness or awareness of kind. In other words, these are the groups for which we precede with the pronoun 'my' such as my family, my nation, my caste, my occupational group etc. Simply put it, it comprises everyone who is regarded as 'we' or 'us'. The members of in-group feel that they share a common fate, adhere to a common ideology, and come from a common background. Important characteristics of in-groups are:

(1) Mutual sympathy towards one another.
(2) Mutual cooperation, help and goodwill.
(3) Respect for mutual benefits and rights.
(4) Sentiment of solidarity and we-feeling.
(5) Feeling of tolerance, compassion and generosity.
(6) Preferential behaviour with the members.

"Birds of the same feather flock together" is an old proverb, which reflect the feelings of in-group to some extent. Individuals having same sex, same language, same past, same interests and aspirations and so on are naturally drawn together and form their own groups.

In-groups may be primary groups but not necessarily. We can feel 'in' with people we have never met or shared personal intimacies with—members of our college alumni group, religious group or nation. One typical consequence of in-group membership is a feeling of distinctiveness and superiority among members, who see themselves as better than people in the out-group. This feeling leads to *ethnocentrism*. It was defined by W.G. Sumner (1906) as "that view of things in which one's own group is the centre of everything and all others are scaled and rated with reference to it." This attitude binds people of one group to the good qualities of other groups. Most groups in society tend to be ethnocentric. Ethnocentrism is an extreme form of the in-group or out-group phenomenon. Sumner said that "in modern nations, ethnocentrism is really the sentiment of patriotism in all its philosophic fulness, that is, in its rationality and its extravagance and exaggeration".

The very existence of an in-group implies that there is an out-group viewed as 'they' or 'them'. *An out-group is a group or category to which people feel they do not belong.* It is defined by the individual with relation to the in-group. For such groups, we usually use the words—they group, other sex, other families, other caste or other occupation etc. We do not identify or affiliate ourselves with such groups, and feel little allegiance with them. We treat most members of out-groups as 'others' or as 'different' from the in-group. We have the feeling of indifference, avoidance, disgust, competition, antagonism, suspicion and scorn towards them. We dislike and ridicule and at times we feel hostile towards them or even come in outright conflict with them. The distinction between in-group and out-group is always a matter of situational definition.

Difference between in-groups and out-groups

The difference between in-groups and out-groups is sociologically important for several reasons:

(1) The in-group tends to stereotype members of the out-group and label them with many epithets such as racists, barbarians, spendthrifts, anti-capitalists, revolutionaries, rich and greedy etc.

(2) Any threat or attack, whether real or imaginary, from the out-group tends to increase the cohesion and solidarity of the in-group.

(3) Sometimes, the difference between in-group and out-group becomes situational and some of them overlap and cause conflict. Our affiliation with a particular in-group may provide us with an identity and a sense of belonging but it also induces conflict and restricts our relationships and interactions with others.

(4) These groups are also important because they affect our behaviour. From fellow members of an in-group, we expect recognition, loyalty and helpfulness. From out-groups, our expectations varies with the kind of out-group. From some out-group we expect hostility, from others, a more or less friendly competition and from still others, indifference in the

form of ethnocentrism, casteism, regionalism and communalism, which are the product of in-group feelings.

We find in-group and out-group feelings at all levels of our life—between families, neighbourhoods, provinces, social classes and castes and between religious groups. The usual attitudes towards out-group members are antipathy, hatred, jealousy and pugnacity. The tales of misery and difficulties of out-groups gladden the hearts of the in-group people.

Primary and Secondary Groups

Perhaps the most fundamental distinction between social groups was made by Charles H. Cooley (*Human Nature and the Social Order*, 1902). This distinction was based on primary and secondary relationships. A primary relationship, according to Cooley, is one in which intimate face-to-face association and cooperation predominate. These relations are based on ties of affection and loyalty, involve many different aspects to people's lives, and endure over long period of times. Explaining the characteristics of primary relationships, K. Davis (*Human Society*, 1949) states: "A new personal relationship can be established, an old one can be abandoned, perhaps the driving force that initiated the relationship may give way to another, but no substitution can be made of one individual for one another in the same relationship." Husband-wife, parent-child, teacher-pupil, friend-friend are a few examples of primary relationships.

Groups that develop on the basis of primary relationships, Cooley termed them as 'primary groups'. He contrasted with the larger and more disparate 'nucleated group' (subsequently referred to more commonly as the 'secondary group', whose members were rarely all in direct contact. (It is to be noted that Cooley himself has never used the term 'secondary group').

Defining primary groups, Cooley writes: "By primary groups, I mean those groups characterised by intimate face-to-face association and cooperation. They are primary in several senses but chiefly in that they are fundamental in forming the social nature and ideals of the individual." As a group, the family embodies all the basic characteristics of primary relationships. Similarly, E.A. Shils (1951) writes: "By primary group we mean a group characterised by a high degree of solidarity, informality in the code of rules which regulate the behaviour of its members, and autonomy in the creation of these rules. The solidarity involves a close identification of the members with one another and with any symbols of the group which might have grown up." These are the groups in which we come to know other people intimately as individual personalities. In such groups, social contacts are intimate, personal and total in that they involve many parts of person's life experience. The social relationships tend to be informal and relaxed. The members are interested in one another as persons. Families, friendship, circles, clique, play groups (sports club), small village, neighbourhood, work team are some of the examples of primary groups. When we find ourselves identifying closely with a group, it is probably primary group.

Characteristics of primary groups

Following are the main characteristics of primary groups:

1. A sense of 'we-ness' (we-feeling) involving mutual identification and shared feeling.
2. Members tend to be emotionally attached to one another.
3. Face-to-face and unspecialised characteristic of association.
4. Intimacy and fusion of individualities.
5. The relations of the members are spontaneous, inclusive, personal and an end in themselves.
6. Spatial proximity – physical closeness of members.
7. Long duration and continuity in the relations of members.
8. Interest of members in one another's sentiments and welfare.

Importance of primary groups

Primary groups are important both to the individual as well as to the society. They are particularly important in shaping the personality, in formulating self-concepts, in developing a sense of worth and in becoming an accepted member of society. In the words of Cooley, primary groups are the "the nursery of human nature". The individual learns the first lesson of loyalty, honesty, sympathy and develops expectations in these groups.

From the point of view of individual: (1) they are primary for the formation of habits and attitudes; (2) they are fundamental to the development of 'social self' and moral knowledge; (3) they impart basic training in social stability, solidarity and cooperation among persons; (4) they play a pivotal role both in the socialisation process and in the development of roles and statuses; (5) they are most efficient humaniser of animal drives (sex, hunger, anger etc.) them any other form of association; and (6) they are the important agency for the development of personality (socialisation) of the individual.

The primary groups are also important from societal point of view. "Primary groups are the basis of all social life" (Gillin and Gillin, 1948). Landis (1958) observed: "From primary groups the individual acquires basic attitudes towards the world around him, people and social institutions. From these groups attitudes of tolerance, kindness, love and generosity are derived." Scholars like Mumford (1962) and Erich Fromm (1965) contend that the strength and vitality of primary groups are the basis of health of society. In an increasingly impersonal world, they are the sources of openness, trust and intimacy. They are also an important source of social control and social cohesion.

Changing scene

In modern society, the importance (functions) of primary groups is decreasing day by day because of the social changes that have taken place in view of scientific and technological revolutions. Many functions of primary groups (rearing, caring and upbringing of child, education, health care etc.) have been taken over by secondary groups and other agencies. The contacts between the group members have become less frequent. The basic social responses are less intense and intimate and the interests have become considerably narrower. Industrialisation, urbanisation, new technology, division of labour and the concept of personal happiness and many other factors have played great role in lessening or narrowing the importance of primary groups, especially family. Though the secondary groups have overshadowed but not destroyed totally the primary groups. These groups still persist in a secondary group dominated modern world, because the human need for intimate and sympathetic association is a continuous one. People living in army camp or college hostel or alone in a metropolitan city feel a great need for primary groups (family and neighbourhood). In the modern society, the functions of primary groups though weakened, yet the primary groups exist because they provide emotional security and mental satisfaction to man.

Secondary groups

The secondary groups are just opposite of primary groups. What makes the relationship secondary is the relatively narrow, utilitarian, task-oriented, time-limited focus of its activities. A secondary group is organised around secondary relationships. These relationship are more formal, impersonal, segmental and utilitarian than primary group interactions. Formal organisations and larger instrumental associations such as trade associations, labour unions, corporations, political parties, international cartel, a club and many others are a few examples of secondary groups. In such groups, one is not concerned with the other person as a person, but as a functionary who is filling a role. In the secondary group not total personality but a segmental (partial) personality of a person is involved. These groups are wholly lacking in intimacy of association as we generally find in primary groups. Defining these groups, Ogburn and Nimkoff (1950) write: "The groups which provide experience lacking in intimacy are called secondary groups." Kimball Young (1942) has termed these groups as 'special interest groups' because they are formed to fulfil certain specific end or ends.

Functions of secondary groups

Following are the main functions of secondary groups:

1. To help in fulfilling various kinds of increasing human needs.
2. To help in bringing social awareness and social change.
3. To help in removing conservatism and superstition through education and rational thinking.

4. To increase social mobility.
5. To help in satisfying various special interests such as sports, dance, music, touring etc.

Characteristics

Following are the main characteristics of secondary groups:

1. Spatial distance between members.
2. Short duration.
3. Large number.
4. Lack of intimacy among members.
5. Formal relationships and partial involvement of personality.
6. Casualness of contact.
7. Impersonal and based on status.
8. Specific aims or interest of formation.
9. Deliberately and consciously formed.
10. Feeling of individualism among members.
11. Voluntary membership.

Classification

Secondary groups have been classified on the basis of culture as under:

(i) Culturally organised groups

(a) Status groups—social classes, castes.
(b) Nationality groups—nations, states.
(c) Residence groups—communities, cities and regional groups.
(d) Attention, interest and purpose groups—religious bodies, publics, institutional groups, trade unions and corporations etc.

(ii) Groups not basically organised by culture

(a) Biological groups – age, sexes and racial groups.
(b) Casual groups – crowd, assemblages, audiences, mobs etc.

Importance of secondary groups

Although primary groups are vital to the health of both individuals and society, secondary groups are also important because they tend to meet specific goals. They help societies function effectively and permit people who do not know one another intimately to perform move effectively in their jobs. Most formal organisations, such as colleges, schools, hospitals, corporations, professional associations and trade unions, are comprised of many secondary groups. (Formal organisations are defined as units employing rational means to attain a set of objectives). The impersonality and formality of the secondary group allows members to focus on skills and specialised interests rather than on personalities. Most jobs, whether they involve driving a bus or performing brain surgery, have clearly defined goals and role expectations, so the personal characteristics of the people fulfilling the role and the public's need for emotional involvement with them are not of great importance. In general, secondary relationships occupy unimportant places in people's lives because their focus is so narrow and they tend to involve little emotional attachment. Though they are quite important for the successful running of societies as in the case of work, one of the dilemmas of life in industrial societies is that so much of people's lives is taken up with secondary relationships.

Difference between primary and secondary groups

The distinction between primary and secondary groups is not always clear-cut. Some special clubs or fraternities become so large and impersonal that they no longer function as primary groups. Many formal secondary group situations involve instances of informality and personal openness. It is seen that at many times primary groups develop from secondary groups and organisations. The composition of an individual's primary and secondary group shifts frequently. The key difference between primary and secondary groups is the quality of the relationships and the extent of personal intimacy and involvement. A primary group conversation usually focuses on personal experiences, feelings, and casual, open sharing, whereas a secondary group conversation is more apt to be impersonal, purposeful, and limited to socially relevant topics.

Comparison of Primary and Secondary Groups

Primary Group	*Secondary Group*
Generally small	Usually large
Personal, intimate and face-to-face association	Impersonal, little intimate and less immediate social contact
Relatively long period of interaction	Less enduring, short duration and temporary
Some emotional depth in relationships	No scope of emotional ties and relationships generally superficial
Formal relationships	Informal relationships
Natural and spontaneous formation	Deliberately and artificially created
No specialised interest	More or less some specialised interest
Relationships end in itself	Relationships goal directed and oriented
Informal social control	Formal social control

Quasi Groups

These groups stand in between the primary and secondary groups. In such groups some characteristics of both these groups are found. Generally, many primary group characteristics, such as intimacy and face-to-face relations, are seen but in other matters they resemble with secondary groups. Bottomore (1975) observed that quasi groups are collection of people which lack organisation and structure and the members do not have much awareness about the existence of their group. In other words, quasi groups are collection of human beings having no structure but are bound on the basis of similar interests and behaviour patterns. They also lack continuity of relationships. In these groups, contacts are direct but the frequency is lesser than in the primary groups and what is more important, emotions are superficial and for the time being. Generally, they have no definite or specific organisation but at times they turn into organised groups. Social classes, status groups, age groups, sex groups, racial groups, crowds, public's, audiences are some of the examples of quasi groups. Although, the various types of these groups have some distinguishing characteristics, it is not unusual for them to overlap or to change from one type to another.

Gemeinschaft and Gesellschaft

Somewhat similar to the concepts of primary and secondary groups are the concepts of *gemeinschaft* and *gesellschaft*. These are German terms and used to represent community and society or association respectively. These concepts were developed by German sociologist Ferdinand Tonnies (1887) to differentiate between urban and rural life or community living and living in the mass society. The concept 'gemeinschaft' is closer to the concept of community. According to Tonnies, it refers to "social relationships whatever function characterised by relative smallness, cohesion, long duration and emotional intensity". It is characterised by a sense of solidarity and a common identity. There is a strong emphasis on shared values and sentiments, a 'we-feeling'. Horace Miner (in *International Encyclopaedia of the Social Sciences*, Vol. 3, 1968) described it as referring to a 'community of feeling' (a kind of associative unity of ideas and emotions) and notes that it derives from likeness and shared life experience. People frequently interact with one another and tend to establish deep and long-term relationships. Social control in gemeinschaft is maintained through informal means such as moral persuasion, gossip, and even gestures.

By contrast, 'gesellschaft' is an ideal type characteristic of modern urban life. It is often conceptualised as a corporate or mass society—a society based on relations or roles and consisting of associational groups. It is characterised by individualism, mobility, impersonality, the pursuit of self-interest and an emphasis on progress rather than tradition. Shared values and total personal involvement become secondary. Tonnies (1987) writes: "Everybody is by himself and isolated, and there exists a condition of tension against all others." Gesellschaft, in short, is the logic of the market place, where relationships are contractual, impersonal and temporary. There is little sense of commonality and social relationships often grow out of immediate tasks, such as purchasing a product.

Largely, as a result of industrialisation, urbanisation, technological revolution, division of labour and population growth, the gesellschaft has replaced the society of tradition with the society of contract. In this society, neither personal attachment nor traditional rights and duties are important. The relationships between men are determined by bargaining and defined in written agreement.

Comparison of Gemeinschaft and Gesellschaft

Gemeinschaft Relationships	*Gesellschaft Relationships*
Personal	Impersonal
Informal	Formal and contractual
Intimate and familiar	Task-specific
Traditional	Utilitarian
Sentimental	Realistic
Emphasis on ascribed statuses	Emphasis on achieved statuses
Less tolerance to deviance	Greater tolerance to deviance
Holistic relationships	Segmental (partial) relationship
Long duration	Transient and fragmented
Relatively limited social change	Very evident social change
Predominance of informal social control	Greater formal social control
We-feeling	They-feeling
Typifies rural life	Typifies urban life

In the end, it may be noted that there is a great deal of similarity between the typologies of C.H. Cooley (primary and secondary groups), Ferdinand Tonnies (gemeinschaft and gesellschaft), Emile Durkheim (mechanical solidarity and organic solidarity) and Robert Redfield (folk and urban continuum). The regular rediscovery, restatement and reiteration of the same dichotomy of social types suggests that the distinction being made is very fundamental.

Reference Groups

Sociologists use the term 'reference group' for such groups that individuals use as a standard for evaluating themselves and their own behaviour. These are the groups to which we psychologically identify with to which we may and may not belong but we may aspire to belong. People do not actually have to be members of the group to which they refer. Mustafa Sherif (1953) defined reference groups as "those groups to which the individual relates himself as a part or to which he aspires to relate himself psychologically". This definition points clearly to the importance of defining the groups with which an individual identifies, whether or not he belongs to them. These are the groups whose values, standards and beliefs guide the person in carrying out his actions and in evaluating himself.

It is not uncommon to orient ourselves to more than one reference group at a time. One's family members, teachers, neighbourhood and co-workers shape different aspects of our self-evaluation. In addition, certain reference group attachments change during the life cycle. We shift reference groups as we take on different statuses during our lives. A reference group may be an actual group, a collectivity or an aggregate, a person or personification of an abstraction.

The term 'reference group' was coined by Herbert Hyman in *Archives of Psychology* (1942) to refer to the group against which individual evaluates his or her own situation or conduct. Hyman distinguished between a membership group to which people actually belong, and a reference group which is used as a basis for comparison and evaluation. A reference group may or may not be a membership group. Later on, Robert Merton and Alice Kitt (1950) refined the concept and provided a functionalist formulation of it. Their work was stimulated by Samuel Stouffer's *The American Soldier* (1949) in which the concept of *relative deprivation* was developed. Merton and Kitt point out that feelings of deprivation were less related to the actual degree of hardship they experienced, than to the living standards of the group to which they compared themselves. Thus, relative deprivation is a special case of comparative reference group behaviour. Merton later distinguished reference groups and interaction groups (in *Social Theory and Social Structure*, 1957).

The originator of this concept, Hyman found in his study of social class that people thought of as their status could not be predicted solely from such factors as income or level of education. To a certain extent, an individual's self-evaluation of status depended on the group used as a framework for judgement. In many cases, people model their behaviour after groups to which they do not belong.

Quite often, an individual is torn between the demands of a membership group to which he belongs but with which he does not identify and the motivational dictates of a reference group of which he is not a member. Social psychologists have termed this position as *marginality*. A familiar example is that of a principal of a private college who is officially a member of the management group but who identifies with the teachers on the college floor. This is a classic dilemma of the *marginal man* (principal) who seeks to join a reference group to which he is excluded and in doing so, he is rejected by the group to which he already belongs.

Types

Sociologists have identified two types of reference groups as described below:

(i) Positive reference groups

These are the ones we want to be accepted by. Thus, if we want to be a film actor, we might carefully observe and imitate the behaviour of film actors. These are the groups, collectivities or persons that provide the person with a guide to action by explicitly setting norms and espousing values.

(ii) Negative reference groups

These groups we do not want to be identified with, also serve as sources of self-evaluation. A person might, for example, try to avoid resembling members of a particular religious group or a circus group. A group rejected by or in opposition to ego's own group, it is 'the enemy' or the negative group.

Importance and functions

The concept of reference group is important for understanding socialisation, conformity, and how people perceive and evaluate themselves, especially in relation to the self. Reference groups perform three basic functions:

(1) They serve a *normative function* by setting and enforcing standards of conduct and belief. T. Newcomb (1953) writes: "The significant thing about a reference group is, in fact, that its norms provide frames of reference which actually influence the attitude and behaviour of a person."

(2) They also perform a *comparison function* by serving as a standard against which people can measure themselves and others.

(3) They serve not only as sources of current evaluation but also as sources of aspiration and goal attainment (as a means of *anticipatory socialisation*). A person who chooses to become a professor or a lawyer begins to identify with that group and becomes socialised to have certain goals and expectations.

Chapter 7

Rural and Urban Communities

Key features

It has been traditional to classify communities as rural and urban, depending upon whether their populations are small and agricultural or larger and industrial or commercial. The physical and social conditions of rural and urban life are also different. Consequently, there are differences in the personality and behaviour of urban and rural people. One of the earliest textbooks, written by Robert MacIver and Charles Page (1949), find that there must be two bases of all communities: (1) the occupation of a territorial area, and (2) the shared possession of community sentiment. For MacIver and Page entire nations can be communities, but territorially separated persons with strongly shared identities and sentiments would not qualify.

Rural Community

A rural community is marked primarily by a small, sparsely settled, relatively homogeneous population that engages primarily in agriculture (although there are exceptions to this rule, especially in industrial societies). The traditional rural community tended to be a *folk society*. Robert Redfield (1941) describes the folk society as "a society, which is small, isolated, non-literate and homogenous with a strong sense of group solidarity . . . . .Behaviour is traditional, spontaneous, uncritical and personal; there is no legislation or habit of experiment and reflection for intellectual ends. Kinship, its relationships and institutions, are the type of categories of experience and the familiar group is the unit of action. The sacred prevails over the secular; the economy is one of status rather than of the market." Today, however, traditional rural community is losing its folk society character and flavour as described above.

Traditional features of rural communities

It would be a mistake to fit all rural communities into one set of image because all rural communities are not alike. Yet certain features have been found common to nearly all kinds of rural communities. These are:

1. Rural society was based predominantly on agriculture. Land was the basic means of subsistence. Nearly all rural population was involved in agricultural way of life directly or indirectly. A substantial part of their income was drawn from agriculture. All faced common problems, performed common tasks and shared common helplessness before the awesome natural calamities (floods, droughts etc.), which man cannot control.
2. The rural way of life used to be quite different from urban life. Thrift was an honoured value and conspicuous consumption was seen as an urban vice. A farmer's status was measured by his lands, his herds, his crops and the inheritance he could pass on to his children. Distrust of city people and disapproval of urban life was a predictable rural attitude. Rural people used to be suspicious of intelligentality and book learning. Their life used

to be simple without any fun and fair in the modern sense of the term. They used to have deep faith in religion and duties.

3. The rural social system was marked with minimum of social differentiation and social stratification. It was mostly based on land and property relations. These relations determined the share of various socio-economic groups and the distribution of agricultural wealth among the various sections of the rural population.
4. There was predominance of primary groups. On one hand, these groups were important in the development of the personality (socialisation) and on the other hand they used to exercise primary control over the lives of the rural people.

Changing rural community

The farm and rural life has played a long and important role in the history of humanity. The agricultural revolution (mechanisation of agricultural activities) that came in 17th and 18th centuries has changed the face of the rural world. Transportation, rationalisation and commercialisation of agriculture has brought rural revolution. Without a revolution in agricultural productivity, there could have been little urban growth. Because of changes in agricultural technology, the rural population is rapidly shrinking everywhere. Moreover, the commercial and industrial development has also provided an urban 'pull'. But rural communities are not transforming entirely on account of urban inputs. In fact, it is the sheer inertia of the agrarian economy which is forcing people to look elsewhere for both livelihood and respect. Thus, it is not that the village is changing in one direction towards urbanisation, but rather the impetus for change is taking place in village itself. "The town is not coming to country, as much as the country is reaching out the town" (Gupta, 2005).

Changing rural India

The village in India, where life was once portrayed as 'unchanging' and 'idyllic', has in recent decades seen profound changes. Dipankar Gupta in his recent article 'Wither the Indian Village' (*Economic and*

Political Weekly, February 19, 2005), while attacking this age old notion that the Indian village is timeless and unchanging, and that the Indian society is essentially rural, wrote that these notions need to be revised. The Indian village is undergoing changes, not just economically, but culturally as well. The agrarian character of the Indian village is fast changing in factual terms. Indian village is not what it used to be. The statistics show the falling rates of growth in agriculture and the increasing exodus from country to town. We have the phenomenon of non-farm employment whose scale has increased tremendously over the years. It is estimated today that about 24 per cent of villagers are engaged in non-agricultural occupations. These statistics do suggest a whittling down of the importance of agriculture as the mainstay of Indian society. Rarely would a villager today want to be a farmer if given an opportunity elsewhere.

Indeed, there are few rural institutions which have not been mauled severely from within, yet there are definite signs of change in rural India. Rural society in India is changing fast. The joint family is disappearing, the rural caste hierarchy is losing its tenacity and much romanticised harmony of the village is now exposed for the sham it perhaps always was. Caste and agriculture no longer exercise their vigorous hold which used to decide matters for India's villages. With the abolition of landlordism, the introduction of adult franchise and the enactment of reservation laws have changed old social relations that dominated the rural India. It would not be out of place to mention here that sociologists, Indian and foreigner, have done a lot of studies on the rural life since 1950s. Rural social transformations such as caste, class and family relations have receive much attention of social scientists.

Urban Community

An urban community is one in which a large number of people are engaged other than the agricultural pursuits, i.e., in the production and collection of food. Such community has a large, densely settled and relatively heterogenous population. The emergence of urban communities has altered human lifestyles and values. The size, complexity and density of urban communities have given rise to new forms of social organisation, new behaviours and new attitudes. Georg Simmel (1950) designated urban life as rational in the sense that it involves quick logical and calculating reactions. He contrasted this to the slow, habitual and simple quality of rural life.

Characteristics of urban community

Urban life and personality are affected by the physical and social conditions of urban living—anonymity, social distance, speed and tension, regimentation, impersonal social interaction, mobility and transiency etc. These conditions produce impersonality, insecurity and segmentation of personality, which appear to be universal characteristics of urbanisation (or urban community) all over the world. Urban mode of life is quite contrary to traditional rural life, though it has affected rural life which is also in the process of change. Its characteristics are represented by the terms 'urbanism' and the process of its expansion is called 'urbanisation'.

1. *Large size and high density of population*: The size of the urban community is much larger than the rural community. Not only this, in urban areas, there is high density of population. Density increases the number of short-term, impersonal and utilitarian social relationships a person is likely to have.
2. *Heterogeneity:* Urban population is heterogenous. It consists of various shades of people—different castes, classes, ethnic groups, religions, etc. They are not all alike. Urban community is noteworthy for its diversity.
3. *Anonymity:* The sheer pressure of number marks for anonymity. Anonymity is a loss of identity and sense of belongingness. The heterogeneity of city life with its mixture of people of all races, castes, classes, creeds, occupations and ethnic origins heightens the sense of anonymity.
4. *Mobility and transiency:* Urban life is dynamic. Social relations are temporary. Therefore, permanency does not develop in urban relations. There is a high rate of geographical as well as social mobility in urban areas. In America, on an average, a person changes his job (occupational mobility) within six years. Consequently, his dwelling (changes of residence), also

changes. Different types of mobility usually mean transiency of contact. As such, urban social relations continue for a very short time. Urban dweller continually makes new social contacts.

5. *Formality of relations:* In urban social life, relations are not intimate and kinship based. Most routine social contacts in the city are impersonal and segmented. Formal politeness takes the place of genuine friendliness. The impersonality of urban life is a necessary and convenient way of urban living.
6. *Social distance:* City people are physically crowded but socially distant. Social distance is a product of anonymity, impersonality and heterogeneity. Occupational differences may be even more important sources of social distance. Urbanites become nigh-dwellers, not neighbours. Apartment dwellers may live for years without any acquaintance with many of the other occupants.
7. *Regimentation*: The city is always in hurry. The life (work and entertainment) in the urban community becomes 'clock regulated'. Order, regularity and the punctuality are the characteristics of urban life. On the streets, his movement is controlled by traffic lights, on railway stations and other places by elevators and escalators.
8. *Segmentation of personality:* Most routine urban contacts are of secondary group rather than primary group nature. Most contacts are instrumental, that is, we use another person as a necessary functionary to fulfil our purposes. We do not necessarily interact with entire persons but with people in terms of their formal roles as postman, bus driver, office assistant, policeman and other functionaries. We thus interact with only a segment of the person, not with the whole person.

Distinction between Rural and Urban Communities

Many scholars have tried to distinguish between the rural world and the urban world. We here are reproducing such differences pointed out by early distinguished sociologists Sorokin and Zimmerman (*Principles of Rural-Urban Sociology*, 1929). This distinction is applicable only on traditional rural communities and the developing industrial urban areas of 19th century and early years of 20th century. After this period much changes have occurred and this distinction has become more or less blurred and defunct:

Criteria		*Rural World*	*Urban World*
1.	Occupation	Totality of cultivators and their families. In the community usually a few representatives of several non-agricultural pursuits.	Totality of people engaged principally in manufacturing, mechanical pursuits, trade, commerce, professions, governing, and other non-agricultural occupations.
2.	Environment	Predominance of nature over anthro-social environment. Direct relationship to nature.	Greater isolation from nature. Pre-dominance of man-made environment over natural. Poorer aid, stone and iron.
3.	Size of community	Open farms or small communities, 'agriculturalism' and size of community are negatively correlated.	As a rule in the same country and at the same period. The size of urban community is much larger than the rural community. Urbanity and size of community are positively correlated.
4.	Density of population	In the same country and at the same period the density is lower than in urban community. Generally, density and rurality are negatively correlated.	Greater than in rural communities. Urbanity and density are positively correlated.
5.	Heterogeneity and homogeneity of the population	Compared with urban populations, rural communities are more homogeneous in racial and psychological traits (negative correlation with heterogeneity).	More heterogeneous than rural communities. Urbanity and heterogeneity are positively correlated.
6.	Social differentiation and stratification	Rural differentiation and stratification less than urban.	Differentiation and stratification show positive correlation with urbanity.

Contd...

Contd...

7.	Mobility and direction of migration	Territorial, occupational and other forms of social mobility of the population are comparatively less intensive. Normally the migration current carries more individuals from the country to the city.	More intensive mobility. Urbanity and mobility are positively correlated. Only in the periods of social catastrophe is the migration from the city to the country greater than from the country to the city.
8.	System of interaction	Less numerous contacts per man. Narrow area of the interaction system of its members and the whole aggregate. More prominent part is occupied by primary contacts. Predominance of personal and relatively durable relations. Comparative simplicity and sincerity of relations. "Man is interacted as a human person".	More numerous contacts. Wider area of interaction system per man and per aggregate. Predominance of secondary contacts. Predominance of impersonal casual and short-lived relations. Greater complexity, manifoldedness, superficiality and standardised formality of relations. Man is interacted as a "number and address".

The above distinction shows that the rural and urban communities used to differ among themselves on the bases of physical and socio-cultural environment, way of life, norms and values, and a large number of other factors such as density of population, birth and death rates, economic activities, caste, class, family and religion etc.

F. Tonnies, in his book *Gemeinshaft and Gesellschaft* (1887) and E. Durkheim in *Division of Labour* (1907) also contrasted the social life of traditional rural communities with that of rapidly developing, industrial urban areas. On the one hand, they stressed family and community as sources of identity and support and, on the other, their relative weakness in urban context where a more individualitic and impersonal way of life was developing. Tonnies used the terms *gemeinschaft* and *gesellschaft* to describe this broad sweep of social change. Durkheim's terms—mechanical and organic solidarity—overlap and complement Tonnies terminology. He described solidarity in traditional (rural) societies as mechanical and in industrial urban societies as organic.

The work of Georg Simmel (1950) also echoes many of the sentiments of Tonnies and Durkheim. Simmel's particular interest in the effect of the urban environment on the individual—eloquently expressed in his essay 'The Mind and the Metropolis'. Louis Wirth (1938), a renowned urban sociologist, made a firm distinction between rural and urban society. He defined the city in terms of three fundamental features, viz., (1) population size, (2) density, and (3) heterogeneity. Social contacts typical of the city were seen by Wirth as impersonal, segmental (narrow in scope), superficial, transitory, and usually of a purely practical or instrumental kind.

Rural and Urban Convergence

Much of the foregoing discussion (historic rural-urban distinction) has become outdated. Today urban and rural differences (dichotomy) of all sorts are rapidly shrinking everywhere in the world, though the speed of this change differs from place to place. The rural-urban distinction has already become less important than occupational distinction. Recent studies show that occupation has become more important than rural or urban residence as a clue to one's personality and way of life. Increasing urban world is beset by problems of community integration and organisation and community planning has become a growing concern in our urban society.

It should also be assumed that urbanisation necessarily brings in its train the situation of anomie (a sense of normlessness or lack of moral guidance to behaviour), disorganised and lack of primary group relationships as observed by earlier writers (Tonnies, Durkheim, Simmel) of urbanism. Some recent studies have found that with the increase in urbanism, primary group relationships within kinship and friendship group increases. When rural people migrate to the city, they rely heavily upon kinship and caste people and other relatives (as we see in India) even if they are distant relatives for social interaction, intimate response, identity and a sense of belonging. The rise of the proportion of secondary contacts with urbanism implies no absolute weakening of primary group life.

Today, with the spread of urban patterns into rural areas, rural life is becoming urbanised. This development is somewhat uneven. Rural areas closer to larger cities show the highest degree of urbanisation. More isolated areas and where farming practices are more traditional show fewer urban influence. But, everywhere, the steady urbanisation of rural society is evident. Not all, but many of rural non-farm people are urban commuters who become a powerful urbanising influence upon rural life.

A new development that has undermined any simplistic rural-urban contrast is the growth of 'commuter villages'. In *Urbs in Rure* (*The City in the Countryside*), R.E. Pahl draws our attention to the commuter invasion of rural areas. Some villages are almost wholly inhabitated by people who work elsewhere. This phenomenon we can easily see in villages situated near Mumbai, Delhi, Chennai, Kolkata etc.

Chapter 8

Socialisation

Key features

The human infant enters this world as a biological organism like all other animals—as a bundle of muscles, bones, vital organs and all other biological parts needed for life. At the time of birth, he is just a human being. A human child cannot survive unaided for at least the first four or five years of life. At this stage, the new-born human baby is helpless. Not only is it physically dependent for the satisfaction of biological drives such as hunger and protection on older members of the species but it also lacks the behaviour patterns necessary for living in human society. In order to survive, the infant has a lot to learn—the skills, knowledge and accepted ways of behaving of the society. It must learn a way of life. This learning, in sociological terminology, is called *socialisation*. Through the process of socialisation, he becomes a social being—with a set of attitudes and values, likes and dislikes, goals and purposes. This process of learning turns the human being into a social being.

Social phenomena are not explainable in terms of original nature (instincts and drives) and capacity (structure of mind) of the human animal. As an animal, man also requires food, protection and sex association but the ways he satisfies these demands of life are quite different from other animals. Not only this, the original nature of human beings of different places, say India, America, Africa or Europe etc., in all essential respects, is the same but still the people differ widely in many respects—manners, language, religion, belief etc. This difference is because of the facts of social learning, i.e., socialisation and culture.

Definitions

Broadly, *socialisation is learning to participate in social roles.* It refers to the way the people learn the habits, attitudes, self-conception, group norms and universes of discourse that enable them to interact with other people in their society, and enact different social roles. Gillin and Gillin (1950) wrote: "By the term socialisation, we mean the process by which individual develops into a functioning member of the group according to its standards, conforming to its modes, observing its traditions and adjusting himself to the social situations." According to Horton and Hunt (1968), "socialisation is the process whereby one internalises the norms of his groups so that a distinct 'self' emerges, unique to this individual." Alex Inkeles (1965) defined it as, "socialisation is the process of learning one's culture while growing out of infant and childhood dependency, leads to internalisation of society's values and goals". According to Anthony Giddens (1977), "socialisation is the process whereby the helpless infant gradually becomes self-aware, knowledgeable person, skilled in the ways of the culture into which she or he is born". In brief, socialisation is a process by which norms and other behavioural regulators are transformed into personality elements. Or, in other words, the process of socialisation has been conceptualised in three ways as under:

1. It is a process of learning (formal and informal both).
2. It is a process of personality formation and the development of self.
3. It is a process of internalisation of social norms (expectations), values, moral codes and ideals of society.

Two viewpoints

It is recognised that the socialisation is not simply a one-way process in which an individual learns how to fit into the society. He may also redefine his roles and obligations and as a result, he affects society. The individual and society both are dependent on each other for their existence. Thus, socialisation can be described from two points of view—as individual learning and as a process of cultural transmission by the community (society) as a whole.

(1) *Objective view:* It emphasises how society interacts and influences the individual. From this point of view, "socialisation is that process by which society transmits its culture from one generation to the next and adapts the individual to the accepted and approved ways of organised social life" (Fichter, 1957). Thus, socialisation is necessary if society is to continue and function effectively. It develops the skills and disciplines needed by the individual.

(2) *Subjective view:* How the individual responds to the society is another view of socialisation process. This view places emphasis on the learning aspect of socialisation. The individual learns the folkways, mores, laws, and other features of culture, as well as the skills and other necessary habits, which enable him to

become a functioning member of the society in which he lives. From this point of view, "socialisation is a process which goes on in the individual while he is adapting to the people" (Fichter, 1957).

Aims and Objectives of Socialisation

The socialisation is mainly aimed at the development of self and the formation of personality. The concept of 'self' refers to the individual as subject (as the source of action and self-reflection), whereas the term 'personality' refers to the individual as object (the object of external evaluation). It is the process through which an individual is moulded into an effective participant of society. The following are the main objectives of socialisation:

1. It inculcates basic disciplines ranging from toilet habits to the method of science. It helps in the learning of self-control.
2. It develops skills and capacities needed to fit into the society.
3. It teaches social roles (responsibilities) and their supporting attitudes.
4. It instils aspirations and satisfies needs of the individual.
5. It helps in the transmission of culture from generation to generation.
6. It develops a sense of identity and the capacity for independent thought and action, for example learning of language.
7. It develops conscience which is one important characteristic product of this process.

Forms of Socialisation: Primary and Secondary

While dealing with the functions of family, Talcott Parsons has analysed two forms of socialisation—primary and secondary. Originally, this distinction was made by Charles Cooley (1909). These two forms of socialisation were defined by him partly in terms of the particular groups or 'agencies' in which they occur. *Primary socialisation* refers to socialisation during the early years of childhood which takes place within the family, peer groups of close friends and closely-knit groups of neighbours. In it two basic processes are involved—internalisation of society's culture and the structuring of the personality. Culture is not simply learned, it is "internalised as a part of personality structure". In this connection, Parsons remarked that families "are factories which produce human personalities". Not only this, 'stabilisation of adult personalities' (marriage relations and emotional security) is also done in the family. *Secondary socialisation* occurs during the last years. It involves learning how to organise and conduct oneself in formal contexts and how to behave towards people who have different degrees of status and authority. The school is an important example of an agency of secondary socialisation, but all formal organisations (Trade Unions and professional associations etc.) influence their members to some degree can be included in this category.

The distinction between primary and secondary socialisation parallels that between informal and formal socialisation. Informal socialisation usually takes place as a part of everyday activity. It affects us unconscionably and must be distinguished from the formal acquisition of specific skills such as reading and writing.

Mechanism of Socialisation

There are numerous sub-processes of the process of socialisation or social learning. The principal ones are the following:

1. *Imitation:* Imitation is copying by an individual of the actions of another. This may be conscious or unconscious, spontaneous or deliberate, perceptual or ideational. It is the main factor in the process of socialisation which works from birth to death. As children grow, they take recourse to imitation. Through imitation, he learns to speak Da Da, Ma Ma, Papa etc.
2. *Suggestion:* Suggestion is a process outside the learner. It is a process of communicating information which has no logical or self-evident basis. A person may 'take a suggestion' not only from the conscious and deliberate persuasion of another but also

without the other person knowing it. It plays a key role in the socialisation of the individual. By it persons are made, unmade and remade. Through suggestion, an educational system moulds the minds of children in the desired direction. Propaganda and advertisements are based on this fundamental psychological principles of suggestion.

3. *Sympathy*: It simply means to feel with another individual. It binds us more closely with our fellow men. Through the sympathetic reaction we enter into a fuller understanding of the feelings and motives of others, for instance, the sight of an ailing person or a disabled person may cause a person to weep or to perform some altruistic act of charity.
4. *Competition*: Competition is a stimulative process in which two or more individuals compete with one another in achieving knowledge. It is particularly important in social learning of children.

Process of Socialisation (Stages of Development)

Socialisation is not confined to childhood; it is a lifelong process. It is no longer regarded as the exclusive preserve of childhood, with the primary agents being the family and school. It is now recognised that socialisation continues throughout the life-course. It begins at birth and continues until death. At each distinct phase of life, there are transitions to be made or crises to be overcome. Some earlier scholars like S. Freud and Jean Piaget have discussed the development process only upto childhood or adolescence. Freud has discussed a series of five stages through which a child develops. These are *oral, anal, phallic, latency and genital*. Piaget's stages of cognitive development are *sensorimotor stage* (birth to 2 years), *pre-operational stage* (2 to 7 years), *concrete operational stage* (7 to 11 years) and *formal operational stage* (11 to 15 years). According to Piaget, the first three stages of development are universal but not all adults reach the formal operational stage. Following Freud, renowned sociologist, Talcott Parsons has also discussed only four stages beginning from the period of infancy (oral, anal and latency) to adolescence period. As said above, the process of socialisation does not stop at adolescence or at a certain age, but it continues till death—the termination of personal existence.

The stages of human development seem at first sight to be biologically determined—from infancy to death—but sociologists do not accept this proposition. They are interested in age stages primarily as social, not biological or chronological categories. The studies of feral and isolated children indicated that they do not develop from stage to stage (as contended by development theorists Freud and Piaget) at all if they do not interact. It is through the association with other human beings that the child develops a consciousness of himself as being different from others. Sociologists study the social construction of age. They believe that the stages of human 'life-course' are social as well as biological. They are influenced by culture and also by material environment of people in which they live. Man's biological nature makes socialisation both possible and necessary. Socialisation cannot occur if man did not have the inborn capacity to learn and use language.

Earlier psychological (psychoanalytic) view of socialisation stressed the internal stimuli, drives and instincts (innate development process), while the sociological view focuses on the way an individual learns to fulfil the requirements of the various social roles he is called upon to play. A person becomes human by internalising the norms and expectations about behaviour of the people with whom he interacts. Sociologists have placed main emphasis on the childhood and adolescence years rather than infancy period. In modern societies, the expectations at different stages of socialisation are changing for men and women both.

Erik Erikson (*Childhood and Society*, 1963) has attempted to integrate biological, psychological and sociological perspectives about 'conception of the life cycle'. He charts eight stages of psycho-social development of the individual as under:

	Stages	Psycho-Social Crises	Significant Social Relations
1.	First year of life	Trust v/s mistrust	Mother or mother substitute
2.	Second year	Autonomy v/s doubt	Parents
3.	Third through fifth years	Initiative v/s guilt	Basic family
4.	Sixth year to puberty	Industry v/s inferiority	Neighbourhood, school
5.	Adolescence	Identity v/s confusion	Peer groups and out-groups: models of leadership
6.	Early adulthood	Intimacy v/s isolation	Partners in friendship; sex competition, co-operation
7.	Middle adulthood	Generativity v/s self-absorption	Divided labour and shared household
8.	The ageing years	Integrity v/s despair	'Mankind', 'my kind'

Now, we shall describe briefly four important stages of socialisation from infancy to old age.

Infancy and childhood (oral, anal and latency)

This is a distinct stage of life which starts from birth to the onset of adolescence, i.e., a period beginning from 0 to 13-14 years of age. In traditional and preliterate societies, 'childhood' as a separate phase of development did not exits. The young child moved directly from a lengthy infancy into working roles within the community. However, in modern societies, long period of childhood has been recognised. Both parenting and childhood have become clearly distinct from other stages than was true of traditional societies.

In the first year of life child's contact with the outside world, including its mother, is channelled through the mouth and lips. The mother is the first parent who begins the process of socialisation. It is from her that the earliest social stimuli to which a child is subjected come. He/She responds to these stimuli by imitating them. At this stage, the child makes no distinction between persons and things—the mother's breast and the nipple of the bottle are equally and solely means of organic satisfaction. Crying, smiling and eye movement in response to others are forms of early social behaviour.

The roles of the mother and the infant are merged at this stage of development.

Near about the second year, the toilet and other training is initiated in many societies. During this period, the child learns how to eat their food and talk in a polite way. The child develops a sense of control over itself and its environment, although it is still dependent on its parents. He starts recognising the family relations. During this stage, the child internalises two roles—his own and that of his/her mother—now clearly separate.

The years from 3 to 5 (phallic stage) are a period of rapid physical development and locomotion, awareness of genital sensations and the appearance of Freudian *Oedipus* complex, in which the boy's attachment to the mother is combined with jealous hostility towards the mother. At this stage, the child learns to 'behave himself' in various contexts of his activity, particularly when interacting with adults. Besides, child also internalises all the four roles of the family, viz., husband-father, wife-mother, son-brother and daughter-sister.

Then comes the latency stage which continues near about 5 years to 12-13 years. By about five, the child becomes a fairly autonomous being, no longer just a baby but almost independent in the elementary routines of life at home. During this period the child acquires informal aspects of culture—folkways, customs, fads and crazes, along with secret modes of gratification and forbidden knowledge. Sociologists have termed this stage as the 'gang stage'. During these years the child shifts his interests more and more from the social world of family to the group life of his/her peers. Social consciousness develops rapidly, the chief interest is in group activities and group loyalty becomes highly important. There is growing revolt against adult domination.

Adolescence

With puberty comes the beginning of adolescence. The biological changes involved in puberty (the point at which a person becomes capable of adult sexual activity and reproduction) are universal. It is a most important stage of socialisation which begins near about 14-15 years till 20-21 years. It is a transition stage from childhood to maturity during which new patterns of behaviour are developed to meet the demands of both the larger and more diversified life of his peers and of the adult society. During this period, the individual is more attracted towards the opposite sex. He feel interested in recreation, films, TV, sports etc. Psychologist G. Stanly Hall wrote that 'adolescence' is 'naturally' a period of psychological 'storm and stress'. But sociologists believe that the emotional experience of youth varies greatly between individuals and across cultures.

Adolescents in traditional societies have less to 'unlearn' than adolescents in modern societies since the pace of change is slower. In traditional cultures, where children are already working alongside adults, this process of 'unlearning' is normally much less severe. In current times, the concept of 'teenager' has become much relevant. Teenagers often try to follow adult ways but are treated in law as children. Teenagers are in between childhood and adulthood.

Adulthood

Adulthood is considered to be attained when a person can support himself or herself entirely independently of the parental family. . . . . Full adulthood implies the ability to form a family of one's own life (Johnson, 1960). It is a period of great stress and strain. During this period, one has to take many life-decisions—about the choice of marriage partners, about the choice of occupation, etc. It is a very critical stage of life. At this stage, the individual marries and starts working for livelihood. As a result, the individual has to assume many new statuses and has to learn roles according to these statuses. When an individual marries, he/she has to face with a new series of accommodations in his personal conduct. The individual has to learn new habits, ideals, customs and notions to adjust with the spouse and his/her family. In due course of events, children may be born and the individual is faced with the new situation and necessity of new adjustments, i.e., those of parent. Since the two parents were themselves brought up by different sets of parents, they will have learned different child rearing techniques and therefore will have to socialise each other to reach agreement about child care practices. All of this learning is a part of adult socialisation.

Another type of socialisation is occupational training, which teaches the attitudes and values associated with an occupation as well as skills. A doctor has to acquire technical knowledge required to practice medicine. A new employee in an office has to learn how to conform to the expectations of the other workers and to the written and unwritten rules. One has to learn the styles of dress, decor and people's conduct in the company of fellow employees.

Adulthood can be bifurcated into two stages—young adulthood and mature adulthood. Young adulthood is increasingly becoming a specific and important stage in the process of human development. This is a period of excitement and sexual development. In modern societies, young adults in their twenties engage themselves in preparing for their professional education, seeking career and finding some job or occupation. Besides this they explore the possibilities of sexual, political and religious affiliation in this crucial period of their life.

The mature adults (middle aged at about the age of 40) often experience a stress of self-evaluation during this period. At this stage, people realise that they have not achieved basic goals and ambitions and have little time left to do so. It is seen that women experience fear and confusion in their middle years. During this period, adults requires the deep internalisation of norms and attitudes that run counter to norms already learned and assimilated.

Old age

This is the final period of transition which occurs mostly between 60-65 years. While old age has typically been regarded as beginning at 60 or 65, but this definition of old age is not universally accepted. At this time many people begin restricting their occupational duties and preparing for retirement. (Norms of retirement differ from place to place). With advancing age, the mind, as well as the body, seems to lose its suppleness. Habits, as well as arteries, harden and refuse the strain of new demands. Those persons, who succeeds in adjusting to these new demands (physical-mental and social both), lead a pleasant life even in the old age. In such individuals socialisation may continue actively to the end of life.

In traditional societies like India, older people were normally accorded a great deal of respect. The elders used to had a major, often the final, say in the family matters and the community as a whole. They had a great role in socialising the younger children in the family. Individuals used to feel themselves to be part of a family and a community. But, now, things are swiftly changing. Older people do not receive that much of respect which they used to be. They are even despised and are left alone to live at their own. No longer living with their children and ejected from the economic arena, it is not easy for older people to make the final period of their life rewarding. At the same time, it is no longer widely accepted that older people should simply sit around passively, waiting to die. Instead, there has been an increase in programmes to socialise the elderly for meaningful pursuits and continued happy living.

Agencies of Socialisation

In general, it may be said that the total society is the agency for socialisation and that each person with whom one comes into contact and interact is in some way an agent of socialisation. Socialisation is found in all interactions but the most influential interaction occurs in particular groups which are referred to as *agencies of socialisation*. The oblivious beginning of the process for the new-born child is his immediate family group, but this is soon extended to many other groups. Other than the family, the most important are the schools, the peer groups (friends circle) and the mass media.

The family

The child's first world is that of his family. It is a world in itself, in which the child learns to live, to move and to have his being. Within it, not only the biological tasks of birth, protection and feeding take place, but also develop those first and intimate associations with persons of different ages and sexes which form the basis of the child's personality development.

The family is the primary agency of socialisation. It is here that the child develops an initial sense of self and habit-training—eating, sleeping etc. To a very large extent, the indoctrination of the child, whether in primitive or modern complex society, occurs within the circle of the primary family group. The child's first human relationships are with the immediate members of his family—mother or nurse, siblings, father and other close relatives. Here, he experiences love, cooperation, authority, direction and protection. Language (a particular dialect) is also learnt from family in childhood. People's perceptions of behaviour appropriate of their sex are the result of socialisation and major part of this is learnt in the family. As the primary agents of childhood socialisation, parents play a critical role in guiding children into their gender roles deemed appropriate in a society. They continue to teach gender role behaviour either consciously or unconsciously, throughout childhood. Families also teach children values they will hold throughout life. They frequently adopt their parents' attitudes not only about work but also about the importance of education, patriotism and religion.

School

After family the educational institutions take over the charge of socialisation. In some societies (simple non-literate societies), socialisation takes place almost entirely within the family but in highly complex societies children are also socialised by the educational system. Schools not only teach reading, writing and other basic skills, they also teach students to develop themselves, to discipline themselves, to cooperate with others, to obey rules and to test their achievements through competition. Schools teach sets of expectations about the work, profession or occupations they will follow when they mature. Schools have the formal responsibility of imparting knowledge in those disciplines which are most central to adult functioning in our society. It has been said that learning at home is on a personal, emotional level, whereas learning at school is basically intellectual.

Peer group

Besides the world of family and school fellows, the peer group (the people of their own age and similar social status) and playmates highly influence the process of socialisation. In the peer group, the young child learns to confirm to the accepted ways of a group and to appreciate the fact that social life is based on rules. Peer group becomes *significant others* in the terminology of G.H. Mead for the young child. Peer group socialisation has been increasing day by day these days. Young people today spend considerable time with one another outside home and family. Young people living in cities or suburbs and who have access to automobiles spend a great deal of time together away from their families. Studies show that they create their own unique sub-cultures—the college campus culture, the drug culture, motorcycle cults, athletic group culture etc. Peer groups serve a valuable function by assisting the transition to adult responsibilities.

Teenagers imitate their friends in part because the peer group maintains a meaningful system of rewards and punishments. The group may encourage a young person to follow pursuits that society considers admirable. On the other hand, the group may encourage someone to violate the culture's norms and values by driving recklessly, shoplifting, stealing automobiles, engaging in acts of vandalism and the like. Some studies of deviant behaviour show that the peer group influence to cultivate behaviour patterns is more than the family. Why do some youths select peer groups which generally support the socially approved adult values while others choose peer groups which are at war with adult society? The choice seems to be related to self-image. Perhaps, this dictum works—"seeing is behaving". How do we see ourselves is how we behave. The habitual delinquent sees himself as unloved, unworthy, unable, unaccepted and unappreciated. He joins with other such deprived youths in a delinquent peer group which reinforces and sanctions his resentful and aggressive behaviour. The law-abiding youth sees himself as loved, worthy, able, accepted and appreciated. He joins with other such youths in a conforming peer group which reinforces socially approved behaviour.

Mass media

From early forms of print technology to electronic communication (radio, TV, etc.), the media is playing a central role in shaping the personality of the individuals. Since the last century, technological innovations such as radio, motion pictures, recorded music and television have become important agents of socialisation. Television, in particular, is a critical force in the socialisation of children almost all over the new world. According to a study conducted in America, the average young person (between the ages of 6 and 18) spends more time watching the 'tube' (15,000 to 16,000 hours) than studying in school. Apart from sleeping, watching television is the most time-consuming activity of young people.

Relative to other agents of socialisation discussed above, such as family, peer group and school, TV has certain distinctive characteristics. It permits imitation and role playing but does not encourage more complex forms of learning. Watching TV is a passive experience. Psychologist Urie Bronfenbrenner (1970) has expressed concern about the 'insidious influence' of TV in encouraging children to forsake human interaction for passive viewing.

Workplace

A fundamental aspect of human socialisation involves learning to behave appropriately within an occupation. Occupational socialisation cannot be separated from the socialisation experience that occurs during childhood and adolescence. We are mostly exposed to occupational roles through observing the work of our parents, of people whom we meet while they are performing their duties, and of people portrayed in the media.

The state

Social scientists have increasingly recognised the importance of the state as an agent of socialisation because of its growing impact on the life cycle. The protective functions, which were previously performed by family members, have steadily been taken over by outside agencies such as hospitals, health clinics and insurance companies. Thus, the state has become a provider of child care, which gives it a new and direct role in the socialisation of infants and young children. Not only this, as a citizen, the life of a person is greatly influenced by national interests. For example, labour unions and political parties serve as intermediaries between the individual and the state. By regulating the life cycle to some degree, the state shapes the socialisation process by influencing our views of appropriate behaviour at particular ages.

Theories of Socialisation

Socialisation is heavily centred upon the development of the concept of *self*. How a sense of self emerges—the awareness that the individual has a distinct identity, separate from other? This problem of the emergence of self is a much-debated one. This is because the most prominent theories about child development emphasise different aspects of socialisation.

Development of self

During the first months of life, the infant possesses little or no understanding of differences between human beings and material objects in the environment, and has no awareness of self. Children do not begin to use concepts like 'I', 'me' and 'you' until the age of about two or after. Only gradually do they then come to understand that others have distinct identities, consciousness and needs separate from their own.

The awareness of self arises in interaction with the social and non-social environment. The social environment is especially important. The development of our personal identity—or self—is a complicated process. The realisation of a distinctive personality is an even more complicated process, which continues throughout life. The child learns to differentiate between various other people by names--Daddy, Mummy and Baby and he begins to use 'I' which is a sign of definite self-consciousness—that he is becoming aware of himself as a distinct human being (Cooley, 1908). As time passes and social experiences accumulate, he forms an image of the kind of person he is—an image of self. This self develops gradually in the child.

How self emerges? This is main focus of the problem of socialisation. Here, we shall discuss views of some celebrated authors.

Freud's theory (psychoanalysis)

Sigmund Freud, the Austrian psychiatrist and founder of psychoanalysis, was not directly concerned with the problem of the individual's socialisation (he has not used the word 'socialisation' anywhere in his writings), he nevertheless contributed amply toward the clarification of the process of personality development. Distinguished sociologist T. Parsons has also adopted Freud's account of personality development to provide the psychological underpinnings of his theory of socialisation. Freud challenged Mead and Cooley's concept of socialised self who saw no separate identity of self and society. Freud believed that rational portion of human conduct was like the visible portion of an iceberg, with the lager part of human motivation resting in the unseen, unconscious focus which powerfully affects human conduct.

Process of personality development

Freud's theory of personality (self) development rests on the following process. He divided the self (human mind) into three parts: (1) the *id*, (2) the *ego*, and (3) the *superego*.

(1) The *id* represents the instinctive desires, which may be viewed as an unsocialised aspect of human nature. It is the obscure inaccessible part of our personality. It is the source of drives (animal impulses of man—hunger, aggression, and sexual drives) demanding immediate satisfaction in some way or the other. These impulses are controlled and partially repressed into the unconscious, while a reality-oriented conscious self, or ego appears.

(2) The *ego* is the acting individual. It serves as the mediator between desires and action representing the urges of the *id* when necessary. It tries to mediate the resultant conflicting demands of the *id* and the *superego*.

(3) The *superego* (the conscience) represents the social ideals (norms, values, traditions, the idea of moral and immoral etc.). It is seen as internalised parental and social authority. The parent is no longer outside telling the child what to do, but is inside the psyche, invisibly overseeing the child's thoughts and

actions, praising what is right and making the child feel guilty for wrong doing. For Parsons, the Freudian *superego* is the key device by which society's values are transmitted to the child. Thus society's norms and values are passed down from generation to generation in this way.

The Freudian theory contends that people possess a number of drives or urges connected with satisfying basic needs, such as the need for food or sexual release. These urges, known collectively as the *id*, seek immediate satisfaction. In society, however, instant gratification is rarely possible, and *id* must be controlled. This control is accomplished by what Freud called the *superego*, the part of the mind that incorporates society's rules. The *id* and the *superego* are in continual conflict. When we are hungry, for example, our *id* urges us to satisfy's our hunger in the quickest way possible. Our *superego*, however, tells us that this is an unacceptable way to satisfy our hunger. Freud stated that normally developing children develop *ego*, which reconciles the demands of the *id* and *superego* as much as possible. Freud presents the relation between the *id* and the *ego* as similar to that between a horse and its rider. The function of the *ego* is that of the rider guiding the horse which is the *id*. But, like the rider, the *ego* sometimes is unable to guide the horse as it wishes and perforce must guide the *id* in the direction it is determined to go or in a slightly different direction.

Evaluation of Freud's theory

Freud's all theories have inspired bitter controversies and numerous interpretations. This theory (development of self) is opposite to the views of Cooley and Mead. Cooley and Mead have demonstrated that the very emergence of the self is a social process and not a psychological process as contended by Freud. They have viewed self and society as two aspects of the same thing, whereas Freud finds that the self and society are often opponents and self is basically anti-social. There is always a clash between the impulses of the self and the restraints of society. Mead and Cooley, on the other hand, viewed self and society as merely different expressions of the same phenomenon. Cooley (1902) writes: "A separate individual is an abstraction unknown to experience . . . . . In other words, 'society' and 'individuals' do not denote separate phenomena but are simply collective and distributive aspects of the same thing." Moreover, it is very difficult to verify empirically the three layers of human mind—*id, ego* and *superego* as suggested by Freud.

Cooley's theory of the 'looking-glass self'

How does a person arrive at a notion of the kind of person he is? According to Charles Horton Cooley (1902), this concept of self develops through a gradual and complicated process which continues throughout life. He pointed out that when we refer to the self, when we use the word 'I' (the social self is referred to by such words as I, me, mine and myself; the individual distinguishes his 'self' from that of others), we usually not referring to our physical body. We use the word 'I' to refer to opinions, desires, ideas, feelings, or evaluations of others with whom we interact. Whether one is intelligent, average or stupid, attractive or ugly, these and many other ideas of the self are learned from the reactions of our associates. Even, the elementary knowledge that one tends to be fat or thin, tall or short is a comparative judgement based on the opinions of others. This process of discovering the nature of the self from the reactions of others has been labelled the *looking-glass self* by Cooley. Looking-glass self simply means how we see ourselves through the eyes of other people. The idea of looking-glass seems to have been taken from Thackeray's book *Vanity Fair* in which it is said: "The world is a looking glass and gives back to every man the reflection of his own face."

> Each to each a looking-glass,
> Reflects the other that doth pass.

Just as we see our face, figure and dress in the mirror which gives an image of the physical self, so the perception of the reactions of others gives an image of the social self. We "know", for instance, that we are talented in some field but less talented in others. This knowledge or perception comes to us from the reactions of other persons. Through play and other group activities, one is also helped to perceive the feelings of others and their feelings toward him.

Stages of formation of self

According to Cooley, there are three steps (stages) in the process of formation of looking-glass self:

1. The imagination of our appearance of how we look to others.
2. The imagination of their judgement of how we look or how we think others judge our behaviour.
3. How we feel about their judgement, i.e., our feelings (self feeling) about their judgements.

We know that we exist, that we are beautiful or ugly, serious or funny, lively or dull etc., through the way other people think of us, of course, but we can imagine how we appear to them and how they evaluate our appearance. We often respond to these imagined evaluations with pride, embarrassment, humiliation or some other feeling. In conclusion, the looking-glass self means that we see ourselves and we respond to ourselves, not as we are and not as other think we are, but as we imagine others think we are.

Evaluation of Cooly's theory

There is a difference of opinion among some scholars about the functioning of the 'looking-glass self'. Several researches have been done to seek empirical evidence of the correlation between one's perception of responses of others and the actual judgements they have made of him. These studies find that there is often a significant variation between individual's perception of how other picture him and the views they actually hold. Clearly, it is our perception of the responses of others and not their mutual responses which self-image, and these perceptions are often inaccurate (Horton and Hunt, 1964).

Theory of G.H. Mead (I and me)

American philosopher and social psychologist George Herbert Mead (1934) developed his ideas about the same time that Cooley did in the early years of the twentieth century. He gave particular attention to the emergence of a sense of self. He emphasised the two-part structure of this self and represented this by the terms '*I*' and '*me*'. He described in detail the whole process of child development and explained how children learn to use the concepts of 'I' and 'me'. The 'I' is the immediate response of an individual to others. It is the unpredictable and creative aspect of the self. People do not know in advance what the action of the 'I' will be. "The 'I' is the unsocialised infant—a bundle of spontaneous wants and desires" (Giddens, 1997). The 'I' reacts against 'me'. The 'me' consists of the attitudes of others that the child adopts and makes his own. Thus, when a parent says things like 'good child' or 'good behaviour' and 'bad child' or 'bad behaviour', such communications from 'significant others' (parents, siblings, playmates, teachers, relatives) become increasingly patterned or organised into that part of the self that Mead calls the 'me'. In other words, the 'me' is the adoption of the 'generalised other', which according to Mead is the 'social self'. Individuals develop self-consciousness by coming to see themselves as others see them. For Freud this is the outcome of Oedipal phase, while for 'me', it is the result of a developed capacity of self-awareness.

In contrast to 'I', people are conscious of the 'me'; the 'me' involves conscious responsibility. It is through the 'me' that society dominates the individual in the form of social control—the domination of the expression of the 'me' over the expression 'I'.

Phases of the development of self

Mead traces the genesis of the self through two stages in child development:

(1) *Play stage*: At this stage infants and young children develop as social beings first of all by imitating the actions of those around them. In their play small children often imitate what adults do. They often play 'house' (Mummy-Papa) or 'school' (Teacher-Student), enacting the role of mother, father, teacher, student or any other person important to them—significant others. Mead calls this process as taking the role of others (role-taking)—learning what is to be in the shoes of another person. By taking the role of these significant others, they can better understand their own roles as children, students, sons or daughters. By practising the roles of others in play, children learn to understand what others expect of them, and they learn how to behave

to meet those expectations. As a result of such play, the child becomes cognisant of himself and obtains a picture of himself by assuming the role of others. However, it is a limited self because the child can take only the role of distinct and separate others. They lack a more general and organised sense of themselves.

(2) *Game stage*: It is the next stage of child development, which according to Mead occurs at about eight or nine, the child starts taking part in organised games. To learn organised games, one must understand the rules of the play, notions of fairness and equal participation. The child at this stage learns to grasp what Mead terms the 'generalised other'—the general values and moral rules involved in the culture in which he or she is developing. This generalised other is an individual's total impression of the judgements and expectations that other persons have toward him. At this stage, the sense of the self in the full sense of term emerges. In the play stage, children are not organised wholes because they play at a series of discrete roles. In Mead's view they lack definite personalities. However, in the game stage, such organisation begins and a definite personality starts to emerge. Thus, for Mead, taking the role of generalised other, rather than that of discrete others, is essential for the full development of self.

Mead's theory of development of self is less cumbersome than that of Freud. It has also been very influential, yet it has been criticised on the ground that the concepts used by Mead such as 'taking the role of other', 'making a gesture to one's self' and the 'generalised other' are not clear enough. Not only this, the concept of self, which is a combination of 'I' and 'me', is also ambiguous. Moreover, the theory of Mead does suggest the method of studying social interaction.

Durkheim's theory of collective representation

Though Emile Durkheim has not directly talked anywhere in his writings about the development of the sense of self or the process of socialisation of the individual, he has definitely described the role of the society in the formation of personality (attitudes, beliefs and behaviour) of the individuals. In his theory of 'collective representation', Durkheim insisted that the individual becomes socialised by adopting the behaviour of his group. He maintained that the individual's thought and behaviour are determined by collective representation. By collective representation, he meant the body of experiences, a system of ideas, patterns of behaviour, attitudes and values held in common by a group of people.

Durkheim's main interest in the relationship of the individual to the group was the group control over the individual. For him, socialisation is a one-way process because he focussed his attention on how society develops and moulds the individual to fit into the group. Durkheim's conception left little room for individual's initiative and freedom in the process of socialisation. This is a great weakness of his theory of collective representation. Durkheim did not recognise any role of the individual in the process of socialisation. How do these representations become a part of the individual or how does collective representation exert pressure over the individual is not fully explained by Durkheim. He utilised his theory of collective representation (theory of socialisation) in explaining the causes of suicide, the social phenomena of religion and the concept of social solidarity etc.

Some Important Concepts Related to Socialisation

Anticipatory socialisation

Anticipatory socialisation refers to the process of socialisation in which a person 'rehearses' for future positions, occupations and social relationships. Sometimes, a person may aspire to belong to a group and, before actually entering the group, he may prepare himself by anticipatory socialisation.

Re-socialisation

Socialisation to a new role or position in life which requires a dramatic shift in attitudes, values, behaviours and expectations learned in the past is known as re-socialisation. This process requires discarding of former behaviour pattern and accepting new ones as part of a transition in one's life. The changes people undergo during adulthood usually require adaptation to new situations. The person has to adopt an entirely new set of meanings to understand his or her new life. The process of re-socialisation occurs throughout the human life cycle. Occupation, marriage and retirement are a few important events of life when a person has to adopt a new set of norms and values. The most dramatic type of voluntarily (or sometimes involuntarily) re-socialisation occurs in institutions like the armed forces, prisons, convents and mental hospitals. People entering these institutions are totally stripped of their old selves. They have to live in a highly controlled social environment under a new set of rules and adopt a new role as a military person, prisoner or mental patient. Goffman (1961) has termed this situation as 'mortification of self'.

Reverse socialisation

Reverse socialisation refers to the process whereby people normally being socialised are at the same time socialising their socialisers. Children, who are viewed as objects of socialisation, function sometimes within the family as agents of socialisation, themselves. They are often very active socialisers of their parents. Sometimes, a baby causes others (mother, father etc.) to change their behaviour patterns. Young people may affect the way their parents (or another adults) dress, eat and even think.

Socialisation, Culture and Personality Development

Personality differs strikingly from society to society. (Personality is viewed as one's total behaviour tendency system). Each society develops a basic personality type which fits the culture. This is shown by renowned anthropologist Ruth Benedict (1934) in her pioneering studies of Dobu and Zuni tribes of North America. Dobu people were found to be distrustful, suspicious and treacherous in stark contrast to the members of the Zuni tribe who were generous, polite, cooperative, confident, trustful and amiable. Where the Dobuan was apprehensive and insecure, the Zuni was secure and serene. This example of difference in personality pattern illustrates the effect of culture on personality. Later on, Margaret Mead's (1963) research on children and adolescence has also established the role of culture in personality formation. Cultural experience shapes personality development. Ralph Linton (1936) writes: "Every culture exerts a series of general influences upon the individuals who grow up under it. These influences differ from one culture to another, but they provide a common denominator of experience for all persons belonging to a given society."

From before one is born until after he is dead, his life is circumscribed by his culture. Each culture provides a set of general influences which vary endlessly from society to society. Culture (1) defines the meaning of situations and thereby indicates the behaviour expected; (2) defines the attitudes one should hold, values one should cherish, and the goals which are worthwhile; (3) provides the myths, legends and supernatural beliefs one will live by; and (4) gives a man a readymade behaviour patterns to carry out all these.

Culture is normally transmitted from generation to generation by adults to children. But, this transmission should not be viewed as a passive process. Socialisation is not a kind of 'cultural programming', in which the child absorbs passively the influences with which he comes into contact. Without active support of the learner successful socialisation cannot take place and the culture cannot be transmitted. The examples of such feral children (children brought up in the company of animals such as the cases of Anna, Isbella or Ramu etc.) who were wholly or largely excluded from social interaction for a period of their lives clearly reflects the role of society in forming human behaviour.

Socialisation and Deviation

Failure in proper socialisation sometimes leads to deviation. Every member of a society is frustrated by the clash of his biological drives (such as sex) with the taboos of his culture. But not everyone becomes a deviant. Why some people become deviant and most persons conform to the norms of the society? Sociologists assume that they are deviant because the socialisation process has failed in some way to integrate the cultural norms into the individual's personality. Where the socialisation process is successful, the individual adopts the norms of the society in which he lives. The approved goals and values of the culture are so internalised that they become his own emotional needs. The taboos of his culture become part of his conscience and he automatically and mechanically acts in the expected manner most of the time. These behaviour norms of the culture and moral values are learned mainly in the family during his childhood and adolescence period. Where family life is conflicting and its atmosphere (or the atmosphere of the neighbourhood and peer group) is charged with the lack of moral values, or where deviation is honoured, children often develop deviant habits.

If men are perfectly socialised, they are constantly motivated to act as required by the social norms. But, for atleast three reasons, men are never perfectly socialised. First, if socialisation is too rigid, it leaves men incapable of dealing with unforseen events; but if it permits some flexibility, then it also allows some personal interpretation of roles. Second, all socialisation makes conflicting demands and, therefore, produces some antagonism to socialising agents, thereby creating a possible source of motivation for social deviance. Thirdly, defects in socialisation process may also lead to deviation. These defects may arise in various ways: through personality dispositions or mental incapacity, through interruptions to social learning, and through incoherence or contradiction in the social environment.

Chapter 9

Individual and Society

Key features

What is the relationship between an individual and society? This is one of the most fundamental questions and the focus of all sociological investigations. It is a question which has baffled many ancient sages and modern thinkers since long even before the term 'sociology' was coined. This question is like a proverbial question or the puzzle whether the hen came first or the egg. In the like manner the question was raised whether the individual came first or the society in which he lived. In the western social thought we find answer to this complex question in the form of two opposing theories: (1) 'The Social Contract Theory' (Hobbes, Rousseau, Lock and Adam Smith), and (2) 'The Social Organismic Theory' (Comte, Spencer, Durkheim). Both these theories have been expressed and explained by many writers over many centuries. Both present one-sided approach to the complex problem and as such both are inadequate to explain the true relationship between man and society because both deny the other side of relationship. Both are based on some or the other erroneous assumptions. We shall here examine in brief the basic assumptions of both the theories.

(1) *The Social Contract Theory*: It is a theory of social order that was most popular in the seventeenth and eighteenth centuries. According to this theory, it is argued that in the pre-social state of nature people enjoyed absolute personal freedom. It emphasised that human beings were set apart from society and individual man and society were separable. It gave more importance to the individual and almost ignored the existence of society.

(2) *The Social Organismic Theory*: This theory rests on the analogy that the human society is like the living organism. Society passes though the process of birth, youth, maturity, old age and death like an organism. Society, like an organism in nature, becomes more complex and differentiated. This theory is also one-sided because it discounts almost entirely the role of the individual in social life.

The inadequacies of the above theories have been proved on the basis of certain factual evidences, such as (1) feral cases, (2) the growth of self, and (3) the man's dependence upon his social heritage.

(1) *Feral cases*: It has been well demonstrated in the studies of *feral children*—children who have grown up in wild in the company of some animals or isolated from societies. Several feral children were reported from different parts of the world: Kasper Hauser (Nuremberg, 1828), Kamla (India, 1920), Anna (America, 1938), Isabelle (Ohio, America) and Aveyron (France). All these cases illustrate to some extent (a) that the denial of society was a denial of human nature; (b) that the traits that we associate with human nature, such as the emergence of individuality or language, are dependent upon the membership in human society. When these children were found, their behaviour was very strange; and (c) that human nature develops in human beings when they are social man, i.e., only when he or she is one

of many men/women sharing a common life. These cases of feral and isolated children emphasise that the development of human personality is dependent to a large extent on the interaction of the individual with the society.

(2) *The growth of self:* The emergence of the capacity for social self is an aspect of the growth of selfhood or personality development. The child does not merely imitate the social usages of adults but in the process of imitation his own social nature is gradually revealed and developed. As the child becomes a self, he discovers thereby that others too are selves. Many sociologists and social psychologists such as G.H. Mead, Sigmund Freud and C.H. Cooley (for their detailed ideas, see chapter on socialisation) have explained in detail the process of the development of selfhood. The process of self-emergence involves the child's continued adjustment to the behaviour of other persons. The self can come to being only in society—only within the give-and-take of group life.

(3) *Man's dependence upon the social heritage:* The individual is neither beginning nor end, but a link in the succession of life. This is a sociological as well as a biological truth. Every individual is the outcome of social relationship which is determined by pre-established mores (norms and values). Our relation to the social heritage is very intimate. It determines our heredity and our mental equipment. It is continuously changing because of our social experiences which evokes and directs our personality. Society both liberates and limits our potentialities. When we use Aristotle's famous phrase that "man is a social animal", we simply mean that society, without the support of the social heritage, the individual personality does not and cannot come into being.

The Individual: A Biopsychological Concept

As a biopsychological concept, the term 'individual' places emphasis upon the traits and characteristics that are in major part biologically determined. It emphasises those aspects of concrete human beings that are original and relatively unchanged by experience. For instance, temperament is in large measure or entirely a matter of original equipment (nature). The native mental capacity of the individual may be determined in the biological structure and may remain unchanged by education and experience. Thus individual is a biological product.

This view of the individual directly or indirectly highlights the importance of biological heritage (heredity) in the development of the personality of the individual. Heredity provides the raw material (the qualities of life) of personality, and this raw material can be shaped in a great many different ways. Some of the similarities in man's personality and culture are due to his common heredity. As far as we know, every human group in the world inherits the same general set of biological needs (oxygen, food, drink, sex, rest etc.) and capacities. Our common heredity thus explains some of our similarities in personality while individual differences in heredity explain some of the individual differences in our personality. What heredity does is to provide the set of needs, capabilities and limitations with which other factors interact in shaping human personality. But, the ways in which these needs are satisfied or coped with vary widely between and within cultures.

All explanations of human behaviour in terms of individual and biological facts are inadequate and have been refuted on many grounds. There is more or less complete denial either of the existence of the biological facts or of their significance. Poverty, crime, integrity, personal achievements and the like are conceived to be socially rather than biologically determined. These phenomena are acquired rather than they are product of original nature. As such, Lombroso's theory of crime, that—"criminals are born, they are not made" is not accepted. Like crime, all social phenomena are learned and product of society. This social determinism does hurt the concrete unity of the human being. The sociological position is that the person is a concrete, individual unity. He is a product and not a sum. Like water, man is compound, not a mixture, i.e., a resultant of the opposed or cooperating tendencies of the hydrogen and oxygen. It behaves as a unit. In like manner the human being is an entity. The individual is an abstraction.

Individual as a Person

The term 'person' is used when reference is laid to the qualities and attributes that are results of social life. It exhibits the human rather than the original nature. Language, for example, is an attribute of the person, not of the individual. It is an organised body of habit responses resulting from social experience. The 'person' is a social product. It simply means an individual with status in the group he belongs. R.E. Park (1921) writes: "The person is an individual who has status. We come into the world as individual. We acquire status and become persons." Park's words are an indication for the role of socialisation in transforming individual into a person. We become socialised largely through role and status.

Individual within Society

There would be no society if there were no people talking to one another, acting and interacting, cooperating with one another. But how to behave in one's society or what is right and what is wrong in the society, all these things one has to learn in the society. Each society has its own special set of rules, its own customs and traditions, its own set of values and beliefs, and each must teach its members to fit into the society. The idea of society implies a mutual give-and-take by the individuals concerned either in the form of mutual glances, waving of hand, greeting, handshake, conversation or the more subtle forms of give-and-take such as letter writing, season or festival greeting, sending and acknowledging of gifts, talking on phone, e-mailing, Internet chatting and participating in public affairs.

The relationship between individual and society can be viewed from three angles (i) functionalist, (ii) interactionist, and (iii) culture and personality.

Functionalist view: How society affects the individual?

What is the relationship of the individual to society? Functionalists regard the individual as formed by society through the influence of such institutions as the family, school and workplace. Early sociologists such as Herbert Spencer, Emile Durkheim and even Karl Marx, who was not a functionalist, examined society as existing apart from the individual. For Durkheim, society is reality; it is first in origin and importance to the individual. Durkheim's keen discussion of the collective consciousness showed the ways in which social interactions and relationships and ultimately society influence the individual's attitudes, ideas and sentiments. He utilised his theory of 'collective representation' in explaining the phenomena of religion, suicide and the concept of social solidarity.

Thus, Durkheim is classed as a 'social realist', a champion of 'sociologism', for he propounded the kind of 'social realism' that gave ultimate social reality to the group, not to the individual. Durkheim's conception left little room for individual initiative and freedom. In contrast to Auguste Comte (known as father of sociology), who regarded the individual as a mere abstraction, a somewhat more substantial position by Durkheim held that the individual was the recipient of group influence and social heritage. In sociological circle, this was the 'burning question' (individual v/s society) of the day.

How is society important in the formation of individual's personality is clearly reflected in the cases of isolated and feral children (children who were raised in the company of animals such as bears and wolves). The studies of feral children, referred to earlier (Anna, Isabelle, Kamla, Ramu etc.), have clearly demonstrated the importance of social interaction and human association in the development of personality.

Interactionist view: How is society constructed?

How an individual helps in building society? For interactionists, it is through the interaction of the people that the society is formed. The main champion of this approach was Max Weber (social action theorist), who said that society is built up out of the interpretations of individuals. The structuralists (or functionalists) tend to approach the relationship of self (individual) and society from the point of the influence of society on the individual. Interactionists, on the other hand, tend to work from self (individual) 'outwards', stressing that people create society. This perspective is sometimes referred to as 'symbolic interactionism'. W.I. Thomas, George Mead and Herbert Blumer were the most influential figures among the interactionists. Other recent approaches, which also place emphasis on individual, are ethnomethodology and phenomenology which is basically a philosophical perspective. Symbolic interactionism emphasises the importance of symbolic means of communication—language, gesture and dress etc. Interactionists fully accept that society does constrain and form individuals but they also consider that there is invariably opportunity for some 'creative' action (W.I. Thomas).

Interactionist Model of Relation between Individual and Society

Source: Mike O'Donnell' *Sociology*, 1997.

A prominent theorist of the last century, Talcott Parsons (1937, 1951) ignored the American symbolic interactionists and tried to attempt a grand synthesis of individual action and large-scale structure in his theory. But, his emphasis was heavily on the large-scale structure (society). He believed that it is the structure of society which determines roles and norms, and the cultural system which determines the ultimate values of ends. His theory was severely criticised by George Homans (1961). In his Presidential address (1964), "Bringing man Back In", Homans re-established the need to study individual social interactions, the building blocks of society.

A recent well-known theorist Anthony Giddens (1984) has not accepted the idea of some sociologists that society has an existence over and above individuals. He argues: "Human actions and their reactions are the only reality and we cannot regard societies or systems as having an existence over and above individuals."

Culture and personality view: How individual and society affect each other? or how individual and society interacts?

Both the above views are incomplete. In reality, it is not society or individual but it is society and individual which helps in understanding the total reality. The extreme view of individual or society has long been abandoned. For sociologists—from Cooley to the present—have recognised that neither society nor the individual can exist without each other and that they are, in reality, different aspects of the same thing. Many studies conducted in the field of social/cultural anthropology substantiate this view. This view was laid down mainly by Margaret Mead, Kardiner and others who maintained that society's culture affects personality (individual) and, in turn, personality helps in the formation of society's culture. These anthropologists have studied how society shapes or controls individuals and how, in turn, individuals create and change society.

Thus, to conclude, it can be stated that the relationship between society and individual is not one-sided. Both are essential for the comprehension of either. Both go hand in hand, each is essentially dependent on the other. Both are interdependent on each other. A few writings of the past and present individualists—Thomas Hobbes (17th century) and John Stuart Mill (19th century) have failed to recognise this interdependency. And today, on the basis of same misunderstanding of the interrelationship, we hear long echoes of this 'threat' of the social order to the individual in our legislative assemblies, UNO and champion of human rights organisations. These institutions and organisations regard every new measure of social security (such as MESA or POTA Acts in India) as a 'blow' to liberty. The same misunderstanding is held by thinkers such as Benjamin Kidd and philosopher Hegel who oppose the above views. In their opinion the individual should be subordinated to society. They say that the individual should sacrifice their welfare at the cost of society. Both these views are extreme which see the relationship between individual and society from merely the one or the other side. But surely all is not harmonious between individual and society. The individual and society interact on one another and depend on one another. Social integration is never complete and harmonious.

Currently, serious students question the utility of this prolonged debate over individual versus society. They perceived the individual and society as different sides of the same coin. Society cannot exist without individuals nor can individuals exist outside the society. "Sociology studies interaction between the self (or individual) and groups, and interaction between the groups. The self may both affect certain groups (and so society) and be affected by these groups. ... Individuals are part of society" (Mike O' Donnell, 1997). It is unlikely that this controversy will ever be solved. Moreover, it is a debate, which is not just confined to sociology, but preoccupies scholars in all fields of the social sciences.

Chapter 10

Status and Role

Key features

Since the influential writing of Ralph Linton (1936), *status* and *role* have become the key concepts of sociology. By status, Linton meant a position in a social system involving designated rights and obligation, whereas by role he meant the behaviour oriented to the patterned expectations of others. Linton went on to state the long recognised and basic fact that each person in society inevitably occupies multiple status and each of these statuses has an associated role.

In every society and every group each member has some function or activity with which he is associated and which carries with it some degree of power or prestige. What the individual does or performs, we generally call his *role*. The degree of prestige or power we refer to as his *status*. Roles are related with the statuses. In a sense, 'status' and 'role' are two words for the same phenomenon. This is why, Linton remarked, "role is the dynamic aspect of status," or the behaviour or tasks associated with or ascribed to a status. In other words, status and role are two sides of a single coin. It simply means that both are closely related and one cannot be separated from the other.

Social status and role are analytic terms; they have a more general quality than the concrete descriptive terms to which they have reference. Sociologist prefers to choose such analytic terms rather than descriptive terms like bus conductor, customer, father or mother etc. After Linton, these two terms have become the basic features of structural-functional theory. Later on many sociologists have refined and added many ideas to these two terms. For instance, R.K. Merton (1968), who is known to be the champion of role theory, departs from Linton's conception of status and role. According to Merton, each social status involves not a single associated role, but an array of roles to which he calls 'role set'.

The concepts of status and role are basic building blocks of social structure or social systems. According to Parsons, 'status-roles' are the sub-units of society. Participation by an actor in social system means that he is 'located' relative to other actors. This is his 'status'. In this position he does various things, and what he does is called his 'role'. For him, 'status-role' is the proper unit of social system. A social system can be thought of as a network of statuses and their associated roles.

What is Status?

Simply defined, a status is a socially defined position in a group or a social system, such as female, student, teacher, child, mother, father etc. A status occupant is expected by other to behave in a special way, relative to specific situation. The relation of the father and the child is reciprocal and gives to each a position in the family group. Position is always relative; status always implies a group. With every status certain privileges, rights and duties are associated.

Most of the sociologists have used the two terms—position and status—synonymously, but some have made distinction between these terms. 'Position' denotes one's situation in the role-structure, which is subjective, while 'status' refers to the evaluative aspect of position—whether others see it as 'high' or 'low'. In this sense, it is an objective term.

Harry M. Johnson (1960) distinguished the three related concepts, viz., 'role', 'status' and 'position'. He defined a *social position* as something filled by an individual member of a social system. The position consists of two main elements: (1) expectations and obligations held by other members concerning the behaviour of the position incumbent; and (2) right or the legitimate expectations of the position incumbent concerning the behaviour of other members. The first element Johnson calls the *role* of a position, while the second element he calls the *status* of a position. It denotes the prestige of a position or an individual.

According to Kingsley Davis (1949), "status is a position in the general institutional system, recognised and supported by the entire society". For Horton and Hunt (1964), "status is the rank or position of an individual in a group". Status in Weber's theory refers to the esteem or 'social honour' given to individuals or groups.

Though generally used synonymously—status and social status—there is a bit difference between the two terms. The term 'status' simple indicates the position a person occupies in a group. Whereas social status is the amount of honour and prestige a person receives from members of the community and from the larger society in a stratification system. It denotes not only the position but relative 'social standing' of a person on publicly recognised scale or hierarchy of social worth. In this sense, it embraces all his particular statuses and roles that determine his social standing in a society. It is the social identity an individual has in a group or society. Social statuses may be very general in nature (such as those associated with gender roles) or may be much more specific (as in the case of occupational positions). Social status of a person is determined by a wide range of factors, facts and conditions such as original nature and physical characteristics, accidental conditions, physique, mentality and temperament. Sex, age, race, caste, class, economic position etc. are also important factors that affect social standing of a person in a society or the community he lives.

Types of Status

Linton (1936) has noted two types of status:

(1) *Ascribed status*: Statuses, which are given to us at birth (age, sex, kinship, race, caste), are known as ascribed status. These are 'assigned' to a person by society without regard for the person's unique talents or characteristics. Such ascribed characteristics cannot be changed by individual effort. These are more or less determined by the cultural situation over which he has no control initially, for example, position or status of a boy or a girl in a family is ascribed in terms both of sex and age. Likewise, Negro or Harijan are ascribed status.

Generally, ascribed statuses are determined on four bases: (1) sex dichotomy (male-female); (2) age difference (child, youth, adult); (3) kinship (son, brother, sister etc); and (4) social factors (divorcee, widow etc). In traditional societies most statuses are ascribed, with one's occupation and general social standing determined at birth.

An ascribed status does not have the same social meaning in every society. For instance, the term 'old man' is viewed as more of an insult in some societies, while respect for the elderly is an important cultural norm in India and other Asian countries. Conflict theorists are especially interested in ascribed statuses (those assigned by birth), since these statuses often confer privileges or reflect a person's membership in a subaltern group.

(2) *Achieved status:* "Any social position held by an individual as a result of his or her personal accomplishments in open formal or market competition with others is known as achieved status" (*Oxford Dictionary of Sociology*, 1994). It is a social position which a person attains through his own efforts, individual choice and competition. This is secured through one's ability, performance and possibly by good or ill fortune. Collector, policeman, husband, father, college graduate, teacher are examples of achieved status. Achieved status requires the individual to make choices, not only of occupation but also of friends, marital partners, place of residence, schools, colleges and organisations (recreational clubs) etc.

The main bases of achieved status are: (1) property (jagirdar, zamindar); (2) occupation (doctor, engineer); (3) education (college graduate, illiterate); (4) specialisation and division of labour (foreman, mechanic); (5) political power (prime minister, president); (6) marital relations (husband-wife, sister-in law etc.); and (7) achievements (good sportsman, musician etc.).

Societies vary considerably in the relative distribution of ascribed and achieved statuses. The ascribed status is more important in a simple and traditional society while in a modern industrial society, greater emphasis is placed on achievement and particularly of occupational positions. In such changing societies, many statuses are open to achievement. Weber argues that ascribed status has rapidly declined as a means of access to economic and political power in modern societies.

Status, Office, Station and Stratum

Kingsley Davis (*Human Society*, 1949) has drawn distinction between a few concepts, which apparently look similar to the basic concept status as under:

Status and office

The term 'status' designates a position in the general institutional system, recognised and supported by the entire society spontaneously evolved rather than deliberately created in the folkways and mores. 'Office', on the other hand, would designate a position in a deliberately created organisation, governed by specific and limited rules in a limited group, more generally achieved than ascribed. Positions of Principal of Jain College or Professor of Psychology in J.N. University are the examples of office, because they refer to a particular position in a particular group or institution. It is to be noted that holding an office may at the same time give one a status and conversely, holding a particular status may help one acquire a certain office. Occupational status is often a status and office both.

Station

A single individual occupies not one but many statuses and offices. 'Station' refers to such a cluster of statuses and offices that tend to be combined in one person as a locus and are publicly recognised as to combined in a great many cases. Whereas a single status or office defines one's position with reference to a limited sector of social interaction, a station embodies one's generalised status (the sum total of one's major position) in the overall social structure.

Stratum

'Stratum' is a term which is used to refer "a mass of persons in a given society who enjoy roughly the same station". Individuals belonging to same stratum tend to have the same outlook toward the world. They used to have like interests, attitudes and problems. Specifying the stratum is one of the most convenient and frequently used ways of giving a shorthand description of a social structure. Every society is commonly divided into some strata.

It may be noted that status is a purely relational term, which means that each status exists only through its relation to one or more other statuses. One status cannot be defined without referring to another. There cannot be a parent without a child or teacher without a student or a doctor without patient. In this sense, all statuses are paired and associated with certain rights and duties to which we call role. Thus, all statuses and roles are usually defined in the contexts of social statuses and roles performed by others. Since statuses are positions in social systems, they exist independently of the particular individuals who occupy them. Indeed, a status can exist even though no one is occupying it at the time, such as the status of President when the current President has died and new one has yet to be elected.

Each person occupies many statuses simultaneously and is expected to perform the roles appropriate to them. A person may be a son, a father, a brother and a police officer and plays roles according to each status. These roles are both complex and different in each case. The playing of them depends on a variety of circumstances, for one is father in relation to one's children, a brother in relation to his brothers and sisters and an uncle in relation to nephews and nieces and so forth. Women have a different status from men, their roles call for 'feminine' behaviour. Feminine role varies with the needs of time and place. The married woman is in a different status from that of the single girl. Her role is different and in many ways she will have a different personality.

Status set

If we take the sum of all of the statuses that we occupy, the result is known as a *status set*. Status set is a complex of many positions a person occupies. A person can be a doctor, father, husband, a citizen, a member of a political party etc. The sum of all these statuses is called status set.

Master status

As written above, each person holds many different statuses. Some may connote higher social positions and some lower positions. Sociologist Hughes (1945) observed that certain statuses are more important than others. A status by which an individual is principally identified in the society is known as *master or key status*. This status dominates others and thereby determines a person's general position within a society. The nature of this key status varies from society to society and varies also from one period of history to another. In India, ascribed status of caste and gender can function as master statuses; they often dominates one's life. They have an important impact on one's potential to achieve a desired professional and social status.

What is Role?

The concept of *role* is by no means a new one. It originally comes from the theatrical setting, referring to the parts which actors play in a stage production. We may illustrate this with the noted writer William Shakespeare's famous lines:

All the world's a stage;
And all the men and women merely players;
They have their exits and their entrances;
And one man is his time plays many parts . . . .

Shakespeare uses the theatre as an analogy for the world as a whole and for the human experience. Actors obviously take on roles but so do the rest of us. In every society individuals play a number of different roles, according to varying contexts of their activities. Stepping into the shoes of Shakespeare, modern sociologist E. Goffman (1959) has proposed *dramaturgical approach* (social life as like a theatre drama) in sociology. He sees social life as through played out by actors on a stage—or on many stages, because how we act depends on the roles we are playing at a particular time.

Role is sociologically important because it demonstrates how individual activity is socially influenced and thus follows regular patterns. There are broadly two approaches to the theory of social roles. The first systematic use of the concept of role was by G.H. Mead in 1934, a forerunner of *symbolic interactionism*. In this usage, roles are analysed as the outcome of a process of interaction that is tentative and creative. A second approach to role theory derives from Ralf Linton (1936), which later on became the hallmark of functionalism. It sees roles as essentially prescribed and static expectations of behaviour, as prescriptions inherent in particular position. These prescriptions derive from the society's culture and they are expressed in social norms that guide behaviours in roles.

According to Ogburn and Nimkoff (1958) a role is "a set of socially expected and approved behaviour patterns consisting of both duties and privileges, associated with a particular position in a group". Some writers, such as Kingsley Davis (1949), have confused the two terms 'role' and 'role performance'. For Davis, role refers to the actual behaviour of a status incumbent. It is acting as a set of duties and privileges as per requirements of his position. H.M. Johnson (1960) and many other writers differing from Davis call it 'role performance'. According to Johnson, "role is expectations and obligations held by other members concerning the behaviour of the position incumbent". Ely Chinoy (1954) agrees with Johnson and uses 'role' to refer to expectations and obligations. What other people anticipate of us or from us and what people actually do (or perform) as status occupant are two different things. Role refers to expected behaviour; it implies a set of expectations both of one's own behaviour and of the reciprocal behaviour by the people in the situation while actually carrying out that role behaviour is known as role performance. In other words, role performance does not always match role expectations. Broadly defined by Alex Inkles (1965) 'role' refers to "the set of expected or normative rights and obligations allowed to and demanded of persons generally felt to be incumbent of a recognised status by others who participate in the same social system". Similarly, Anthony Giddens (2000) states: "Roles are socially defined expectations that a person in a given social position follows. . . . It is the expected behaviour of an individual occupying a particular position." In this light, a role may be understood as a set of norms and expectations applied to the incumbent of a particular position. Roles not only refer to expectations about activities that are performed, they also refer to the beliefs and values attributed to performers. With every role some sets of ideas, beliefs, values, norms, attitudes along with expectations are attached.

Much of social interaction is guided by *role expectations*. Social life acquires a great deal of predictability as a result of the development of shared situational expectations among individuals with special social identifications. Roles are often paired so that members of society not only hold these expectations above others, but they also can develop themselves and know that they are capable of playing *reciprocal roles*, even prior to experience. Thus, for example, it is expected that persons labelled as teachers will act in a very special way in the presence of students seeking knowledge.

Role Conflict

The clash of expectations concerning some aspects of a role have usually been called *role conflict* (Faris, *Handbook of Modern Sociology*, 1964). The term 'role conflict' has been used in various senses. It takes several different forms—role collision, role confusion, role incompatibility, inadequate role preparation, or failure in role performance. Several roles may conflict with one another or a single role may carry conflicting duties and pressures. When two individuals have roles which are in conflict in some respect, it is called *role collision*. When the same individual plays two or more roles (role of an employee and housewife) which have contradictory expectations, it is called *role incompatibility*. When there is a lack of agreement among group members about the expectations for a given role, it is called *role confusion*. For instance, when a person defines his or her role in one way while those in related roles define it differently. Role conflict can occur when someone simply has difficulty satisfying expectations because their duties are unclear, two difficult, or disagreeable. Ill-defined roles, such as parent or friend where the scope is very wide, becomes at many times the casualty of role conflict.

As Linton pointed out in his early discussion of the concept of role, every individual fills more than one role at a time. This is one reason for the discrepancy between the way a person ought to behave and the way he actually behaves. Violation of one role requirement often occurs in the course of conformity to another. Modern society is full of conflicting role demands. For example, the expectations associated with two different roles—role of employee and role of parent or role of military officer and role of military subordinate—are contradictory and produce strain in the person called upon to resolve the contradictions. When this involves roles associated with two different statuses, such as employee and parent, the situation is known as *status strain* or 'inter-role conflict'. When the conflicting roles are both associated with the same status—military officer, for example, the result is known as *role strain*, or 'intra-role conflict'.

To minimise or resolve the effects of role conflict, a variety of ways are resorted to. The first is to choose which role is most important and then violate the expectations associated with the other role. For instance, the primary loyalty of the Nayars of Malabar goes to the state (military duty) than to the conjugal family. The second way is to leave one of the conflicting statuses (a person might quit a job if it interferes to much with his parenting responsibilities). A third response is to engage in *role segregation*, the practice of separating various role partners from one another. A fourth response involves what Goffman (1959) called *role distance*. It refers to 'some disdainful detachment' of the performer from the role he or she is performing. This is one method for minimising role strain associated with a disagreeable role. Military officials use role distance in similar ways when they refer to people as 'soft targets' and civilian casualties as 'collateral damage'.

Role Set

It is generally assumed that there is one fairly clearly defined role appropriate to each social position, but the facts of social reality are much more complex. There are, indeed, frequently many roles related to any one social position. For any social position there is what Merton (1957) calls "a complement of role-relationships in which persons are involved by virtue of occupying a particular social status". This means that each status carries with it a role set consisting of a collection of roles performed in relation to different role partners. Thus, the various roles associated with occupying a particular status when combined is known as role set. Merton illustrates the idea of role set with an example of a medical student. He writes, the status of medical student entails not only the role of a student vis-à-vis his teachers, but also an array of other roles relating him diversely to other students, physicians, nurses, social workers, medical technicians, and the like. Similarly, the school teacher who by virtue of his position has roles to play vis-à-vis his pupils, his colleagues, his head master, parents, members of the school board, professional associations and so forth. There is possibility for a considerable degree of conflict in such a role set, for what the parent feels should constitute the education of his child is not necessarily what the school board considers it should be and the head master may have his views, so may be professional associations and other organisations.

Merton has distinguished role set from 'multiple roles'. He writes: "The role set differs from what sociologists have long described as 'multiple roles'. By established usage, the term multiple role refers not to the complex of roles associated with a single social status, but with the various social statuses in which people find themselves—for illustration, the statuses of physician, husband, father, professor, church elder, conservative party member and army captain. (This complement of distinct statuses of a person each of these in turn having its own role set. I would designate as a status set)."

Distinction between Status and Role

Status is a concept in sociology, role is a concept in social psychology; status is a structural phenomenon, role is behavioural phenomenon; status depends upon social structure, role depends upon the personalities and capabilities of individuals. Although status and role are usually found together, it is possible to imagine situations involving status without role and role without status. People occupy statuses, they play roles. The norms, however, are attached to the statuses. Since the norms are constantly changing in a changing society, statuses too—as well as roles—are dynamic phenomena. Statuses and role may, however, change in relative independence of each other. New statuses arise in society and old ones disappear.

The concept of 'status' is often combined with the notion of 'role' to produce the idea of a 'status role'. Each status in society is accompanied by a number of norms. This group of norms is known as a role. A status of husband is accompanied by the role of husband, a status of teacher is accompanied by the role of teacher.

The concepts of status and role are central to sociological study. These along with the two other elements—groups and social institutions make up social structure just as a foundation, walls, ceilings, and furnishings make up a building's structure. As written elsewhere in the book in sociology man's all social actions and interactions are analysed in terms of status and role.

Chapter 11

Social Stratification

Key features

All human societies, from the simplest to the most complex, have some form of social inequalities in terms of unequal distribution of power, privilege, prestige and wealth between individuals and social groups. We all are not equal. Some people are rich and some are poor. Some are respected and others are despised. Some are powerful and others are powerless. The egalitarian society remains a dream though men have always longed for an egalitarian society. It is dreamed that in an egalitarian society, there will be no rich and poor, no haves and have-nots, no exploitation and oppression and the phrase like 'power to the people' will become a reality.

How inequality develops, and how it persists generation to generation? Why are some groups in a society more wealthy or powerful than others? These are some of the questions which have led sociologists to study social inequality. To describe social inequalities, sociologists have used the term *social stratification*. Stratification is a term that refers to all forms of inequalities based on age, gender, ethnicity, caste, class etc. We can compare social stratification to layers of a rock in the earth's surface, one on the top of each other. While rock's layers are quite rigid (subject to minimum change) but such rigidity is not found in social structure.

What is Social Stratification?

No problem in sociology has received more attention in the last about five-six decades, and probably no other has been subject of confusion than social inequality and stratification. It is still a dominant concern among sociologists of today. Not only this, it is probably the most difficult and confused area within sociology. There is no general agreement about what constitutes social stratification, or social inequality. This is why, social stratification has been variously defined but the main contention of all the definitions is the differentiation of a given population into hierarchical ranked superposed classes along some dimension of inequality. It involves the division of population into unequal layers (upper and lower layers) or strata based on income, wealth, gender, ethnicity, power, status, age, or some other characteristic. Its basis and very essence consists in an unequal distribution of rights and privileges, duties and responsibilities, social values and privations, social power and influences among the members of a society.

According to Raymond W. Murry (1946), "social stratification is a horizontal division of society into 'higher' and 'lower' social units". For Talcott Parsons (1954), "stratification in its valuational aspect is the ranking of units in a social system in accordance with the standard of the common value system". (*Essays in Sociological Theory*, 1954) Kurt B. Mayer (*Class and Society*, 1955) defined it as, "an arrangement of positions in a graded hierarchy of socially superior and inferior ranks". In his text, Mike O' Donnel (1977) defined it as, "Stratification is the division of society or group into hierarchically ordered layers. Members of each layer are considered broadly equal but there is inequality between the layers". A renowned theorist of late twentieth century Anthony Giddens (2000) writes: "Stratification can be defined as structured inequalities between different groupings of people." The term 'stratification' in sociology is usually applied to the phenomena of structured social inequality which arise as unintended consequences of social processes and relationships. It is a hierarchical ordering of people in a society differentiated according to power, privileges and status. The term 'structured' indicates an arrangement of elements—the inequality is not random but follows a pattern, displays relative constancy and stability and is backed by ideas that legitimise and justify it.

In brief, the term 'stratification' refers to the system of ranking of persons that a society adopts. In this system, rank of some strata is higher, some lower. Their sum constitutes the stratification system of that particular society. It indicates the location of a person in society.

Distinguishing Features of Social Stratification

The above description reveals the following characteristics and features of social stratification:

1. Division of society into permanent groups or categories on the basis of income, wealth, ethnicity, gender, age, caste and class.

2. Involves the hierarchical ordering of these groups or people. In certain industrial societies, particularly the USA, hierarchy of social groups has been by a hierarchy of individuals.
3. Relationship of superiority and subordination among the people.
4. Unequal distribution of power, privilege and status.
5. Members of a particular stratum have a common identity, similar interest and a similar lifestyle.

Social Differentiation and Social Stratification

"A society does not exists as a single entity, a monolith rigidly moulded and solidly integrated. It is rather made up of knots and nodes, of clusters constantly changing groups of people in ever fluctuating relationships with other people" (Bierstead, 1957). It is in reference to this diversity within society that sociologists use the term 'social differentiation'. It is generally used to refer diversity between men and women, caste and class, city and village etc. In another sense, social differentiation simply means role differentiation or division of labour which is essential for the survival and stability of society. Some type of division of labour and specialisation is necessary in human and animal society both. In animal society, it is determined by heredity but in human society the patterns of social behaviour are determined by culture instead of heredity. In brief, Social differentiation is meant the manner in which people recognise that society is subdivided, with individuals occupying different statuses according, for example, to age, sex, occupation, ethnicity and related characteristics in modern pluralistic societies.

The term 'social differentiation' is closely associated with that of social stratification but both are not synonymous terms. Social stratification involves differential ranking (a feeling of superiority or inferiority), i.e., how roles are ranked and their incumbents unequally rewarded. When social differences are based on hierarchy, sociologists refer to it as social stratification. It is a special type of social differentiation, signifying the existence of a systematic hierarchy of social positions whose occupants are treated as superior, equal or inferior relative to one another in socially important respects. To put it differently, whenever we have stratification, we have social differentiation, but not the other way round. It is an undisputed fact that social differentiation is a universal phenomenon of human society but there is some controversy about whether stratification is universal. For instance, the difference in sex is universal. In no society do males and females do the some things, occupy the same statuses, share identical interests, conforms to the same norms or aspire to the same kinds of achievement.

Characteristics of Stratification

M. Tumin (1969) listed five basic attributes of the phenomenon of stratification:

1. *It is social:* It means its character is patterned. The adjective 'social' indicates here five things: (a) The make-up of any system of stratification is dependent upon conventionally ascribed meanings and socially defined criteria and prescriptions. In simple terms, it is different from outward biological caused inequalities. Although difference in such factors as strength, intelligence, age and sex can serve as bases on which statuses or strata are distinguished, such differences in biological traits do not become relevant in patterns of social superiority and inferiority until they are socially recognised and given importance. These differences never by themselves sufficient to explain why some statuses have more power, prestige and property than others. To determine who is the 'fittest' and who is having property and power is always a matter of complex social and cultural meanings. (b) Norms and sanctions are key factors in shaping and maintenance of the system. The 'social' aspect of stratification also suggests that the distribution of rewards in any community is governed by 'norms' or conventional rules. (c) The norms have to be taught anew to each generation. For this, there is a need to socialise each generation. There is no evidence that any kind of mentality—slave, ruling or otherwise (in Indian

context, caste mentality)—is biologically inherited. (d) Like all other social systems, this system is also likely to be unstable, because socialisation is never identical throughout the society. Because of this reason, among others, every system of stratification is continuously changing. (e) To say that stratification is 'social' also implies that this system is always connected with other aspects of society, such as politics, kinship, marriage and the family, economics, education and religion. For instance, the connection of stratification with politics is the phenomenon of power, by which the sons of the ruling elite (king or jagirdar) succeed their parents. Such connections of stratification can be seen with other institutions of society.

2. *It is ancient:* It has been found in all past societies and in all times. This fact has been established by historical and archaeological records. Even, in animal groups, such as the bees and aunts, there is distinction based upon physical structure and physiological functions. In every animal aggregation there are individual differences that go to determine relative status. Stratification was present in small wandering bands. Both age and sex in combination with physical strength played important part in stratification.

   As said above, the system of stratification is unstable and subject to change. As such, we see, this ancient system, which was primarily based on ascriptive characteristics, is now changing in the modern industrial society and becoming more and more achievement-oriented.

3. *It is universal:* There is no society which is flat. Social scientific research has revealed that inequality exists in all societies—even the simplest of cultures. Among the Bushmen of America, who hunt, gather their food and live in small bands of 50 to 100 people, stratification is present though in a very rudimentary form. The good hunter is distinguished from the poor one and is generally accorded more prestige or higher standing in the community. There is no real equality among the members of most primitive societies. In the simplest human societies, there are age groups, sex divisions, privileged classes and other

divisions that make organisation necessary and possible. In brief, there is no society known which does not make some distinction between individuals by making them on some scale of value. The most universal is that between men and women. A sort of stratification is even found in the so-called socialist countries (erstwhile Soviet Union and the modern China).

4. *It is diverse in its forms and amount:* Though stratification system is found in all societies but its bases, forms and amount differ from place to place, and from time to time. At the one extreme, we find the caste system in traditional India, with its more than 5,000 sub-castes, which is based on ascriptive system and have the extreme of total inequality. On the other hand, the 'kibbutzim' (the agricultural communal cooperatives) of Israel represents the extreme form of total equality. Open class system, which is an another major form of stratification system, is based on achieved qualities. In between the caste system and class system, we find the mixtures of these types also in many countries. Occupation, wealth, income, education, race/ethnicity, family and heritage used to remain the main bases of stratification.

5. *It is consequential*: The consequentiality of stratification simply means that the most important, most desired, and often scarcest things of human life, that is power, property, evaluation and psychic gratification are all distributed unequally. All the 'most entitled' to enjoy larger amount these can be classified into two: (1) life chances, and (2) lifestyles. Under *life chances*, we include such things as rates and incidences of infant mortality, longevity, physical and mental illness, childlessness, marital conflict, and divorce. *Lifestyles* refer to such things as the kind of house and neighbourhood one lives in, the recreational facilities, the cultural products, the kind of books, magazines and TV programmes to which one is exposed and the relationships between parents and children. All these things depend upon one's place in stratification or class situation. Life chances are much more involuntary and impersonally determined, while lifestyles reflect differences in preferences, tastes, and values.

> Different social strata have different chances of enjoying and suffering the unequal distribution of rewards, power, privilege and status in society as members of different group.

Social Stratification and Social Inequality

There are writers like Tumin (1969) who think that there is no difference between stratification and social inequality. For them, these two terms are synonymous. But, there is a band of other scholars, like Haralambos and Holborn (2000) who have made distinction between these two phenomena. For such scholars, a society can exhibit inequality without being stratified—for example, by affording truly equal opportunity to all but distributing rewards based upon performance. Thus, it is possible for social inequality to exist without social strata. Stratification is systematic and is based on identifiable social processes through which people are sorted into categories such as caste, class, race and gender.

For Haralambos, social stratification is a particular form of social inequality and it refers to the presence of social groups which are ranked one above the other, usually in terms of the amount of power, prestige and wealth their members possess. Those who belong to a particular group or stratum will have 'consciousness of kind'—a common identity, like interests and a similar lifestyle. The Indian caste system provides the best example of social stratification system.

On the other hand, the term 'social inequality' simple refers to the existence of socially created inequalities. It is not biologically based, for example, whites might claim superiority over blacks. There is probably no relationship between genetically based and socially created inequality in traditional Hindu society. Social inequality is a condition in which members of a society have different amount of wealth, prestige and power. It entails unequal rewards or opportunities for different individuals within a group or groups within a society. If equality is judged in terms of equality of opportunity, or equality of outcome, then inequality is a constant feature of the human condition. In a nutshell, the difference between social stratification and social inequality can be exhibited as under:

Differentiation of Characteristics	+	Differentiation of Prestige	=	Social Stratification
Differential Rewards and Opportunities	+	Class Consciousness	=	Social Inequality

Many scholars of different political persuasions regard equality of opportunity as a pre-condition for a fair society. Of course, equality of opportunity does not guarantee equality of outcome. It simply means that people will achieve jobs suitable to their intelligence and talents, regardless of social background. Marxists want a different kind of equality from this. They want resources to be distributed in terms to need rather than competition. There are people who are influenced by both views. Perhaps, there is no issue other than inequality, its causes and consequences particularly as they relate to social class, gender, ethnicity and locality, which has been debated hotly by social scientists in the 20th century and this debate still continues. It has become more important in the wake of liberalisation and globalisation.

Principal Forms of Social Stratification

Concrete forms of social stratification are different and numerous. However, sociologists have grouped majority of these into four basic systems of stratification: slavery, estates, caste and class. These are sometimes found in conjunction with one another.

1. *Slavery:* The term 'slave' is used to denote "a man whom law and/or custom regards as the property of another". Slaves are in lower condition and have no political rights. The legal conditions of slave ownership have varied considerably between different societies. Slavery is an extreme form of inequality. Its basis is economic. It has existed almost in all agrarian societies where slaves become an asset in production. In the 18th and

19th centuries, slaves were used exclusively as plantation workers and as domestic menials in the United States, South America and the West Indies. In India, this institution existed in the form of 'bonded labour'.

2. *Estates:* Estates were categories in feudal systems, especially in Europe during middle ages. They were less rigid than castes and allowed some mobility. In an estate system men are assigned to their strata according to their birth, military strength and landholdings. Unlike castes, estates were created politically by man-made laws rather than religious rules. Each estate had its own code of appropriate behaviour. The normal divisions were three-fold: (a) the *nobility* [the first (highest) estate], which was composed of aristocracy and gentry; (b) the *clergy* (the second estate), which had lower status but possessing various distinctive privileges; and (c) the *commoners*, which include everyone else from peasants to artisans. In an estate system, the people of various strata were identified by the rights they had and the duties they were expected to perform.
3. *Caste system:* The Indian caste system provides an example of a peculiar type of social stratification based on ascription. It is a system of inherited inequality as the guiding principle in social relationships. A caste may be defined as an endogamous group whose members follow by tradition a single occupation, or certain cognate occupations and who are held together by definite social rules of behaviour, and by common ceremonial or ritual observances. The system of caste is based on the assumption that each person is preordained a place and occupation in society at birth. Contact between persons of different strata (castes) is 'impure' and intermarriage between castes is forbidden. Even the most trivial acts of life, such as sipping water or eating, are governed by rules of each caste. Caste system derives its authority from the Hindu belief in the principles of *karma* and rebirth. Accordingly, individuals who fail to abide by the rituals and duties (*karma*) of their caste, it is believed, will be reborn in an inferior position in their next incarnation. The caste system is an illustration of social closure

in which access to wealth and prestige is closed to social groups, which are excluded from the performance of purifying rituals.

The concept of caste is sometimes used outside the Indian context where two or more ethnic groups are largely segregated from one another, and where notions of racial purity prevail. Modern Weberians, such as John Rex, argue that the apartheid system in South Africa was a form of caste system.

4. *Social class:* The above three systems of stratification—slavery, estate and caste system—are mainly associated with agrarian societies. In the modern industrial societies, where machine energy has replaced human and animal energy as the primary source of economic production, an entirely new set of social stratification has developed, which is known as social classes.

Social Class

A social class is made up of people of similar social status who regard one another as social equals. Each class has a set of values, attitudes, beliefs and behaviour norms which differ from those of the other classes. According to Giddens (2000), "a class is a large-scale grouping of people who share common economic resources, which strongly influence the type of lifestyle they are able to lead". Horton and Hunt (1968) writes: "A social class is defined as a stratum of people of similar position in the social status continuum." A stratum is a collectivity of people occupying similar positions in the hierarchical order.

Max Weber has defined class in terms of life chances and said, "a class is a number of people sharing one or more causes of life chances". By life chances he meant "the typical chances for a supply of goods, external living conditions, and personal life experience". Karl Marx, an another main theorist of class, has written much about social class but nowhere he has defined it in certain exact terms. From his writings, it appears that for Marx, "a class is a group of people who stand in a common relationship to the means of production", to the political-power structure, and to the ideas of the time, a relationship which necessarily brings it into conflict with some other group having divergent ideas and different interests with respect to the economic and political structures" (Lopreato and Lawrence, 1972). This statement presents the Marx's basic notion of class. Thus, he defined class in economic terms.

Thus, a social class is an aggregate of people who have same status, rank or common characteristics (lifestyle). This aggregate of people is identified on the basis of their relationship to the economic market who have differential access to wealth, power and certain styles of life. Ownership of wealth together with occupation are the chief criteria of class differences but education, hereditary prestige, group participation, self-identification and recognition by others also play an important part in class distinction.

Characteristics of class system

The following are the principal characteristics of class system:

1. A system of hierarchy of status.
2. A system of social ranking based primarily on economic position.
3. A system marked by unequal distribution of wealth and power.
4. A system more mobile than caste system.
5. A system in which status is achieved by one's own efforts rather than ascribed, assigned or inherited.
6. A system having some degree of permanency of the class structure.
7. A system based on stratum (class) consciousness and solidarity.
8. A system having distinctive mode of life (lifestyle) and cultural expressions of each class.
9. A system based on the recognition of superiority and inferiority in relation to those who stand or below in the social hierarchy.
10. A system in which boundaries between classes are fluid and are less precisely defined.
11. A system in which social classes act as sub-cultures—each social class is a system of behaviour, a set of values and a way of life.

Divisions of social classes

How many classes are there? Classes are not sharply defined status groups like castes. Social status varies along a continuum. The several social classes may be viewed as points on this continuum. Consequently, the number of social classes is not fixed, nor do any definite boundaries separate them. Earlier scholars of social class broke up the status continuum into three main classes—upper, middle, and lower. Later scholars found this division unsatisfactory and often used a six-fold classification by breaking each of these three classes into an upper and lower section. Warner and associates (1941, 1942) used this classification in their study of a New England town. The most commonly used classification is of J.H. Goldthrope who developed it in his study *Social Mobility and Class Structure in Britain* (1980). Goldthrope identifies eleven social class categories, which may be compressed into three major social classes—service, intermediate and working. This classification was later on severely criticised by feminist writers. They contend that the Goldthrope's class scheme inadequately represents the class position of women. Recently, Giddens (2000) developed a four-fold classification that exist in western societies. These are an *upper class* (the wealthy, employers, and industrialists, plus top executives); a *middle class* (which includes most white-collar workers and professionals); and a *working class* (those in blue-collar or manual jobs). In some of the industrialised countries, such as France or Japan, a fourth class—*peasants* (people engaged in traditional types or agricultural production)—has also until recently been important. In addition to these four classes, there is one more class known as *underclass,* which is composed of ethnic majority and underprivileged minorities. Members of the underclass have worse working conditions and living standards than the majority of the population. In Indian context, we can keep 'dalits' in this category.

Significance of social classes

The importance or the significance of social classes is reflected in the functions which they perform for societies that can be grouped as under:

(1) *Determining life opportunities:* Opportunities and rewards of a person are greatly affected by his class position. Wealth and income confers power and members of the upper class have more power than lower class people. This helps them attaining leading positions in the political, educational and cultural spheres. Major types of mental disorder and physical illness, including heart disease, cancer, diabetes, pneumonia and bronchitis, are all move common at lower levels of the class structure than towards the top (Waitzkin, 1986).

(2) *Colouring personality development:* Social classes act like sub-cultures, the personality development of the child is affected in many ways by social classes. His goals, interests and habits are affected by the needs of social world he lives in. His moral standards are equally class-typed. Studies of child development and socialisation show that there is a lot of difference in the personality make-up of lower-class and middle-class groups.

(3) *Assigning social responsibilities and privileges:* Social classes provide their members with distinctive sub-cultures that prepare them for specialised functions in society. It is said that the social class is useful as an efficient means of role allocation in the society. Through role allocation, a society fixes social responsibilities of persons. Champions of functional theory of stratification (Davis and Moore, 1945) claim that society requires a variety of occupational roles, and one's social class background equip a person with the skills and attitudes desirable for his occupational function. A lot of unpleasant work must be done in any society, and someone must be persuaded to do it. The class system compels someone to do such unpleasant jobs. This position has been sharply criticised, and it is said that social class may be dysfunctional. It hinders social adjustment and it may make it difficult for the individual to make the best use of his potential abilities.

(4) *Shaping life-adjustment patterns:* Social class affects the way people deal with virtually every aspect of reality. The way people handle life situations varies with social class. The lower class tends to be radical in political action connected with economic benefits. But this class is conservative in accepting

social changes while the opposite tends to be true of the upper class.

(5) *Explaining many group differences:* Social class affects the style of life of its members. As said above, social classes act like sub-cultures and, therefore, the groups which live differently, also think and behave differently. This is why, we see great diversity in the outlook and behaviour of different social classes. A band of sociologists are of this view that many other kinds of group differences—racial, religious, regional—are really class differences.

(6) *Defining the conventional morality:* Social classes do not merely differ in etiquette or mode of behaviour; they also differ in more judgements. In his study of sex behaviour, Kinsey (1948) has shown how sex mores differ between classes. Premarital sex experience, which is viewed as 'natural' by the lower classes, is generally condemned by the middle classes. For them it is degenerating and 'unnatural'. On almost every point of moral conduct, class-typed mores differ.

(7) *Cultivating class ethnocentrism:* Social class directly or indirectly helps in developing stereotypes and prejudices against other than one's own class. People at every class level tend to see those above themselves as snobbish, pretentious, exploiters and those beneath as either disgusting or pathetic, delinquents etc. Members of one class judge members of other classes in terms of their own expectations and values. The feeling of 'us' and 'them' begins with the family which later on paves the way for the formation of class ethnocentrism.

Determinants of social class

Different criteria have been adopted for making distinction between various classes. Those criteria vary with time, place and circumstances. There was a time (in feudal and medieval times) when birth was the main criterion used in determining the status of a person in the society. In modern times, this criterion has not much relevance, though, it still persists in some or the other form. Following are the main criteria (attributes) used in the determination of social class:

(1) *Wealth and income:* Possession of substantial amounts of wealth is the main characteristic distinguishing the upper class from other class groups in society. Persons having more wealth and income generally have higher social position and respect in society. Wealth and income (money), though necessary for upper-class position, yet one's class position is not directly proportional to his income. A prostitute has less social status than a professor though her income is far greater than the professor. In spite of all its weaknesses, wealth and income are an important determinant of social class, partly because of the way of life it permits or enforces (a social class is basically a way of life), and partly because it suggests about one's family life and way of life. Upper-class children have a better chance, and for their grandchildren, a secure upper-class status is practically assured. Wealth and income, over a period of time, usually gains upper-class status. In his analysis of class divisions, Karl Marx argued that social class is based entirely on wealth.

(2) *Occupation:* Occupation is an exceedingly important aspect of social class and as such it is another determinant of class status. It is a well-known fact that some kinds of work are more honourable than others, e.g., doctors, engineers, administrators, professors and lawyers hold a higher position than a car mechanic or manual worker. The high-prestige occupations generally receive the higher incomes, yet there are many exceptions. Occupation is also one of the best clues to one's way of life, and therefore to one's social class membership. It affects many other facets of life (values, beliefs, marital relations) other than determining the social class.

(3) *Education:* There is a close reciprocal relationship between social class and education. To get a higher education one needs money plus motivation. Upper-class children already have money for the finest schools and colleges. They also have family tradition and social encouragement. One's amount and kind of education affects the class rank he will secure. Thus, education is one of the main levers of a man's social class.

(4) *Prestige:* It refers to the respect and admiration with which an occupation is regarded by society. Prestige is independent of the particular person who occupies a job. Sociologists have tried to assign prestige rankings to various occupations.

Besides wealth, occupation and education, there are certain other criteria which help a person to attain higher social status in the society. These are family background, kinship relations, location of residence etc., but education, occupation and expanded income are the most fairly visible clues of social class. With these are associated most of the other behaviour characteristics which make one 'belong'. Most of the social scientists have used these three criteria in dividing people into social classes for research purposes.

Difference between class and caste systems

In Max Weber's phraseology, caste and class are both status groups. While castes are perceived as hereditary groups with a fixed ritual status, social classes are defined in terms of the relations of production. A social class is a category of people who have a similar socio-economic status in relation to other classes in the society. The individuals and families which are classified as part of the same social class have similar life chances, prestige, style of life, attitudes etc. In the caste system, status of a caste is determined not by the economic and the political privileges but by the ritualistic legitimation of authority. In the class system, ritual norms have no importance at all but power and wealth alone determine one's status (Dumont, 1958).

Class system differs in many respects from other forms of stratification—slavery, estate and caste system. In earlier textbooks such as written by MacIver, Davis and Bottomore, it was observed that caste and class are polar opposites. They are antithetical to each other. While 'class' represents a 'democratic society' having equality of opportunity, 'caste' is obverse of it. Following are the main differences between class and caste systems:

1. Castes are found in Indian sub-continent only, especially in India, while classes are found almost everywhere. Classes are especially the characteristic of industrial societies of Europe and

America. According to Dumont and Leach, caste is a unique phenomenon found only in India.

2. Classes depend mainly on economic differences between groupings of individuals—inequalities in possession and control of material resources—whereas in caste system non-economic factors such as influence of religion [theory of *karma*, rebirth and ritual (purity-pollution)] are most important.
3. Unlike castes or other types of strata, classes are not established by legal or religious provisions; membership is not based on inherited position as specified either legally or by custom. On the other hand, the membership is inherited in the caste system.
4. Class system is typically more fluid than the caste system or the other types of stratification and the boundaries between classes are never clear-cut. Caste system is static whereas the class system is dynamic.
5. In the class system, there are no formal restrictions on inter-dining and inter-marriage between people from different classes as is found in the caste system. Endogamy is the essence of caste system which is perpetuating it.
6. Social classes are based on the principle of achievement, i.e., on one's own efforts, not simply given at birth as is common in the caste system and other types of stratification system. As such social mobility (movement upwards and downwards) is much more common in the class structure than in the caste system or in other types. In the caste system, individual mobility from one caste to another is impossible. This is why, *castes are known as closed classes* (D.N. Majumdar). It is a closed system of stratification in which almost all sons end up in precisely the same stratum their fathers occupied. The system of stratification in which there is high rate of upward mobility, such as that in the Britain and United States is known as open class system. The view that castes are closed classes is not accepted by M.N. Srinivas (1962) and Andre Beteille (1965).
7. In the caste system and in other types of stratification system, inequalities are expressed primarily in personal relationships of duty or obligation—between lower- and higher-caste

individuals, between serf and lord, between slave and master. On the other hand, the nature of class system is impersonal. Class system operates mainly through large-scale connections of an impersonal kind.

8. Caste system is characterised by 'cumulative inequality' but class system is characterised by 'dispersed inequality.'
9. Caste system is an organic system but class has a segmentary character where various segments are motivated by competition (Leach, 1960).
10. Caste works as an active political force in a village (Beteille, 1966) but class does not work so.

New dynamics of class

Some sociologists argue that class today has become relatively unimportant in the so-called modern post-industrial societies, especially the societies of the western world and North America because of the weakening of the reproduction of classes through the impact of global processes. The modern changes (privatisation, liberalisation, proletarianisation, de-industrialisation, globalisation etc.) suggest that the capacity for social production of both classes (capitalist and proletariat) has been reduced. Indeed, the 1980s and 1990s have seen the emergence of a new culture known as an *enterprise culture* through which it is said that anyone can, given initiative, skills and a bit of luck, 'get on' and 'do well'.

It is not surprising to find people saying (Abercrombie and Urry, 1983) that class identities have lost their meaning in the modern world, that class itself has lost importance as a determinant of social position and reward, that new social movements—such as the peace and human rights movement, the environmental movement, vegetarianism, alternative medicines (healing through yoga and indigenous herbs) and technologies and feminism—have all replaced the allegiances and respect that the labour movement once commanded. These new movements proclaim the demise of traditional class structure or *decomposition of class*. Moreover, class identities have been said to be eroded through the new importance of 'consumption'.

In the post-modern consumption-oriented society, identity is derived more by what we consume than by the work we do (or do not do).

How far the above assertion is true? The above view of class decomposition is highly exaggerated. There is not much truth in it. The basic class structure is still alive and well. Anthony Giddens (2000) argues: "Thus picture is far from accurate. The influence of class may be less than Marx supposed, but there are few spheres of social life left untouched by class differences." The degree to which traditional class distinctions and inequalities have been eroded has been much exaggerated. Secondly, where there are significant changes, they are primarily a result of the growing impact of globalisation (economic process) that is forcing a restructuring of class at national level throughout the capitalist industrialised world. Instead of total decomposition of class, what we observe is the change in the class structure. The global processes (such as the decline of manufacturing industry) have altered the context within which class reproduction occurs. Membership of the upper class, which was previously based on ownership of property—land, businesses, and financial organisations—is now replaced by professionals (doctors, engineers, lawyers, chartered accountants, managers and administrators, etc.). Likewise, the structure of middle and lower classes has also changed because of the change in the structure of occupations. Many new shades of occupations have cropped up. As a result of these changes, the working class is contracting relative to other classes and a rootless and disaffected underclass is developing. Not only this, the feminisation of certain jobs has also affected the class structure.

Processes of Stratification

The basic processes that generate, shape and sustain systems of stratification as identified by Tumin (1969) are: (1) differentiation, (2) ranking, (3) evaluation, and (4) rewarding.

(1) *Differentiation of statuses:* Status differentiation is the process by which social positions, such as father, mother, teacher and employer, are defined and distinguished from one another by

assigning to each a distinctive role—a set of rights and responsibilities. All roles involve a good deal of teaching, learning, motivating and sanctioning. This process is indispensable to any society if it is to continue for a long time.

Status differentiation operates most effectively when (1) tasks are clearly defined; (2) lines of authority and responsibility for roles are clearly distinguished; (3) effective mechanism exists for recruiting and training a sufficient number of persons to assume the statuses; and (4) adequate sanctions in the form of rewards and punishments exist to motivate individuals to conscientious performance.

(2) *Ranking of statuses:* Statuses can be ranked on three criteria: (i) *personal characteristics* such as intelligence, beauty or strength; (ii) *trained skills and abilities* such as manual dexterity, knowledge of law, command over language etc; and (iii) *consequences or effects* upon others and upon society. Actors provide entertainment, judges ensure justice, policemen preserve order.

(3) *Process of evaluation:* This process involves assigning to various statuses different places on a scale of value or worthiness. Several different kinds of evaluational judgements, such as superior/inferior, better/worse, more/less need to be distinguished.

(4) *Process of rewarding:* Rewarding involves the allocation of various amounts of the good things in life to statuses which have been differentiated, ranked and evaluated. In every society there are rules or norms that determine how rewards will be distributed. These rules can be very variable and operate in such a way that large portions of a population may live in poverty while others can enjoy comfort or luxury in great proportion. They can call for relatively equal allocation to all. But, some inequality in rewards is, of course, characteristic of every known society.

Classical Theories of Social Stratification

Why are societies stratified? The question has been widely debated. Earlier sociologists like Spencer (one of the champions of the evolutionary approach) believed that society developed through an evolutionary process, and those who profited from natural selection—"*survival of the fittest*"—came out on top. Accordingly, superior people (fittest) would have more wealth, power, education, and become leaders in the society, whereas inferior people would remain in the bottom rank of society. This view was challenged by later sociologists. Modern sociology has developed two main approaches to the study of social stratification—structural-functionalist and conflict perspectives. These approaches have been explained later on under the heading 'Modern Theories of Stratification'.

Marxian perspective

The whole Marxian perspective about social stratification revolves round the concept of social classes. No theorist stressed the significance of class for society and for social change more strongly than Karl Marx. Marx viewed class differentiation as the crucial determinant of social, economic and political inequality. According to Marx, there is always a dominant and a subordinate class—a ruling class and a subject class. The former (ruling class) is the class which owns the means of production (e.g., land and machinery) and the latter (subject class) sells its labour to survive. The ruling class survive its power from the ownership and control of the forces of production. The relationship between these classes has always been exploitative in all phases of history (feudal or any types of ancient societies) with an exception of a simple primitive society. Marx believed that primitive societies were non-class societies. In such societies, there was simple equality and as such there was no stratification based on class.

In Marxian view, the ruling class exploits and oppressed the subordinate class. As a result, there is a basic conflict of interest between the two classes. This conflict between social classes has been continuous since the dawn of history. We find echo of these views in these lines: "*The history of all hitherto existing society is the history of class struggles*." Marx viewed history is an outgrowth of class struggle. From a Marxian perspective, systems of stratification derive from the relationships of social classes to the forces of production. According to a Marxian view, a class is a social group whose members share the same relationship to the forces of production.

Though Marx analysed stratification in all types of human societies, but his main focus was on the societies of 19th century Europe. During this period, Europe was under the spell of modern industrial capitalistic mode of production. The society was divided into two main classes—industrialists or capitalists—those who own the means of production (factories and machinery etc.) and working class—those who earn their living by selling their labour to them. For these two classes, Marx used the terms *bourgeoisie* (capitalist class) and *proletariat* (working class). Marx contended that those who own the means of production always try to maximise their profit at the cost of workers. The lower the wages paid, the higher the profit made by the capitalist. The wages paid to the workers for their labour are well below the value of the goods they produce. The difference between the value of the wages and commodities is known as *'surplus value'*. This surplus value is appropriated in the form of profit by the capitalists. Marx argued that capital, as such, produces nothing. Only labour produces wealth.

Thus, in the capitalist society, the relationship between the bourgeoisie and the proletariat is one of mutual dependence and conflict. It is a relationship of exploiter and exploited, oppressor and oppressed. According to Marx, the oppression and exploitation of the proletariat will inevitably lead to the destruction of the capitalist system. But, for this, the working class must first develop *class consciousness*—a subjective awareness held by members of a class regarding their common vested interests and the need for collective political action to bring about social change. Marx differentiated between class consciousness and false consciousness. For Marx, *false consciousness* is a belief that the upper class is superior and has the right to rule. It gives a false picture of the nature of the relationship between social classes.

Criticism

Commenting on the theory of Marx, T.B. Bottomore (*Classes in Modern Society*, 1965) has observed: "For the past eighty years Marx's theory has been the object of unrelenting criticism and tenacious defence." This observation remains true even today. Marx's analysis of class is seen as too simplistic. Critics argue that even in Marx's own time the class structure of capitalist societies was becoming more complex rather than a bio-polar system as envisaged by Marx. Marx is also criticised for exaggerating the importance of class and particularly class conflict. His prediction about future classless society seems to many unlikely and unachievable. In modern societies, the consciousness and behaviour of the working class has proved much more 'moderate' and open to compromise than Marx hoped. Marx's class analysis is sometimes seen as loaded with political and ideological bias. It is also said that his analysis is quasi-religious wishful thinking in the garb of scientific analysis. Today, Marxism is seen as "the God that failed" later.

Current scientific interest in class has shifted from Marxian theory of class warfare to the struggle for individual mobility. Current technological, economic and governmental changes have changed the face of the so-called capitalist society and we are advancing toward a middle class society.

Max Weber's theory

Max Weber, the great German sociologist, though developed his analysis of stratification around the views of Marx, but insisted that no single characteristic (such as class) totally defines a person's position within the stratification system. Weber argues that the evidence provides a more complex and diversified picture of social stratification. He argued that social stratification is a reflection of unequal distribution of power. Since power can be derived from different kinds of resources—a system of social stratification presents more than one dimension according to which a man has a standing.

Like Marx, Weber also sees class in economic terms, yet Weber argues that the actions of individuals and groups could not be understood solely in economic terms. He identified three analytically distinct components of stratification: class, status and party. Thus, in Weber's opinion, these three criteria are to be used to differentiate people in modern society: *class power* (economic) based on relationship to the means of production, *status* (social) differences, founded on esteem (social honour) given to individuals or groups by others, and *party power* (political), derived from one's dominance over a political, legal or administrative system. Weber did not accept this Marx's view that party and status are merely functions of class. Now, we will discuss Weber's ideas about class, status and party in brief.

Class

Although Weber accepts Marx's view that class is founded on objectively given economic conditions, he differed from Marx on the precise definition of class and the role of economic factors in class formation. Weber's most detailed discussion of class is found in *Wirtschaft and Gesellschaft* (1921-22) but he did not give any 'definitive statement' about classes anywhere. For Weber, a class as a group of individuals who share a similar position in a market economy and by virtue of that fact receive similar economic rewards. At other place, he defined, "a class is a property class where its members' "class situation" is primarily determined by property differences". He used property or the lack of property as the basic distinction in all "class situations". He made distinction between economic class and social class. According to Weber, economic class is a person's situation in the economic market—both the commodity market (buying/selling) and the employment market. This situation gives rise to different life chances. Qualifications or credentials, experience, skills largely determine the types of jobs people are able to obtain. The better qualified and experienced can usually command greater rewards. Social class includes economic class. Members of the same social class share similar chances of social mobility. Thus, a man from a low social background would tend to have poor chances of social mobility. Members of a given social class, therefore, share a common socio-economic situation. This difference in the definition of class led to a fundamental disagreement between Weber and Marx about the class structure of capitalist society.

Weber differed with Marx not only about the definition of class but about the member of classes also. He indicated four main classes:

(1) upper, (2) petit bourgeoisie (small businessmen and professionals), (3) middle (propertyless white-class workers) and, (4) manual working class against Marx's two social classes: the bourgeoisie (owners of property and wealth) and the proletariat (working class). However, he agreed with Marx that the most powerful class in capitalist society is that of the owners of property and wealth (the upper class). He also agreed with Marx that a second class, the petit bourgeoisie, was likely to become less important. Contrary to Marx, however, Weber gave great emphasis on propertyless white-collar employers (civil servants and professionals). He referred to them as 'technicians' and considered them as a distinct and numerically expanding class.

Status

While class forms one possible basis for group formation, collective action and the acquisition of political power, Weber argues that there are also other bases for these activities, e.g., status and party. In particular, groups form because their members share a similar 'status situation'. Whereas class refers to the unequal distribution of economic rewards, status refers to the unequal distribution of social honour or prestige they are accorded by others. According to Weber, any factor might be the basis of shared honour or status—religion, caste, ethnic group membership, taste or whatever. The main expression of status group membership is style of life or lifestyle. Membership of a status group gives exclusive right to certain opportunities and privileges as we find in the estate or caste system as discussed earlier (Weber has regarded caste system as status groups). While distinguishing between ascribed and achieved status, Weber states that ascribed status has rapidly declined as a means of access to economic and political power in modern societies. He regards economic and career opportunities as increasingly open to competition in modern society.

Pointing out difference between status and class, Anthony Giddens (2000) states: "Whereas class is objectively given, status depends on people's subjective evaluations of social differences. Classes derive from economic factors associated with property and earnings; status is governed by the varying *styles of life* groups follow." Marx regarded status distinctions primarily as a product of class stratification. In modern societies, an individual's status is usually derived from his economic or class situation. Finally, in a telling contrast between status group and class membership, Weber argues that whereas status groups are 'communities', classes are usually not. It has been a central problem of Marxism that the working class as a whole has not become an active political community. In many societies class and status situations are closely linked. However, those who share the same class situation will not necessarily belong to the same status group. For example, the neo-rich people are sometimes excluded from the status group of the privileged because their tastes, manners and dress are defined as vulgar. Thus, status groups may create divisions within classes.

Party (Power)

For Weber, party is a further and distinct political dimension of stratification. Weber defines 'parties' as groups which are specifically concerned with influencing policies and making decisions in the interests of their membership. Parties are concerned with the acquisition of social 'power'. He did not regard political power as a function of economic factors as Marx did. In modern societies, according to Weber, parties live in a house of power. In other words, they are an important source of power. They can influence stratification independently of class and status. Marx tended to explain both status differences and party organisation in terms of class. In contrast to Marx, Weber argued that party and status identities could cut across class lines. Weber insisted that, although economic factors could certainly affect political ones, the reverse was also true. In Weber's view, then, each of us has not one rank but three. A person's position in a stratification system reflects some combination of his or her class, status and power.

Weber's analysis of classes, status groups and parties suggest that no single theory can pinpoint and explain their relationship. The interplay of class, status and party in the formation of social groups is complex and variable. In conclusion, it can be said that in rejecting

Marx's polarised analysis of the class structure (Marx attempted to reduce all forms of inequality to social class) and replacing it with a finely graded version, Weber attempted to reformulate Marx's theory of stratification. Yet, the basis of Weber's perspective is power conflict. On this fundamental point, Weber and Marx were in agreement. Since the standpoints are similar in many ways, though complementary in others, some theorists like Erik Olin Wright (1978, 1985), Frank Parkin (1971, 1979) and W.G. Runciman (1990) attempted to combine the two traditions in their own way. Wright has reformulated Marx's concept of capitalist economic control. He has also incorporated some ideas of Weber in his theory of class. According to Wright, there are three dimensions of control over economic resources in modern capitalist production. These include: (1) control over the physical means of production, mainly land, factories and offices; (2) control over investment capital; and (3) control over labour power. These dimensions are the bases that allow us to identify the major classes. Critics of Wright argue that there is little difference between this analysis of contradictory class locations and Weber's analysis of the new white-collar classes. In contrast to Wright, Parkin's theory of class leans heavily on Weber than on Marx. Parkin agrees with Marx that ownership of property (means of production) is the basic foundation of class structure. However, according to Parkin, property is only one form of *social closure* (a process whereby groups try to maintain exclusive control over resources), which can be monopolised by a minority and used as a basis of power over others. Besides property or wealth, other characteristics such as ethnic origin, language and religion as used by Weber may be used to create social closure.

It is argued that the models of class structure presented so far are incomplete. Class models based on ownership (Marx) and those on personal marketability (Weber) tend not be effectively combined. A third area of distinct concern has arisen in recent class theory, that of control. This has focussed particularly on the rise of white-collar management. W.G. Runciman (1990) has developed an ambitious class scheme to integrate differences of ownership, marketability and control in a single model of class. His unifying concept is that of economic role which he considers to be the basis of class. Assessing the power of economic roles, Runciman constructs a seven-part class model: upper class, upper-middle class, middle-middle class, lower-middle class, skilled working class, unskilled working class and underclass. Runciman's analysis of class in terms of economic power combines elements of neo-Marxist and neo-Weberian analyses.

Contemporary sociologists have also debated the political consequences of the new system of social stratification ushered in by industrialism and information technology. Gerhard Lenski (*Power and Privilege*, 1966) maintains that "the appearance of mature industrial societies marks the first significant reversal in the age-old evolutionary trend toward ever increasing inequality". Other writers—most notably F. Hunter and C.W. Mills—contend that industrial societies have produced a new type of *power elite,* who controls the destiny of modern nations such as America.

Modern Theories of Stratification

The theories of these early writers—Spencer, Marx and Weber—have a strong influence on the two main prevailing modern theories of stratification—Structural-Functional Theory and Conflict Theory that we are dealing with in the following paragraphs:

Structural-functional theory

This theory of stratification has been put forward by Davis and Moore (1945) and, separately by Talcott Parsons (1954), who derives it in fact from Spencer and Durkheim. Structural-functionalists have refined Spencer's notion that society, like any other organism, is self-regulating and self-maintaining and that it consists of interrelated parts that serve a function in maintaining the system as a whole.

According to modern structural-functionalists, stratification is necessary or inevitable for society to function. It serves 'vital functions' in complex society, particularly in an industrial society where it inevitably occurs. Functionalists are primarily concerned with the function of social stratification, i.e., how stratification systems help to maintain order and stability in society.

These writers have argued that inequality is inherent in any society and that the particular rewards a society gives to its members are the result of their 'functional' utility. In modern society power is placed in the hands of people who are capable of being leaders. Society rewards those who serve as leaders by giving them wealth. Wealth and status, both scarce resources, provide power, so those who serve society by providing scarce skills become the powerful people. Thus, inequality is created by the needs of society, not by the desires and needs of individuals (Davis and Moore, 1945). This means that an unequal distribution of rewards is necessary for the successful functioning of societies characterised by a division of labour. Under the division of labour people perform set tasks on a regular basis. Some of these tasks are more closely tied to societal requirements than others and must therefore be differentially rewarded in order to attract sufficient people who are capable of performing them.

Davis and Moore begin their most celebrated article "Some Principles of Stratification" (1945) with the observation that stratification exists in every human society. They regard social stratification as a 'functional necessity' and see it as a solution to a problem faced by all social systems. They argue that all societies need some mechanism for insuring effective role allocation and performance. This mechanism is social stratification which they see as a system which attaches unequal rewards and privileges to the different positions in society. Unequal rewards and privileges motivate individuals to compete for more societally important positions.

Davis and Moore asserted that in all societies there are positions (or tasks) that objectively have more functional importance than others. Such positions (or tasks) must be filled with properly talented and trained persons. These positions need special skills if they are to be performed adequately. It is necessary that the more talented persons be attracted to those occupations which require their skills. While anyone can perform unskilled tasks, only the talented can perform certain skilled ones; consequently, persons with specialised skills must be rewarded with money, prestige or power. They argue that differential rewards are functional for society, because they contribute to the maintenance and well-being of social systems. The possession of greater wealth, prestige and power marks a section of society as a class. Given this, and given the existence of the human family, class privileges will be inherited by one generation from another. But, there will also be certain amount of social mobility; those who are unsuccessful at performing the tasks required of them may lose their class position, while others with exceptional abilities may rise.

Like many functionalists, Talcott Parsons (1953) sees social stratification as both inevitable and functional for society. It is inevitable because it derives from shared values which are a necessary part of all social systems. It is functional because it serves to integrate various groups in society. His theory of stratification is based mainly on the role of common values in the maintenance of social systems. He believes that order, stability and cooperation in society are based on value consensus. His theory of stratification is based on the following assumptions:

(1) Power and prestige differentials are essential for the coordination and integration of a specialised division of labour.
(2) Social inequality is also essential, without this how members of society could effectively cooperate and work together.
(3) Inequalities of power and prestige benefit all members of society since they serve to further collective goals which are based on shared values.
(4) High rewards are necessary to motivate people to do functionally important jobs.
(5) Achievement values have replaced ascriptive criteria in industrial society and a merit system placed people in occupations.
(6) Occupations are arranged in a hierarchy of material rewards and social prestige according to their functional importance to society.
(7) There is a consensus about the importance of occupations.

Parsons has been strongly criticised on all above points. Sociologists of Marxian followings have seen stratification as a divisive rather than an integrating force. These sociologists believe that it is an arrangement whereby some gains at the cost of others. They have also questioned Parsons' view that stratification systems derive ultimately from shared values.

Criticism

Functionalist accounts were criticised heavily in a long-running debate popularly referred to as the *Davis-Moore debate*. The critics of this view put forward the following counter-arguments: (1) That functional importance of positions cannot be specified (Tumin) and the theory is circular, because high-paying jobs are defined as functional or of more importance simply because they are high paying. (2) That they dispute the argument that some tasks are more vital or important to a society than others. Many occupations which afford little prestige or economic reward can be seen as vital to society. The manager is no more vital than the manual labour, (like sweeper) for the one cannot operate without the other. (3) That the conflict and the influence of power as aspects of stratification are under-emphasised. (4) That the significance of wealth and property is ignored. (5) That the extent to which inequality reflects achievement is exaggerated. (6) That the consensual element is over-emphasised. (7) That the theory favours social stability (status quo) rather than change. (8) That it ignores the inheritance of class position. (9) That stratification is not beneficial to society but actually it may hinder the efficient working of a social system by preventing those with superior, innate abilities from performing certain tasks which are the preserve of a privileged class. (10) That they question the need for large income differentials as a means of attracting men of talent to skilled occupation. Critics argue, in fact, that if occupations require special skills, they will usually give more intrinsic satisfaction than those which do not, so that there should be less need to offer higher rewards, not more. (11) That they cast doubt on the implicit assumption that actual differentials of reward do reflect differences in the skills required for particular occupations.

(12) The final criticism is that a society without social classes is, in principle, possible if it possesses a value system, which encourages a commitment to equality and public service. It is said that this theory has been exposed as an ideological justification of existing patterns of inequality, especially in America that was concerned to deny the reality of social class. To conclude, it may be written that Davis and Moore theory pivots on the causes and consequences of social stratification for society. There is little or no concern in it for the personal experiences of individuals who constitute the society.

Criticising severely Davis and Moore's views in his book entitled *The Rise of the Meritocracy* (1961), Michael Young argues that no evidence supports the idea that the stratification is based on the principles of meritocracy and that is functional for society. He pointed out many dysfunctional possibilities of the stratification systems. For instance, he argued that in a meritocracy, "talent and ability are efficiently syphoned out of the lower strata. As a result, these groups are in a particularly vulnerable position because they have no able members to represent their interests".

Some scholars like Eva Rosenfeld (*Social Stratification in a 'Classless' Society*, 1974) tried to investigate the truth of the functionalist's claim that stratification is inevitable. From her research of the Israeli 'Kibbutzim' system (a system which tries to translate the idea of an egalitarian society—a society without social inequality), Rosenfeld notes that even in this system authority and prestige are not equally distributed. The position of 'leader-manager' in the Kibbutzim carries authority and commands higher prestige than the lower stratum that consists of the 'rank and file'. This study clearly lends some support to the functionalists' claim that social stratification, at least in terms of power and prestige, is inevitable in human society.

Conflict theory (Marx's theory)

Conflict theory begins principally with the writings of Karl Marx that we have discussed in detail in the previous section. Conflict theorists reject outrightly the above functional view of stratification. They argue that inequality develops as a result of people's desire for scarce resources, and close knit groups compete with one another to gain possession of these resources. According to this view, resources are not rewards for talent but are acquired through inheritance, coercion or exploitation. Inequality results when one group acquires more resources than other groups. According to Marxian analysis, social class depends on similarity of economic interest, i.e., the individual's relation to the means of production.

Social theorists in the 19th and early 20th centuries were concerned with conflict in society. Functionalists of the mid-20th century neglected conflict in favour of a unitary concept of society and emphasised social integration (stability and order), social equilibrium and the harmonious effect of common values. Some sociologists in the 1950s and 1960s attempted to revive what they called 'conflict theory' against the dominant theory of functionalism of the time, drawing on Karl Marx, George Simmel to this end. Those identified with the conflict school, such as Robert Lynd, C. Wright Mills, Lewis Coser and Ralf Dahrendorf, see society as a collection of various institutions—economic, political, educational—that are generally poorly integrated with each other. The unequal distribution of property, power and prestige is seen as representing a special privilege enjoyed by an elite. Social stratification or social inequality is thus conceived by these theorists as a major source of continuing conflict in a society. They see conflict as inherent, natural and predictable in any social organisation. They believe that human beings are prone to conflict over such scarce resources as wealth, status and power. They are not concerned much about how parts of an organisation (society) fit together or how they sustain each other; rather, they inquire into the sources of tension and strain and view these as natural products of social interaction. The functionalists (or equilibrium theorists) study the positive functions of social inequality or stratification, the conflict theorists are more concerned with the negative functions. Conflict theorists reject the functional view (Durberman, 1976), arguing that inequality develop as a result of people's desire for scarce resources, and close-knit groups compete with one another to gain possession of these resources.

Synthesis of functional and conflict approaches of stratification

Neither functional nor conflict theory gives us a full understanding of how stratification systems develop. Some sociologists have attempted to synthesise these two approaches of stratification (Dahrendorf, 1951; Tumin, 1963; Lenski, 1966). Researches in this field suggest that stratification has a variety of causes, some based on conflict and some on cooperation (functions). A stratification system based on religion may stress feelings of community and selflessness. Others, based on landownership or accumulation of money, may tend to emphasise competition and the efforts of individuals that may lead to conflict. It is becoming increasingly apparent that stratification is influenced by a great many factors.

Gerhard Lenski has offered a view of stratification which synthesises certain elements of the functionalist and conflict approaches. He believes that each of these perspectives is valid under certain conditions and that different stages of technological development lead to different systems of stratification. Essentially, Lenski agrees with functionalists that the key resources of a society are allocated as rewards for persons who occupy important roles. Consequently, a definite and rigid social class system develops, such as a ruling class, a merchant class and a peasant class. Such unequal allocation of resources leads to the societal tension and conflict discussed by Marx and by Dahrendorf and other conflict theorists. Yet, in Lenski's view, inequality does not necessarily increase with industrialisation. To maintain their power and privilege, the elites share a position of economic surplus with the lower classes as and when such situation arises.

Feminisation of Stratification

Feminist sociology challenges the methodological assumptions of conventional class analysis for failing to treat women as a distinct socio-economic group with specific disadvantages and life chances.

Studies of stratification were for many years 'gender blind'. They were written as though women did not exist, or for purposes of analysing divisions of power, wealth and prestige, women were unimportant and uninteresting. Yet gender itself is one of the most profound examples of stratification. There are no societies in which men do not, in some aspects of social life, have more wealth, status and influence than women (Giddens, 2000).

Most researches fail to provide the connection between economic subordination of women and its expressions through the family and personal life. According to radicalists, it is the place of women in relation to economic production which ultimately determines male/female differences. In this sense, it can be argued that 'gender' is analogous to class relationship. Yet class divisions are so marked in modern societies that there is no doubt that they 'overlap' substantially with gender inequalities. Generally, the economic position of a woman is 'read off ' from her husband, since majority of women are in a position of economic dependence on their husbands, it follows that their class position is most often governed by the husband's class situation. How far this approach is correct, is a matter of continuous debate. Since the last decade, female-headed families (either by choice or death, divorce, separation) are increasing everywhere, especially in USA and western societies. As such, the position of women should be studied independent of their husbands/fathers. Some scholars have suggested that the class position of a woman should be determined without reference to the household or domestic circumstances.

In her survey of the literature Gaye Tuchman (*Hearth and Home: Images of Women in the Media*, 1978) showed that women were portrayed in only two significant roles: the domestic and the sexual (including the romantic). In contrast, males appeared prominently in spheres of employment, family, polity and other areas of social life. Clearly, the media were presenting men as dominant and women as subordinate. Tuchman describes this as a 'symbolic annihilation' of women. This reflects something akin to the real undermining of women in society.

Social Stratification in Post-Industrial Societies

Marx's two-fold classification of class (bourgeoisie and proletariat) is no more applicable in the post-industrial societies. New systems of social stratification, which have recently emerged, are not associated with the means of production or not necessarily based upon the possession of wealth. In the post-industrial societies the majority of the labour force is engaged in the provision of services, technical and professional workers increase in numbers, and scientific knowledge becomes crucially important in the direction of economic, political, and social affairs (Daniel Bell, *The Coming of Post-Industrial Society*, 1973). Some social scientists have argued that a *managerial class* has emerged that possesses power independent of those who technically own means of production. The numbers of *technocrats* have also grown at an amazing rate in post-industrial societies. In addition, the ranks of the lower white-collar class, such as sales and clerical people, computer operators and other non-manual workers, have drastically expanded. (This accounts about the post-industrial societies is also applicable to some extent on the changing Indian society.)

The changes in the social stratification systems of post-industrial societies have prompted some commentators to foresee a new society. Dahrendorf (1959) believes that we are entering a *post-capitalist era* where ownership of property is no longer a prerequisite to membership in the upper classes. Rather, he contends that those who exercise control in the political and economic realms now constitute a governing class. Daniel Bell envisages a period in which those who possess knowledge will increasingly gain in power. Utopians, such as Herbert Marcuse, Immanuel Wallerstein, Melford Spiro, and Paul Goodman foresee different futures for post-industrial civilisation.

Chapter 12

Social Mobility

Key features

The phenomena of social stratification and social mobility are closely related. A fundamental characteristic of systems of stratification is the extent to which they are open or rigid (closed). How much opportunity a person gets to move from one position to another in society? The study of such movement is the study of social mobility.

What is Social Mobility?

The term *social mobility* refers to movement of individuals or groups from one position of a society's stratification system to another. This is a situation where individuals or groups rise or fall from the stratum to which they have been assigned. The rise of a person from a very poor background to the presidency (e.g., A.P.J. Abdul Kalam,

President of India) or to some other position of great prestige, power or financial reward is an example of social mobility. Mobility runs both ways—up and down. Thus, it is a movement up or down in the social ladder or in social status. Some people fail to maintain their social class rank into which they are born because of loss of wealth or income, acceptance of a lower-status occupation and adopt a lower-status pattern of life. These are the symptoms and processes of downward mobility. In contrast to this, persons who gain in property, income, status or a change in the job of higher rank indicates upward mobility. Lipset and Bendix (1960) defined social mobility as "a process by which individuals move from one position to another between such hierarchical arrangements that are to be found in each society".

Thus, "social mobility is a movement up or down the social class hierarchy" (Mike O'Donnell, 1997). It involves change of one's position in the social status hierarchy but does not necessarily involve any structural change in the hierarchy itself. According to Anthony Giddens (2000), "social mobility refers to the movement of individuals and groups between different socio-economic positions".

The amount of social mobility is often used as an indicator of the degree of openness and fluidity of a society. Stratification systems, which provide little opportunity for social mobility, is termed as 'closed' (caste system), whereas that with a relatively high rate of social mobility as 'open' (class system).

Types of Social Mobility

Social mobility can be studied from many angles. It has many dimensions, viz., direction, time and place etc. From the point of view of direction, it can occur in any one of the directions: from lower to higher (upward mobility), from higher to lower (downward mobility), or between two positions at the same level (horizontal mobility). In addition to the three directions in which movement can take place, there is dimension of time also. That is, changes can occur between generations (inter-generational mobility) or within one generation (intra-generational mobility). Geographical movement involves moving from one place or location to another (neighbourhood, towns or regions). This is known as *lateral mobility*.

1. *Horizontal mobility:* It refers to the movement of a person from one social position to another of the same rank. "A man moving from one job to another but at much the same level of prestige or income is known as horizontal mobility" (Inkeles, 1965). In brief, moving from one job to another job of equal rank is called horizontal mobility.
2. *Vertical Mobility:* It refers to the movement of a person from one social position to another of a different rank. It may involve moving upward (job of higher rank) or downward (job of lower rank) in a society's stratification system. Each of these illustrates vertical mobility. Downward mobility is less common than upward mobility. According to Inkeles (1965), "movement from one stratum to another up or down any one of the possible stratification hierarchies is called vertical mobility".

Most sociological analyses focus on vertical rather than horizontal mobility. The amount of vertical mobility in a society is a major index of the degree of its 'openness', indicating how far talented individuals born into lower strata can move up in socio-economic ladder. Many researches have been conducted since the pioneering study of Pitirim Sorokin (*Social Mobility*, 1927). To mention a few, the studies by David Glass (1949), Blau and Dunken (1967), Lipset and Bendix (1960), Erikson and Goldthrope (1993) and Featherman and Hauser (1978) are well known in this field. In India, social mobility (especially mobility in caste structure) studies were initiated by M.N. Srinivas (1950) and later on many other scholars like A.R. Desai (1961), Yogendra Singh (1977), K.L. Sharma (1976) and Andre Beteille (1965) carried on such researches.

Vertical mobility can take three forms: (a) inter-generational, (b) intra-generational, and (c) structured.

(a) *Inter-generational mobility*: When changes occur from one generation to another, it is known as inter-generational mobility. This type of mobility involves changes in the social position of children relative to their parents. Thus, a bus conductor, whose father was an engineer, provides an example of downward inter-generational mobility. A film star, whose father was a farmer, illustrates upward inter-generational mobility.

(b) *Intra-generational mobility:* When mobility occurs within one generation, it is called intra-generational or career mobility. It involves changes in person's own social position within his or her adult life. Persons can move up or down the social scale in the course of their working life. A man who enters as a school teacher and eventually becomes an inspector of schools of a district is an example of intra-generational upward mobility. Downward intra-generational mobility is not much common.

(c) *Structural/stratum mobility:* These terms refer to the vertical movement of a specific group, class or occupation relative to others in the stratification system. For example, modern information technology has made machines and computer technicians more important in society. They are receiving more respect previously reserved for lawyers and scientists. An influx of immigrants may also alter class alignments, especially if the new arrivals are disproportionately highly skilled or unskilled. Even in the rigid caste system of India, we are witnessing this change through the process of *sanskritisation* (propagated by M.N. Srinivas), whereby a low-status group (the sub-caste) attempts to improve itself through structural mobility. Srinivas cited an example of Toddy tapper caste known as *Nadars* (South India), who have tried to improve their social standing through emulating the customs, values and style of life of higher castes.

Open and Closed Class Systems

A system in which people are ranked strictly according to individual ability and performance is known as an *open class society*. An open system implies that the position of each individual is influenced by the person's achieved status. In an open class system, competition among members of society is encouraged. In contrast to this, a system in which status is theoretically based strictly on heredity, is known as a *closed class society*. Caste provides an example of closed class society or stratification system. An individual automatically belongs to the caste of his parents and, except in rare instances, spends the rest of his life in that status (now some changes are occurring in this situation). By comparison with class system (which is known as open system of stratification), the rate of mobility in caste system is altogether absent. In this system, there is little or no possibility of individual mobility. In such societies, social placement is based on ascribed characteristics, such as caste, race or family background, which cannot easily be changed.

No class system (or stratification system) is entirely open or closed. Modern industrial societies tend towards the open class system, while traditional agricultural societies often had caste or estate systems, which restricted social mobility. Negro-white relationships in America are often cited as a caste situation, although the class differences within each caste make the caste-class concept and designation more useful because it can be used as a measuring stick to determine the freedom of movement in different societies.

Factors Affecting Social Mobility

Social mobility depends both on the individual and on the structure of the society in which he lives. Individual mobility is of little use when society allocates its rewards on the basis of ascribed status. On the other hand, an open society is of little help to the individual who does not want to face competitive struggle. In some societies the ambitious youth may find only one or two possible channels of mobility open to him, while in many others there may be hundreds of possible routes to higher social status.

It would be incorrect to assume that the degree of social mobility and means of obtaining mobility are the same in all class systems. At many places mobility opportunities are affected by structural factors, such as labour market changes which lead to the rise or decline of an occupational group within social hierarchy. Continuous immigration is also a significant factor in shaping a society's level of inter-generational and intra-generational mobility.

Education, occupation and income are the main factors that help in lifting one's class status. In brief, the following are some of the major factors which speed up the process of social mobility: (1) increased technology and substantial change in occupational structure; (2) the growth of large industries and corporations; (3) an increased standard of living; (4) cultivating class-typed modes of behaviour; (5) manipulating associational membership; (6) growth of urban areas; (7) the maintenance of split labour market; (8) differential fertility; (9) open educational opportunities; (10) social and cultural factors like developed sense of protestant (or secular) ethic; (11) intelligence and talent; and (12) a strategic (planned) marriage system.

Consequences of Social Mobility: Functions and Dysfunctions

It is generally held that social mobility is a *sine qua non* of modern democratic culture. We at many times say that a closed class society hinders the fulfilment of individual personality and deprives society of the contributions of many talented people. Mobility brings new opportunities and greater outlets for potential ability but has its own penalties also. It brings emotional strains and threatens patterns of friendship, residence and family ties. It exacts its price from those who compete and aspire for upward social mobility in the following forms:

1. *Status insecurity:* An open class system grants a person a chance to rise but charges him with the fear of failure. There is no guarantee that he will not fall down below his ancestral status. His obligation is not merely to maintain his status but to improve. In the process of improving, he falls pray to status anxiety. Nervous breakdowns among such ambitious persons are not uncommon.
2. *Strain of new role adjustments:* Upward mobility requires the unlearning and re-learning (de-socialisation and re-socialisation) of a great many minor role adjustments. Learning new patterns of speech, etiquette, manners, dress

pattern etc. according to new role puts a heavy strain on the mobility-oriented persons.

3. *Disruption of primary group relationships*: Social mobility often requires geographical mobility. Frequent movements means the disruption of established social relationships, neighbourhood relationships, family friends relationships, working place persons relationships etc. Even the marriage of the mobile couple is sometimes threatened. Upward mobility not only disrupts primary group relationships but this may sometimes lead to loneliness and isolation. Some sociological studies suggest that mental illness may sometimes be the price for either upward or downward social mobility.

The other side of the picture is more confusing. Is a high rate of social mobility worth the cost? If a complex, changing society does not permit upward mobility to the talented and ambitious young people, it runs the risk of turning them into rebels and revolutionaries (as we are witnessing in India these days). A high rate of mobility may tend to stabilise a social order by providing an encouraging outlet to talented persons who are dissatisfied with their social status. Such discontented individuals may turn their energies to seeking personal advancement rather than to social revolution. High mobility has certain other undesired consequences. For instance, it may tend to undermine established traditions and develop in the old people a cranky conservatism. It may lead to anomie for persons who move rapidly through a succession of statuses and roles (Tumin, 1957).

Marx believed that high rate of social mobility would tend to weaken class solidarity. Classes would become increasingly heterogeneous as their members ceased to share similar backgrounds. Class identification and loyalty would weaken since it would be difficult for mobile persons to feel a strong consciousness of kind with members of the class in which they found themselves. As a result, the intensity of class conflict and the potential class consciousness would be reduced. Ralf Dahrendorf (1959) believes that this situation has arrived in modern (Western-American) societies. He argues that as a result of high rate of social mobility, the nature of conflict has changed. He remarked "the better the opportunities for mobility in a society, the lower the chance of class-like behaviour among its members". Concluding his ideas, he notes that "although mobility diminishes the coherence of groups as well as the intensity of class conflict, it does not eliminate either".

A number of sociologists have attempted to assess the effects of mobility on social order. For example, Frank Parkin (1968, 1972) has seen the relatively high rate of upward mobility as a 'political safety-valve'. It provides opportunities for many able and ambitious members of working class to improve their situation. The upward mobile persons pose no threat to social stability. Similar conclusions have been drawn from studies of downward mobility (persons moving down into the working class) that the downward mobility did not lead skidders to reject the social order and so threaten the stability of society. Contrary to this assumption, an Indian sociologist K.L. Sharma (1997), while analysing downward social mobility, notes, "downward mobility lends greater fluidity to the social structure than upward mobility".

Barriers to Social Mobility

The greatest barrier to social (class) mobility springs from the fact that social classes are sub-cultures which fit the child for participation in the class (in Indian context, caste) sub-culture to which he/she has been socialised. The average low-class (caste) child does not have the ambition and study habits needed for upward mobility because he has little chance to learn them in his sub-culture. The process of growing up in a class (caste), thus, sets forces in motion which hold one in the same class position.

The followings are the main barriers which hamper or hinder channels of social mobility:

1. Birth and father's position.
2. Social discrimination.
3. Differential access to education, training and motivation.
4. Rigid educational requirements (educational degree of any kind).

5. Lack of development of the necessary qualities.
6. Lack of inherited wealth.

These and many other factors act as impediments in the free flow of persons into their most suitable and desired niches.

Social Stratification and Social Mobility in India

Social stratification found in India is identified as the caste system. It is associated chiefly with the traditional Hindu culture of the Indian sub-continent. Hindu society in traditional India was divided into four strata: four *varnas* and a fifth group, the outcaste, whose members were known as 'untouchables'. It is said that the castes or *jatis* are the outcome of ancient *varna* system. The *varna* consists of four categories (Brahmin, Kshatriya, Vaishya and Sudra), each ranked differently in terms of social honour. Below these four groupings are the 'untouchables'. They are excluded from the performance of rituals which confer religious purity. Each *varna* is sub-divided into castes (*jatis*) and sub-castes, which in total number were about three thousands. *Jatis* are occupational groups. They are ranked in terms of ritual purity. The Brahmins or priests, members of highest caste, personify purity, sanctity and holiness. They are the source of learning, wisdom and truth. Only they can perform the most important religious ceremonies. At the other extreme, untouchables are defined as unclean, inferior and impure, a status which affects all their social relationships. In general, the hierarchy of prestige based on notions of ritual purity is mirrored by the hierarchy of power. . . . . Inequalities of wealth were usually linked to those of prestige and power (Haralambos, 1981).

Let us briefly examine the chief characteristics of Indian caste system. Kingsley Davis (*Human Society*, 1967) lists seven features which distinguish Indian castes from other types of groups (social classes):

1. Hereditary caste membership.
2. Closed system of stratification (restricted social mobility).
3. Endogamy (marriage within one's own caste or sub-caste).

4. Commensal restrictions (feeding and social intercourse).
5. Common traditional occupation determined by one's birth.
6. Hierarchical arrangement of castes.
7. Caste ethnocentrism.

Almost similar features of caste system have been mentioned by J.H. Hutton (*Caste in India*, 1963) and G.S. Ghurye (*Caste and Class in India*, 1950). Caste determines one's status, identity, education and occupation and one must marry within his own caste (or sub-caste). Although individuals are debarred from moving between castes, caste as a whole can raise in status by changing its customs to imitate a higher caste. This process of change is termed as *sanskritisation* by renowned Indian sociologist M.N. Srinivas. In the caste system there was no possibility of an individual moving up or going down in the hierarchy since he belonged to the group in which he was born. Any social mobility was only possible in terms of the group as a whole in one area. Such a mobility, though rare, did happen.

Srinivas asserts that mobility characteristic of caste results only in 'positional' changes of particular sections of a caste and did not lead to 'structural' changes in the system as a whole. He writes: "A low caste was able, in a generation or two, to rise to a higher position in the hierarchy by adopting vegetarianism and teetotalism and by sanskritising its ritual and pantheon... however, the mobility associated with sanskritisation results only in posititional changes in the system and does not lead to any structural change... a caste moves up above its neighbours, and another comes down, but all this takes place in an essentially stable hierarchical order. The system itself does not change." For instance, Sudra continues to be a Sudra but because he has adopted vegetarianism etc., he may move up slightly in the scale of *jatis* within the given *varna*.

Many studies relating to the social mobility in India are centred on the mobility in caste structure. Srinivas who initiated such studies emphasised sanskritisation and westernisation as conceptual tools for understanding mobility in caste system. He holds that 'corporate mobility' stills remains basic at the caste or *jati* level, as familial mobility does not obtain public recognition. The concept of sanskritisation is 'cultural bound', it covers only socio-cultural aspects of change and confines to 'group mobility' of a caste only. It does not take note of mobility that takes place at the familial and individual levels and also the motives and factors that underlie such mobility. Moreover, the concept of sanskritisation only pinpoints cultural mobility and does not throw much light on structural mobility. Therefore, the utility of the concept of sanskritisation to understand social mobility in India is limited. This concept has been severely criticised by Indian and many western sociologists on different grounds. For example, Yogendra Singh (1973) notes: "I do not think that cultural mobility as visualised by Srinivas can bring about structural changes." K.L. Sharma (1980) argues: "The efforts to move up in caste hierarchy without corresponding economic elevation have failed." Moreover, change within or between castes does not necessarily constitute mobility within the caste system (Lynch, 1968). To understand mobility in a better way in caste structure, K.L. Sharma (1980) suggested that mobility is to be analysed at three levels: individual, familial and group levels. These three levels of mobility encompass the entirety of mobility in caste structure. It would also help us to understand the social mobility at structural level.

Studies have shown that there are two kinds of stratification existing side by side in the villages as well as in the urban areas, namely, caste hierarchy and class hierarchy. Till recent decades there was a correspondence between the class hierarchy and the caste hierarchy in the villages of India. Landowners were largely from the higher castes—Brahmins, Rajputs or Jats. The tenants were the middle caste non-Brahmins and the agricultural labourers were from the lower castes—the Harijans or other Dalits. Thus, there was correspondence between the caste structure and the class structure. Since independence, this close relationship between caste hierarchy and class hierarchy in the villages has been disturbed due to the philosophy of socialism and democracy. Many legislations have been passed to bridge the gap between the rich and the poor, between the upper castes and the lower castes. Due to some welfare measures (reservations etc.) and economic development, we observe some mobility in the caste system. But such changes do not affect the hierarchy of the caste system in any significant manner. Even, when a person changes his occupation or becomes a collector of a district or even the chief minister of a province, he continued to be a member of the caste in which he is born.

Because of new measures of ameliorations, new middle classes have emerged. Lowest castes like Harijans, who were till recently propertyless labourers, have now changed their position by becoming tenants and in some cases they have become landowners. This trend we also observe in the class structure of urban areas. In the towns and cities, many Harijans and members of other Dalit castes have become clerks, teachers, professors, administrators or other professional people. Not only this, they have achieved positions of high rank such as chief secretary, minister and the like. With the purchase of land by the dalits, the class system has dissociated itself from the rigid caste structure. Similarly, in the recent decades, power has shifted from the traditional elite who belonged to higher castes, such as Brahmin, Kshatriya or Vaishya, into the hands of new popular leaders belonged to the non-*sawarna* castes. Thus, the convergence between caste, class and power in the traditional system of stratification in India has now been altered in the recent decades.

Modern Trends in Social Stratification and Social Differentiation in India

There is a clear trend toward class decomposition in India. Members of social classes (and even castes) become less similar to one another. There is a progressive social differentiation, i.e., even people from the same backgrounds become increasingly dissimilar to one another. Members of bourgeoisie become divided between owner and managers, the working class becomes divided according to the region they live in, their level of skills and a growing diversity of lifestyles and consumption pattern. The middle class also becomes increasingly heterogeneous with divisions between professional, administrative and technical workers and between state employers and those working in private industry. A survey conducted between 1986 and 1994 by the National Council of Applied Economic Research

(NCAER) in New Delhi had already found that India's consumers could be divided into five classes, not three: (1) the very rich, of six million people (or one million households), (2) the 'consuming class' of some 150 million (half the conventional estimate), (3) the 'climbers' (a lower-middle class of 275 million), (4) the 'aspirants' (another 275 million who in America or Europe would be classified as 'poor'), and finally (5) the destitute (210 million). Of course, the numbers have gone up by another 100 million or so in the decade since the survey was conducted, but the relative balance amongst these five classes, despite some progress in all of them, is unlikely to have changed dramatically. This change can be attributed to the economic transformation of India since liberalisation and globalisation after 1991. Shrinking jobs in public sector, and consequent privatisation, has also affected class structure in India. All these changes have helped in swolling up in the ranks of middle class.

Chapter 13

Processes of Social Interaction

Key features

There are sociologists like R. E. Park and E. W. Burgess (1921), who defined sociology as the study of social interactions and social processes. These sociologists viewed society as an ongoing process, as a series of interactions between human beings, each person stimulating another person and responding to the stimuli from the other persons. Interaction refers to an action done in response to another person's action. It is defined as interpersonal action. It becomes a social action when it is oriented to others or taking others into account. Social action is an action done by a social actor. It is always a response to another actor or an attempt to secure such a response. Social action becomes social interaction when the response occurs. It is an action that affects the recipient in someway and usually intended by the actor to result in a reaction back to him. When social interaction becomes continuous and repeated many times, it leads to some result, and then it becomes a social process.

Social interaction is the essence of social life. Without interaction there would be no social or group life. It is the basic ingredient of social relationships which are the basis of the formation of society. This is why, it is often said that society is rooted in social interaction. 'Social interaction consists of that behaviour by which an individual influences the overt actions or the state of mind of another.' Study of processes of social interaction helps us to understand the pattern of social relationships or so to say society which is the real subject matter of sociology. Man becomes *social animal* only when he interacts with other members of society (family, community and many other groups).

What is Meant by Process?

Before examining social process, we should know what is meant by process. A process is a sequence of steps by means of which transition is made from one condition to another. In this sequence, each step is the outgrowth of what precedes and in turn give rise to that which follows. It is a group of activities, each of which has a meaning in relation to all others. For example, the process of digestion includes various steps involved in the organism's transformation of food into the various elements of the body tissue. Process is essential to being: interaction is a necessary part of reality. Separate and disparate planets do not make a solar system. Life cannot be understood merely through inert, nonacting and isolated aggregate of cells. Every natural process involves the reciprocal interaction of diverse elements. Where there is no interaction, there is no process. So diverse elements and mutual interactions are the two essential factors that constitute any natural process. The processes have no beginning, and no end. No beginning because there were antecedent actions, and no end because there is continuity.

Explaining Social Process

A social process is a group of related activities involved in the transition from one social condition to another. According to Horton and Hunt (1968), "the term 'social process' refers to repetitive forms of behaviour which are commonly found in social life." Ginsberg (1956) stated: "Social processes mean the various modes of interaction between individuals or groups." MacIver and Page (1949) observe: "Social process is the manner in which the relations of the members of a group, once brought together, acquire a certain distinctive character."

The essential elements of social process are:

(1) Sequence of events or elements
(2) Repetition of events
(3) Relationship between the events
(4) Continuity of events
(5) Social result

The concept of interaction has become one of the fundamental and most nearly universal ideas almost in each of the fields of knowledge—physical, biological and social. But it should not be inferred that interaction as it takes place in the inorganic or organic order is the same in all respects as is interaction in the superorganic (human-social) realm. It is also the core datum of sociology. It has been defined as "any event by which one party tangibly influences the overt actions or the state of mind of the other" (Sorokin, 1928). It is a reciprocal and interdependent activity. Defining social interaction, Gillin and Gillin (1948) wrote: "By social interaction we mean the mutual or reciprocal influence, resulting in the modification of behaviour, exerted through social contact and communication which, in turn, are established by interstimulation and response." This definition emphasised on two main conditions of social interaction: (a) social contact, and (b) communication. Social contact is the first place of interaction. It rather initiates interaction. Social contact refers to the connection between persons and groups.

For social contact social proximity (mental contact) and not the physical proximity (bodily contact) is essential. Social contact differs from physical or bodily contact. Mere physical contact (proximity) of individuals does not constitute a group. This is why, it is said, "where there is contact of human minds, there association exists; where there is no contact, there is a state of isolation". Social contacts may be direct or indirect and positive or negative. Direct contacts involve immediate presence of persons (face to face) in the exchange of ideas or things. Other contacts are indirect as we find in the case of the writer and the recipient of a personal letter. Such contacts may be established through any means of communication (telephone, TV, Internet). Positive contact means associative interaction which leads towards assimilation through tolerance, compromise or cooperation. Negative contact means disassociative interaction, which gives rise to the feeling of hatred, rivalry, jealousy, indifference or lack of response.

The other condition for social interaction is communication. Society can only be conceived of through communication. It has a central place in society. It may vary from writing a letter to a friend, to all the modern methods of communication. Means of communication may be language, script, gestures, words or symbols etc. Language is a symbolic communication because it consists of conventional cues or signs. Gestures and facial expressions like speech and language play a significant part in communication at human level. Hand-shake, head-nodding, waving the hand are good examples of gestures. Communication in either form of material or sensory medium is a necessity for social contacts. Communication plays an important role in personality formation, transfer of social heritage and social experience from generation to generation.

Classification of Social Processes

Social process may be classified in three ways:

1. By the number of persons involved, i.e., one-with-one; one-with-group; and its reverse, group-with-one, and group-with-group.

2. By the degree of intimacy of the individual and groups in interaction. For example, primary, secondary and tertiary or marginal groups.
3. By the nature or types of the processes.

There are, of course, hundreds of social processes—political process, educational process, industrial process, economic process, religious process and various others. The specific social processes are very numerous. Among those of more general nature are association, cooperation, conflict, accommodation, assimilation, domination, exploitation, differentiation etc. These processes may be grouped into two main categories: (i) integrative/conjunctive/associative, and (ii) disintegrative/disjunctive, disassociative.

Integrative or conjunctive or associative processes

These are the processes which bring the individuals and groups together. Such processes produce unity among members of a group or society. Co-operation, accommodation and assimilation are the examples of integrative or associative processes. According to Max Weber, "a social relationship will be called associative if and in so far as the orientation of social action within it rests on a rationally motivated adjustment of interests".

Disintegrative or disjunctive or disassociative processes

These processes are quite opposite to the integrative processes. They breed contempt, tension and bring disunity among the members of a group or society. Competition, rivalry and conflict are the main disintegrative processes. Max Weber has also included 'communal' relationship under this category. For him, "a social relationship is 'communal' if and so far as the orientation of social action, whether in the individual case or on the average, is based on the subjective feelings of parties whether affectual or traditional that they belong together". Such relationships may be seen in religious brotherhood, personal loyalty and in national community.

We shall here discuss only five fundamental types of interactions (social processes), viz., co-operation, competition, conflict, accommodation and assimilation.

Co-operation

It is a basic process of social life. Its nature is associative. Society cannot exist without co-operation. Co-operation generally means working together in the pursuit of common goals or common interests. It is a joint activity carried out for shared rewards. It is a coordinated effort to reach mutual goals. Co-operation implies a regard for the wishes of other people. Men may also find that their selfish goals are best served by working together with their fellows. Co-operation involves sacrifice, effort, subordination of private interests and inclination to the joint ends of the community, the existence of social constraint. The tendency to co-operate seems to be fundamental. It is found in animals as mutual aid (Kropotkin and Kohler), in primitive people (Mead), in children and in civilised adults.

Definitions

According to Merrill and Eldrige (1952), "co-operation is a form of social interaction wherein two or more persons work together to gain a common end". Fairchild (*Dictionary of Sociology,* 1944) observes: "Co-operation is the process by which individuals or groups combine their effort, in a more or less organised way for the attainment of common objective." Defining co-operation, Robert A. Nisbet (1974) wrote: "It is joint or collaborative behaviour toward some goal in which there is common interest." It may be:

(1) spontaneous/directed (planned as in bureaucracy)

(2) voluntary/involuntary

(3) contractual/traditional (joint family)

(4) large/small in scale

Elements

Following are the main elements of co-operation:

(1) Two and more than two persons.

(2) Common end or goal.

(3) Joint activity.

(4) Conscious effort.

(5) Restrain over ego-centered drives.

Types

Co-operation may be personal or impersonal, and direct or indirect, in character. There are many modes of co-operation in social life. Its principal types are: (i) deliberate primary group co-operation, and (ii) indirect secondary group co-operation.

Deliberate primary group co-operation

Co-operation by members of small groups (family, recreation groups, work associates) is very common in our society. The nature of this type of co-operation is personal and direct. Playing together, worshipping together, tilling the fields together are the instances of direct personal co-operation. In the direct co-operation individuals do *like* things together.

Indirect secondary group co-operation

This type of co-operation is found in the secondary groups such as large organisations, industry, government, trade unions etc., consumer and producer co-operation are its good example. The nature of such co-operation is generally indirect and impersonal. This type of co-operation is based on the renowned principal of division of labour and specialisation. In such activities people do *unlike* tasks for fulfilling a common goal/end. Indirect co-operation is the main characteristic of modern society. The individual of modern industrialised society increasingly separated from face-to-face direct co-operation.

Importance

"Society is co-operation crossed by conflict". These words of MacIver and Page (1956) clearly highlight the importance of co-operation in society. The authors have equated society with co-operation but at the same time they have not ignored the incidence of conflict which takes place from time to time in society. All progress of mankind is attributed to the co-operative efforts in various fields but conflict is also necessary for the upliftment of society lest the people may become inert and life become inactive and eventless. Co-operation is a universal phenomenon found since birth to death. Rearing, caring and protection of the child is not possible without the help and co-operation of mother or any other person. Even on death some persons are required to carry the dead body to the cremation ground. All social groups—from the smaller family to the large international organisations—are based on the co-operation of their members.

Competition

Competition is an elementary, universal and impersonal form of social interaction. It is elementary in the sense that it is basic to all other forms of interaction. Each individual is involved in countless ways of which he is generally unaware in a vast web of competitive relationships. This lack of awareness on the part of the competing units gives competition its impersonal character. Of the various concrete expressions, the most obvious is *struggle for existence*. Every form of life is in constant struggle for life with the impersonal forces of nature that exist everywhere in the natural world. There is a ceaseless struggle between each form and its foes. In human society, the struggle of existence is seldom a brute struggle for the means of life as we find in the animal world. The typical struggle in human society is for livelihood rather than for the means of existence. The human struggle is for economic security and for place, power and status. It is present almost in every walk of life.

Definitions

Competition is the struggle for possession of rewards which are in limited supply—money, goods, status, power, love—anything (Horton and Hunt, 1964). It is a process of seeking to obtain a reward by surpassing all rivals. In the words of Biesanz and Biesanz (1964), "competition is the striving of two or more persons or groups for the same goal which is limited so that all cannot share it". According to Sutherland, Woodward and Maxwell (1961), "competition is an impersonal, unconscious, continuous struggle between individuals or groups for satisfaction which, because of their limited supply, all may not have".

Regarding competition one important point to be kept in mind is that the attention of the competitors is always focused on the goal or reward and not on themselves. When there is a shift in interest or focus from the objects of competition to the competitors themselves, it becomes rivalry which may sometimes lead to conflict in hard cases.

Characteristics

(1) *Competition is a culturally patterned process:* It is present to some degree in all societies but it differs greatly from society to society. The fiercely competitive Kwakiutl society (a tribe of North America) and the relatively non-competitive Zuni (a pubelo Indian group of New Mexico) society offer an example of a striking contrast. American society though competitive, yet this competition is sharply limited.

(2) *Competition is impersonal:* Impersonal means, the competition is usually not directed against any individual or group in particular. Competition may be personal when the competitors know one another but generally its nature is impersonal.

(3) *Competition is unconscious:* Competition takes place on the unconscious level. Competitors at many times are not aware about other competitors and even if they are aware, they do not pay any heed to the activities of their competitors. Candidates, appearing for IAS or any other competitive examination, do not know one another and their whole attention is focused on their studies (reward or goal) rather than on competitors.

(4) *Competition is universal:* Competition, though an important characteristic feature of modern society, is found in all societies—primitive, traditional, modern or in pre-historic eras and in every age.

(5) *Competition is continuous:* It is a never ending process. It goes on consciously or unconsciously all the time. It is unstable and frequently yields either to co-operation or to conflict.

(6) *Competition is restrained:* It implies that there are rules of the game to which all competitors must follow. When the competitors break the rules or when it turns into cut-throat competition (unrestricted), the situation transforms into conflict.

(7) *Competition is for scarce goods (rewards):* If the object of competition is in abundance (unlimited) quantity or sufficient in supply, there would be no competition. There is no competition for sunshine and air, which are unlimited.

Types

There are mainly two types of competition:

(1) *Personal competition:* When two competitors contest for election to office, it is called personal competition. In this competition, competitors know each other.

(2) *Impersonal competition*: When contestants are not aware of one another's identity as we find in university or civil service examinations, it is called impersonal competition.

Importance

Competition is indispensable in social life. It is sociologically significant for the positive and negative effects it produces in social life. It performs many useful functions in society. Some of the main functions are: (1) It serves the function of allocating scarce rewards among the competitors. (2) It has the additional function of stimulating both individual and group activity in a manner to increase the total productivity of the competitors. It furnishes motivation to excel or to obtain recognition or to achieve reward. (3) It assigns place to each individual in the hierarchical social system. It determines who is to perform what function. (4) It tends to enhance one's ego and helps in satisfying it. (5) It is conducive to progress and welfare of the society. It spurs individuals and groups to exert their best efforts to fulfil their goals. (6) It increases efficiency.

Competition has negative functions also. For example: (1) It shapes the attitudes of competitors when persons or groups compete, they normally develop unfriendly and unfavourable attitudes towards one another. (2) It may turn into conflict if it is too acute and sharp (cut-throat competition). Unfair competition has the most disintegrating effects on the individual and the society both. (3) It may create emotional disturbances. According to H.T. Mazumdar (1966), it may lead to neurosis through frustration. (4) Unlimited competition may lead to monopoly. People try to protect themselves through their association.

Early sociological thinkers such as Herbert Spencer saw competition as a necessary mechanism for achieving social progress—a view that was very much in line with the emergent modern capitalist system and its beliefs in competition as an engine that promotes low prices and high efficiency. It is the main driving force of modern capitalistic societies. It is widely prevalent in every sphere of modern life and in its every activity. In its approach to urban life, the Chicago School of Sociology (Park and Burgess) stressed the role of competition in urban growth patterns as various ethnic, class, racial, and other groups compete for space.

Max Weber saw competition as a peaceful form of conflict. Karl Marx also saw its relationship to conflict but in a less peaceful light. Marx argued that competition among capitalists, among workers, and between capitalists and workers were major sources of contradiction and struggle.

Accommodation

The antagonistic state of affairs produced by conflict is for a brief time and impermanent. Life cannot go long if individuals or groups are engaged in conflict continuously. It must be resolved as early as possible for making life peaceful and worth living. The conflicting parties arrange for alternatives to conflict to bring about termination of hostilities or conflicting relationships and to enable some form of co-operation. The cessation of hostalities usually occur by means of two social processes of interaction—*accommodation* and *assimilation*.

The term 'accommodation' is derived from experimental psychology, where it denotes how individuals modify their activity to fit the requirements of external social world. Although accommodation has its origin in conflict situation, still it is radically different type of interaction. In a conflict situation there are always forces operating to its cessation because conflict does not continue indefinitely. The forces making for peace, as those making for war, are continuously operative. The transition from a state of war to a condition of peace may come in numerous ways. After sometime conflicting parties come to certain terms. This state is known as *accommodation*.

Definitions

Accommodation is a form of social interaction in which 'we get used' to the factors that are likely to lead to conflict either by force of habit, or sheer inertia, or a desire to 'live and let live'. It simply means adjusting oneself to the new environment. For adjustment (physical or social), one has to adopt new ways of behaving. In this process of adjustment, persons are required to take a sequence of steps by which they are reconciled to changed conditions of life through the formation of habits and attitudes made necessary by the changed conditions themselves. It involves conscious and tentative forms of subordination and superordinations. Now, we will cite some definitions of the prominent sociologists.

According to Gillin and Gillin (1948) "accommodation is the term used by sociologists to describe a process by which competing and conflicting individuals and groups adjust their relationships to each other in order to overcome the difficulties which arise in competition, contravention or conflict".

J.M. Baldwin notes: "Accommodation denotes acquired changes in the behaviour of individuals which enable them to adjust to their environment."

Park and Burgess (1921) observe: "Accommodation is a natural issue of conflicts. In an accommodation the antagonism of the hostile elements is temporarily regulated and conflict disappears as a overt action. Even though it remains latent and may become active again with a change in the situation."

Accommodation is "a process of developing temporary working agreements between conflicting individuals" (Horton and Hunt, 1964).

Accommodation refers to "a permanent or temporary termination of rivalrous parties to function together without open hostility atleast in some respects" (Cuber, 1968).

"Accommodation is a term used by the sociologists to describe the adjustment of hostile individuals or groups" (Ogburn and Nimkoff, 1958).

Nature

Accommodation is both a condition and a process. As a condition, accommodation is the recognition and acceptance of a set of relationships that defines the status of person in the group or of the group in a more inclusive social organisation (Reuter and Hart, 1933). The state of accommodation does not represent a state of complete harmony. It is rather an acceptance of conditions in order to avoid or terminate conflict. In reality, this state represents the fact of equilibrium between individuals and groups. Conflict, out of which accommodation directly or indirectly arises, does not entirely disappear in accommodation. It continues to exist as a kind of potential opposition. In some cases, conflict appears in a disguised or sublimated form. Indifference, reticence and cynicism are some of the forms of accommodation. As a process, it refers to the adjustment by means of which overt conflict is resolved and competition restrained within fixed limits. The glaring example is the adjustment between husband and wife that enables each to realise personal wishes in a measure and with a minimum of friction and to carry on a tolerable common life. The person, who goes to a new social situation, has to develop new habits and interests in accord with the new situation and his/her accommodation to it is then underway. The example of Indian bride is most appropriate to cite here. In order to accommodate herself in the family of her husband, she has to make many adjustments. For adjustment conscious efforts are made by persons to develop working arrangements among themselves and try to make their relations more tolerable.

Characteristics

From the above description, we may sum up the characteristics of accommodation as follows:

(1) It is the natural result of conflict (Park and Burgess, 1921). Even if conflict disappears as an overt action, it remains latent as a potential.

(2) It is a universal process.

(3) It is a continuous process. It changes with the changing environment.

(4) It is a state in which the attitudes of love and hate coexist (Ogburn and Nimkoff, 1958).

(5) It is generally a subconscious process.

(6) It is an agreement to disagree (Jones, 1949).

(7) It involves changes in habits, attitudes, patterns of behaviour, techniques, institutions and traditions etc. according to the changed conditions of life.

Forms/Methods

Accommodation takes a number of forms. Some are deliberately planned, others arise as unplanned products of group interaction. It may be brought in many different ways. The more important of these are described below:

Yielding to coercion

Coercion means the use of force or the threat of force to terminate a conflict. It usually involves parties of unequal strength, the weaker party yields and submit itself to the wishes of the stronger group, because of the fear of being overpowered. This happens only when the parties are so unequal in power that resistance seems useless or impossible.

Compromise

Compromise is the adjustment of the opposed wishes of people in which each contender gives up part of his demands. When all the parties are of equal strength or powerful enough so that none of them want conflict, they may compromise their differences. It involves a limited surrender by all groups in order to end or avoid conflict. In compromise, each party agrees to make some concessions and yields to some demands of other in order to reach an agreement. In this type of accommodation the spirit of 'give and take' prevails. Politics may be seen as a continual round of shifting power positions and changing compromises. Illustrations of compromise in labour-management disputes are numerous. Family differences are often settled through compromise.

Arbitration and conciliation

The techniques of arbitration, mediation and conciliation are generally used in arranging compromises. These involve the third party to bring about an end of the conflict between contending parties. Such techniques are often helpful in breaking deadlocks of hostile relations. The labour-management conflicts usually are resolved through the intervention of an arbitrator or a mediator. The UNO frequently serves in the role of arbitrator at an international level. The great difficulty with arbitration is the securing of a mediator who has the confidence of both sides in the controversy.

Arbitration differs from mediation in that a definite decision is handed down by the arbitrators and the decision is regarded as binding. In the mediation, the suggestions made by the mediator have no binding force. Compromise is rarely an ideal solution because it does not last long.

Toleration

Where compromise is unacceptable yet agreement not absolutely necessary, people or groups may use toleration as an alternative to conflict. In this form of accommodation, interacting parties may agree to disagree. People accept each other's right to differ without demanding settlement. Each party holds its position, but respects the fact that the other party has an opposing viewpoint. Religious conflict, such as the demolition of Babri Masjid, is a classic example of this situation. Both parties to this issue 'tolerate' each other, despite the fact that the basic issue is not eliminated.

Conversion

In this form of accommodation, one of the acting parties accepts and adopts the views of the other on the ground that it has been wrong and its opponent is right. Conversion is frequently related to religious beliefs but it may also occur in politics and other fields.

Rationalisation

Accommodation through rationalisation involves plausible excuses or explanations for one's behaviour instead of acknowledging the real defect in one's own self. Recently, the American government has justified its attack on Iraq on the ground that Iraq has nuclear weapons.

Superordination and subordination

The fundamental pattern of accommodation is of reciprocal superiority (superordination) and subordination. The whole web of relationships between two persons is commonly complex series of subordinations in which one or the other is subordinated according to the character of the situation in which they are jointly involved. For example, in legal matters, the physician is subordinate to the lawyer whereas in medical matters the lawyer assumes the subordinate role. The organisation of all societies is essentially the result of such a type of accommodation. From family to larger groupings (political, economic or religious), we can see such types of relationships.

Accommodation by subordination is effective under two conditions. The first is that the dominant party should be so strong as to force the other to submit. The second condition under which subordination as a form of accommodation may be successful is that relationships of subordination should be socially sanctioned as a part of the social structure and heritage of society. The hierarchical structure of military organisation, with the clearly defined superior and subordinate ranks or the familial relationships between parents and children, are good examples of such type of accommodation.

Truce

A truce is an agreement to cease rivalrous interaction for a definite or indefinite period of time. The purpose is usually to give both parties time to review the issue in the light of proposals or suggestions for settlement. This form of accommodation is temporary, usually giving way to a more permanent form.

Displacement

Displacement involves termination of one conflict by replacing it with another. Use of a 'scapegoat' is a displacement technique; the problem of a group (a nation or a village) may be blamed on an individual or on a minority or on imperialists, etc.

Institutionalised means

The structure of various societies may provide institutionalised means for release of tensions. They work as safety valves for resolving of hostility. These means may provide us a form of accommodation in bringing about termination of antagonistic relationships. Community sports, wrestling and other tournaments (cricket matches between India and Pakistan), special feast days, religious and other festivals are its few examples.

Accommodation and adaptation

Accommodation is to be differentiated from adaptation although both are forms of adjustment. Whereas 'adaptation' may be defined as structural change in the organism which takes place through biological variation and selection. The term 'accommodation' is reserved for functional changes in the habits and customs of persons and group changes which are transmitted socially rather than biologically.

Adaptation is a biological concept. Accommodation is an outcome of conflict, while the adaptation is a natural issue of competition. Adaptation is an end result in the process of biological evolution. It refers to the biological process of selection which operates through a series of generations and tends to produce organic forces better and better fitted to their environing circumstances. As a condition, it refers to the biological state of a species. Accommodation is not a selective process and involves no change in the organic type. It is a learning process that fits the person to the environing social conditions by way of changes in habits, sentiments and ideas. As a process, accommodation is a mode of transition from one prior condition, usually one of conflict, to another. It involves a sequence of steps by which persons are reconciled to the changed conditions of life.

The distinction between accommodation and adaptation is well illustrated by Park and Burgess (1921) in the difference between domestication and training. Domestication is a specific type of adaptation. It is a matter of selection, through generations, of variants and the gradual production of a new biological form. Training, on the other hand, is a specific form of accommodation. The tamed animal acquires a set of habits that allow it to live in association with man, it undergoes no organic change in so doing.

Importance

Accommodation is one of the familiar and commonplace facts of everyday life. The situation into which a child is born is never one that satisfies the wishes of his original nature. He has to accept the arrangements that characterise the particular group and culture. Such accommodations are a part of the social heritage. They are accepted without question by the persons born and reared in the society. All through the life, the process of accommodation goes on, changing the person to the changing surroundings. It involves changes in habits, attitudes, patterns of behaviour, techniques, institutions and traditions etc., according to changed conditions of life.

Society can hardly go on without accommodation. It checks conflicts and brings unity between opposing elements. Our society is by and large a complex of competing interests. It is also a fact that the competing individuals or groups are not always having equal power and resources. One may dominate and the result is conflict at many a time. It may be harmful to both the opposing parties if the conflict is not checked and hence accommodation comes to play. Besides, accommodation creates a background for another social process, namely, assimilation.

Assimilation

A term synonymous with acculturation, used to describe the process by which an outsider, immigrant, or subordinate group becomes indistinguishably integrated into the dominant host society (*Oxford Dictionary of Sociology*, 1994). Acculturation, on the other hand, is a process of culture change set in motion by meeting of two autonomous cultural systems. It modifies cultures, without a complete blending of the two cultures. Acculturation, therefore, implies modification but not complete assimilation. Assimilation is different from accommodation whereby the subordinate group simply conformed to the expectations of the dominant group. Assimilation implied that the subordinate group actually came to accept and internalise the values and culture of the group. In accommodation, the mental distance and 'inactive intolerance' continue. In assimilation, the psychological distance is completely overcome and perfect identity of shared experiences is a precondition. Accommodation is a first step to assimilation. Assimilation is also different from the analogous process of amalgamation, which is a biological phenomenon. It is a process of cross-breeding to the production of hybrid offspring and the blending of racial stocks through inter-marriage and intermating. Assimilation, on the other hand, is a cultural, social and psychological phenomenon. On one hand, it involves the fusion of cultural heritages, and, on the other hand, the modification of sentiments and attitudes and the gradual incorporation of the strangers into the cultural group. The two processes are thus quite different from each other. One is biological, the other is sociological; one is a fusion of cultures, the other is blending of racial stocks. Like socialisation, accommodation is also a process of learning.

Definitions

According to Park and Burgess (1921), "assimilation is a process of interpenetration and fusion in which persons and groups acquire the memories, sentiments, attitudes of other persons or groups and by sharing their experiences and history are incorporated with them in a cultural life".

Ogburn and Nimkoff (1958) write: "Assimilation is the process whereby individuals or groups once dissimilar become similar, i.e., become identified in their interests and outlooks."

Horton and Hunt (1964) defined it as, "the process of mutual cultural diffusion through which persons and groups become culturally alike".

According to Schaffer and Lamm (1992), "assimilation is the process by which a person forsakes his or her own cultural tradition to become part of a different culture".

Summarising the above views about assimilation, it may be said that assimilation is a process of fusion or blending, whereby cultural differences tend to disappear and individuals and groups once dissimilar become similar. It results in the modification of attitudes, values, patterns of thinking and ultimately behaviour. Husbands and wives, starting marriage with dissimilar backgrounds, often develop a surprising unity of interest and purpose. In the long run they become more or less similar in their attitude toward life and family.

Nature

Assimilation takes place slowly, gradually and to a considerable extent without conscious effort and direction. The speed of the process of assimilation depends upon the nature of contacts. If the contacts are primary, assimilation occurs naturally and rapidly but if they are secondary, i.e., indirect and superficial, the result is accommodation and not assimilation. It takes quite sometime before individuals or groups dissimilar become similar i.e.; become identified in their interests and outlook. Children are gradually assimilated into adult society as they grow up and learn how to behave. Assimilation occurs through the mechanisms of imitation and suggestion.

Assimilation is a matter of degree. Complete assimilation of an individual into a culture takes considerable time and is seldom if ever achieved within his lifetime. Such a person exhibits behaviour that reflects elements of both cultures. He has been labelled as a 'marginal man'. In large society, complete assimilation is perhaps hypothetical.

Assimilation is a two-way process when it happens between two cultural groups. Each group contributing varying proportions of the eventual blend. The alien group not only contribute to the host culture but retain many of their own ways. As a result, there is *cultural pluralism* which may reflect incomplete assimilation. Should the minority group be forced to assimilate the culture of the majority group is a very controversial question.

Forms

The process of assimilation takes place mainly at three levels: (i) individual, (ii) group, and (iii) culture.

Individual level

A socialised individual when enters or joins a new group having different cultural patterns, he or she has to adopt new patterns of values, habits, customs and beliefs of the other group in order to be fully accepted by the new group. In course of time, he or she becomes assimilated into the second group. An Indian woman after marriage starts with dissimilar backgrounds and develops a surprising unity of interests and identify herself with the family of her husband. The tendency is to conform to other's behaviour pattern and differences in time may largely disappear.

Group level

When two groups with dissimilar patterns of behaviour come in close contact, they inevitably affect each other. In this process, it is generally seen that the weaker group would do more of the borrowing from and would give very little to the stronger group. For instance, when we came in contact with Britishers, being a weaker group, we have adopted many cultural elements of the Britishers but they have adopted a very few cultural elements from Indian society. The adoption of elements of dominant culture paves the way for total absorption, if not checked, of the new cultural group with the dominant culture. Similarly, immigrants in America or Britain usually adopt the material traits (dress pattern, food habits etc) easily in order to adjust themselves in the new cultural environment.

Culture level

When two cultures merge to produce a third culture which, while somewhat distinct, has features of both merging cultures. In western countries chiefly but also in developing countries to some extent, rural and urban cultures which were radically different are, with rapidly increasing communication, merging as differences continue to disappear although they still exist.

Types

Two types of assimilation have been identified: Cultural assimilation and structural assimilation.

Cultural assimilation

Assimilation, as said above, is a two-way process: persons (such as immigrants) must want to be assimilated and the host society must be willing to have them assimilate. The immigrant must undergo cultural assimilation, learning the day-to-day norms of the dominant culture pertaining to dress, language, food, recreation, games and sports. This process also involves internalising the more critical aspects of culture such as values, ideas, beliefs and attitudes.

Structural assimilation

It involves developing patterns of intimate contact between the 'guest' and 'host' groups in clubs, organisations, and institutions of the host society. Cultural assimilation generally precedes structural assimilation, although the two sometimes happen simultaneously.

Conducive factors

Factors that contribute or aid to assimilation are:

(1) *Tolerance:* Without the attitude of tolerance assimilation is not possible. Tolerance requires the feeling of sacrifice and elimination of strong prejudices. It is a democratic virtue which fosters sympathy.

(2) *Intimacy:* Frequent close social contacts and communication are a prerequisite for the start of assimilative process. Intimacy dissolves the walls of ultra-individualism which separates man from man.

(3) *Cultural homogeneity:* Culturally homogenous groups easily assimilate the values and goals of one another. Mutual similarity creates mutual affinities which bring two individuals or groups nearer to each other.

(4) *Equal economic opportunity:* Equal economic opportunities are required to fill the gap of disparity in wealth. It implies that any increase in the availability of opportunities or equality in their distribution would create conditions favourable to the growth of assimilative process.

(5) *Association:* Various associations, clubs, and other places of public meetings help in the assimilative process. When people live in the same vicinity, meet and come together, there is every possibility of the start of the process of assimilation.

(6) *Amalgamation or inter-marriage:* Amalgamation, though a biological process of cross-breeding, helps in cultural assimilation. Through inter-marriages members of different racial stocks come together and adopt the cultural traits of other group.

Hindrances

There are certain factors which retard or hinder the process of assimilation. Some of these are:

(1) *Cultural dissimilarity:* Extreme differences in cultural background act as the most powerful impediment in the way of assimilation. Language and religion are usually considered to be the main constituents of culture. Same religion and language often help in early and speedy assimilative process. Customs and beliefs are other cultural characteristics, which can aid or hinder assimilation. When two cultures (or groups) share many common elements, assimilation is accelerated; the absence of such factors acts as a barrier to the process.

(2) *Physical differences:* Differences in physical traits and skin colour present a formidable barrier to assimilation. This we can see between white and Negro (black) races in which discrimination is practised almost everywhere in the world. Physical differences are extremely visible and can be eliminated only by generations of inter-marriage between cultural groups concerned.

(3) *Feeling of superiority and inferiority:* Such feeling, along with the exploitation of the weaker section (minority group) of the population by stronger one, are contradictory to the assimilative process.

(4) *Prejudice:* Stereotypes and ethnocentrism both can operate as barriers to assimilation. Prejudices (prejudgement) may create a social distance between the alien and dominant cultures.

(5) *Isolation:* The absence of communicative interaction is isolation. It is a situation deprived of social contacts. Isolation signifies detached position or the act or process of attaining a detached position. It may be spatial separation or organic.

Importance

Assimilation is a process of mutual interchange or diffusion of culture through which persons and groups come to share a common culture. It is a process of decreasing differentiation and increasing unification among people. It reduces group conflict by blending differing groups into larger, culturally homogenous groups. Anything which binds people into a larger group will tend to reduce rivalry and conflict between them. A study by Sherif and Sherif (1953) shows that even there are no real differences or issues to fight over, conflict still tends to develop wherever separate group identity is recognised. Assimilation removes some but not all possible pressure toward conflict.

The importance of assimilation rests primarily in its elimination of boundary lines as two groups, formerly distinct, assume a common identity. Boundaries help in developing 'in' and 'out' group feelings or the feeling of *ethnocentrism* (the attitude that one's own culture is superior to others, that one's own beliefs, values and behaviour are more correct than others). Boundary determination is accomplished through various means such as separate unions, using some distinctive marks (*Tilak* on the forehead by Hindu males and red *Bindi* and vermilion by Hindu females), initiation ceremonies etc. To lessen the effect of boundaries, systematic linkage is suggested. Systematic linkage is a process by which groups avoid isolation while maintaining their separate identities.

Integration

Integration, literally, means to make up whole out of parts. It presupposes diversities and the idea is to bind the parts together. Ogburn and Nimkoff (1958) observed: "Integration is a process of creating a single unit by joining different parts." Integration is a process of establishing unity between the constituent parts of a structure which though different have organisation in their relationships. The different parts of this structure are so systematically related to each other that the emerging whole becomes greater than the sum of parts. Thus, integration is more than collection of parts. In this connection, Gillin and Gillin (1948) aptly remarked: "Integration is organisation, rather than homogeneity." It does not preclude differences between different parts altogether.

When we apply this view to society, it only means that different constituent groups that make the society, do not lose their identity. It is thus different from the concept of assimilation in which different groups (religious, racial or ethnic) submerge their identity to make a homogenous society. In assimilation, a person forsakes his or her own cultural traditions and forget his/her own history to become part of a different culture.

The term 'integration' is fundamental in functional theory. According to this view, it is "a mode of relations of the units of a system by virtue of which, on the one hand, they act so as collectively to avoid disrupting the system and making it impossible to maintain its stability, and on the other hand to 'co-operate' to promote its functioning as a unity". (Parsons, 1954). According to Parsons, there are four 'functional exigencies', which must be met by a social system in order to survive as a coherent entity. These are goal attainment, adaptation, integration, and pattern maintenance. Other scholars have used this term more loosely as a synonym for *social consensus*. In their view, integration is a process that involves a *consciousness of the kind* (Giddings) as well as generally socially constructive efforts of different groups and sub-groups to attain a common goal and a maximum level of solidarity, identification and involvement. The main aim of integration is to maintain a harmonious and active relationship between various structural components of society.

Methods

How various elements of society are held together, and how they integrate with each other. The following are two methods of integration:

(1) Integration by commonly held views.

(2) Integration by interdependence in the division of labour.

The first method is commonly known as the assimilationist approach. According to this, all groups (religious, racial, linguistic or ethnic) should conform in major public to what they take to be the established way of life (Indian or British or American way of life). They do not believe in multi-culturalism or pluralism. Assimilationists consider that minority groups (generally immigrants) should adopt themselves to the dominant culture of the society. There are people who even insist on assimilation in the area of public life and personal taste. Such people in cricket game expect that a true 'Indian' person would support the Indian team rather than say, the Pakistan team. This view tries to strike at the very roots of a person's identity as he or she seeks to gain full acceptance as an 'Indian' or 'American' or 'Brit-isher'.

The other method is generally known as the integrationist approach, which emphasises pluralist or liberal-pluralist view. According to this view, a variety of cultural groups can and do exist in a society (say, Indian society) within a common legal and democratic framework. In cultural pluralism various groups maintain their distinctive cultural patterns, sub-systems and institutions. Whereas an assimilationist seeks to eliminate ethnic or racial boundaries, pluralist (integrationist) wants to retain them. Pluralists argue that groups can co-exist by accepting their differences. However, basic to cultural pluralism are beliefs that individuals never forget or escape their social origin, that all groups bring positive contributions that enrich the larger society, and that groups have the right to be different but equal. Cultural pluralism may be expressed with the formula:

$$A + B + C = A + B + C$$

The alphabets ABC represent the various groups with their distinctive cultural patterns, institutions etc.

We can designate these two views as 'Indo-conformity' process and 'melting pot' process. Melting pot process represents the integrationist view in which each group contributes a bit of its own culture and absorbs aspects of other cultures such that the whole is a combination of all groups. Indo-conformity process is equated with 'Indianisation', whereby the minority loses its identity completely to the dominant (Hindu) culture. After independence integrationist policy has been adopted in India. Integration comes about when feeling of different race, religion, ethnicity etc. becomes insignificant and everyone can freely and fully participate in the social, economic and political mainstream.

Education serves the latent function of promoting social and political integration by transforming a population composed of diverse racial, ethnic and religious groups into a society whose members share—to some extent—atleast a common identity (Touraine, 1974). From a functionalist perspective, the common identity and social integration fostered by education contribute to societal stability and consensus.

Social planning is the most effective method of achieving integration in a complex and rapidly changing society like India. For this purpose, programmes of social planning are to be launched. The avowed objective of all social planning is welfare and establishing harmony and unity in the society.

Conflict

Georg Simmel (1955) writes: "There probably exists no social unit in which convergent and divergent currents among its members are not inseparably interwoven. An absolutely centripetal and harmonious group, a pure 'unification', not only is unreal, it could should have no real life process . . . . society, too, in order to attain a determinate shape, needs some quantitative ratio of harmony and disharmony, of association and competition, of favourable and unfavourable tendencies."

It is said that human beings are for the most part quite selfish and that chaos and strife are both common and natural. This is why conflict is the fundamental form of disassociative interaction or oppositional oriented relationship. It is inherent in all social relationships and is also inevitable and universal. Bottomore (*The Study of Conflict,* 1962) observed: "Conflict is an intrinsic part of our social life, sustaining, modifying or destroying the social groups in which it takes place." Whenever and wherever there is a difference in the motives and interests (desire for prestige, economic benefit, power and defeat or destruction of the enemy) of different persons, there is bound to be some kind of conflict. It may be destructively or constructively directed. It may be between individuals, between groups of individuals or between two societies (or nations) depending whether the contradictory interests involved are personal or of group or of the whole community or nation.

Definitions

An analysis of the literature reveals that the term 'conflict' is defined in a number of ways. Followers of Georg Simmel, like R.E. Park, have seen conflict as one of the central forms of interaction. Simmel (1955) writes: "If every interaction among men is a sociation, conflict must certainly be considered as sociation." Park and Burgess (1921) likewise treat conflict as a distinct form of competition. They wrote: "Both are forms of interaction but competition is a struggle between individuals or groups of individuals who are not necessarily in contact and communication while conflict is a contest in which contact is an indispensible condition."

According to Max Weber (1968), "a social relationship will be referred to as *conflict* in so far as action within it is oriented intentional to carrying out the actor's own will against the resistence of the other party or parties". Thus, the social interaction of conflict is defined by the desire of each participant to impose his will upon the other's resistence. These sentiments are well echoed in the words of A.W. Green (1956) who defined it as "the deliberate attempt to oppose, resist or coerce the will of another or others". As a process it is the antithesis of cooperation in which a deliberate attempt is made to thwart the will of others. Gillin and Gillin (1948) wrote: "Conflict is the social process in which individuals or groups seek their ends by directly challenging the antagonist by violence or threat of violence." To sum up, it may be said that conflict refers to the struggle in which competing parties, attempting to reach a goal, strive to eliminate an opponent by making the other party ineffectual or by annihilation.

Characteristics

On the basis of foregoing discussion, the following characteristics (nature) of conflict, in brief, may be cited:

(1) It is a *universal* process found in every society.

(2) It is the result of *deliberate and conscious* efforts of individuals or the groups.

(3) The nature of the conflict is *personal and direct.* In conflict the incumbents or participants know each other personally.

(4) It is basically an *individual's* process. Its aim is not directly connected with the achievement of the goal or an objective but is rather directed to dominate others or to eliminate the opponent.

(5) Conflict is of brief duration, temporary and *intermittent* in character. But, once begun, the conflict process is hard to stop. It tends to grow more and more bitter as it proceeds. Being temporary, it gives way to some form of accommodation.

(6) It is a process loaded with *impulsiveness* of human emotions and violent passions. It gains force and then bursts open. Unlike fighting of animals, generally in human groups, the spontaneous

fighting is inhibited. It is often avoided through the process of accommodation and assimilation.

(7) It may be *latent or overt.* In the latent form, it may exist in the form of tension, dissatisfaction, contravention and rivalry. It becomes overt when an issue is declared and a hostile action is taken.

(8) It is *mostly violent* but it may take the form of negotiations, party politics, disputes or rivalry.

(9) It is *cumulative;* each act of aggression usually promotes a more aggressive rebuttal. Thus, termination of conflict is not easy.

(10) It tends to be *more intense* when individuals and groups who have close relationships with one another are involved.

(11) Groups previously in conflict may co-operate to achieve a goal considered important enough for them to unite despite their differences.

(12) It may emerge as a result of opposing interests.

(13) It has both disintegrative and integrative effects. It disrupts unity in a society and is a disturbing way of setting issues. A certain account of internal conflict, however, may serve indirectly to stimulate group interaction. External conflict can have positive effects by unifying the group.

Conflict and contravention

Contravention is the mild form of conflict in which contending parties (groups or individuals) strive to prevent each other from achieving the objective through indirect attacks on the opposite party. It does contain antagonism and hostility like conflict. The establishment and fostering to temporary political parties during national elections with the express purpose of dispersing votes and confusing the electorate is an illustration of contravention.

Forms

In all societies there are at least two sorts of conflict. First, there is conflict between men contending for positions of power. Second, there is conflict between the powerful and the powerless. Conflict can be distinguished in so many ways. It may take place between persons or individuals and groups. Conflict between persons is a most direct and immediate form of conflict. It may involve intense personal animosities. It may take the form of a brute struggle on the physical level to destroy or eliminate the opponent. Personal conflicts arise on account of various motives—envy, hostility, betrayal of trust being the most predominant.

Group or corporate conflict

It takes place between two societies or groups within a society. When group loyalties and needs take precedence over personal individual feelings, it is group conflict. In such conflict, individual feelings become irrelevant. Groups attempt to impose their will on other groups in order to gain power, prestige, wealth and commodities of value. Such conflict is impersonal. Communal or race riots, religious persecution, labour-management disputes, and wars between two or more nations are some of the examples of corporate conflict.

Heractitus once said: "All is incessantly changing and war is the father of all things." War is the most characteristic and spectacular form of group conflict. In the first instance, it grows out of a clash of interests such as to destroy or weaken the competitor group, to snatch the land or to steal the women or the property. Primitive warfare has often operated selectively between the occupying peoples and the invading hordes. In the later culture development over population has often been at the base of national conflict, although the direct and inciting causes often seem for removed.

Simmel (1955) distinguished four types of conflict: (i) war; (ii) feud or fictional strife; (iii) litigation; and (iv) conflict of impersonal ideals. Simmel attributed war to a deep-seated antagonistic impulse in man. For him, antagonistic impulse is a foundation of all conflicts. Feud is an intra-group form of war which may arise because of injustice alleged to have been done by one group to the other. Litigation is a judicial form of conflict when an individual or group asserts its claims to certain rights on the basis of objective factors. Conflict of impersonal ideals is a conflict carried on by the individuals not for themselves but for an ideal. In such a conflict each party attempts to justify truthfulness of its own ideals.

Direct and indirect conflict

Direct conflict occurs where individuals or groups thwart or impede or restrain or injure or destroy one another in the effort to attain the goal. Indirect conflict occurs where individuals or groups do not actually impede the efforts of one another but nevertheless try to attain their ends in ways which obstruct the attainment of the same end by others.

Gillin and Gillin (1948) have classified conflict in five groups: (i) personal conflict, (ii) racial conflict, (iii) class conflict, (iv) political conflict, and (v) international conflict.

Causes

Earlier scientists like Darwin saw conflict as inherent in the principles of struggle for existence and survival of the fittest, while for Malthus, the champion of population theory, reduced supply of the means of subsistence is the cause of conflict. Some sociologists like Ratzenhofer and Gumplowicz regard it as underlying social evolution and progress. According to Ratzenhofer, the struggle for life takes the form of conflict in interests. For Gumplowicz, it represents a primordial feeling of 'syngenism' – a feeling of belonging together. There are two main approaches which have analysed the causes of conflict in their own way:

(1) *Psychological approach:* This approach tries to look for the causes of conflict in human nature and posits a 'fighting instinct'. This is exemplified in the views of Simmel, Freud and Lorenz. According to Freud, there is an innate instinct for aggression in man which is responsible for conflict in human society. Recent biological and anthropological studies have generally supported the notion that there is an 'aggressive instinct', resulting from natural selection. This theory has been criticised on various grounds. It is said that the theory which depends upon a permanent and constant aggressive instinct cannot explain the cycle of conflict and absence of conflict. It only explains the propensity to engage in aggressive behaviour.

(2) *Sociological approach:* This approach is based on a theory of interests i.e., conflict occurs, for example, when territory is invaded. This approach has its roots in the Marxist tradition. This tradition assumes that social life is shaped by groups and individuals who struggle or compete with one another over various resources and rewards. These shape not only the patterns of everyday life and interaction, but also large patterns such as racial, ethnic and class relations. Marx argues that most conflict is economic and rests on the unequal ownership and control of property.

There are many other causes of conflict, which may be briefly stated as under:

(1) *Individual differences:* No two men are alike in their nature, attitudes, ideals, opinions and interests. These differences lead them to some or the other sort of conflict to fulfil their individual interest. Because of these differences, they fail to accommodate themselves with each other.

(2) *Cultural differences:* Culture differs from society to society and also group to group. These differences sometimes cause tension and lead to conflict. The religious differences have often led to wars and persecution in history. In India, often, communal conflicts broke out which are the results of religious differences.

(3) *Clash of interests:* The interests of different people or groups occasionally clash. For example, the interests of workers clash with those of the employers which leads to conflict in the form of strike, *bandh* or *dharana* etc. among them.

(4) *Social change*: All parts of society do not change with the same speed. This causes 'lag' in the parts which may cause conflict between different parts of the society. Conflict of generations (parent-youth) is the result of such social changes.

Role (functions) of conflict

Conflict has always captured the attention of the people and the society. As other forms of social interaction, it has both positive and negative effects. Conflict both terminates and commences to serve the interests of man in society. Cooley (1902) maintained: "Conflict of some sort is the life of society, and progress emerges from a struggle in which each individual, class or institution seeks to realise its own ideals of good." Simmel (1955) observed that a conflict-free harmonious group is practically an impassibility. There is no denying the fact that society requires for its formation and growth both harmony and disharmony, association and disassociation. Georges Sorel (1908) felt that a social system was in need of conflict if only to renew its energies and revitalise its creative forces. His arguments that violent confrontations can be noble and civilizing and that there is nothing to suggest civilized men and women will ever wholly renounce violence to advance estimable causes. Mack and Young (1959) write: "At its most rudimentary level, conflicts result in the elimination or annihilation of the opponent. In human society, however, most conflicts end in some sort of agreement or accommodation or in the fusion of the two opposing elements." It is said that the origins of the state, social organisation and many social institutions are the result of war and struggle.

Generally, conflict is regarded as disintegrative and its dysfunctions are highlighted but conflict plays constructive role also and it has positive functions for the individual and society both. For instance, inter-group conflict is a patent source of inter-group co-operation. It helps in unifying a society or a group when some external aggression occurs. Conflict prevents the ossification of the social system by exerting pressure for innovation and creativity. Horton and Hunt (1964) have distinguished the effects of conflict as under:

Integrative effects	*Disintegrative effects*
Define issues.	Increases bitterness.
Leads to resolution of issues.	Leads to destruction and bloodshed.
Increases group cohesion.	Leads to inter-group tension.
Leads to alliance with other groups.	Disrupts normal channels of cooperation.
Keeps groups alert to members' interests.	Diverts members' attention from group objectives.

As a form of interaction, sociologically significant both from the point of view of personality (individual level) and from that of social organisation both self-consciousness and group-consciousness are the result of conflict. At the individual level, every problem in the life of the person is a conflict. Conflict plays a corresponding role in group organisation. Groups reach the maximum of unity and solidarity in overt conflict. External conflict (conflict with another group) tends to integrate the group. On the one hand, it provides the members with an external outlet for their hostilities and resentments and thus removes a lot of internal tensions. On the other hand, it compels each member to co-operate and forge unity to face the external threat. While external conflict separates a group from its enemies, it also promotes alliances with other groups. Georg Simmel (1955), an early analyst of social conflict, writes: "A state of conflict pulls the members so tightly together and subjects them to such a uniform impulse that the most completely get along with or completely repel one another." Lewis A. Coser (*The Functions of Conflict*, 1956) has also analysed the role of conflict in promoting unity in detail. Thus, the above discussion about the role (functions) of conflict may be summed up as under:

(1) Conflict determines the status of the individual in the social organisation. Rivalry, war and other forms of personal struggle determine superiority and subordination of men and groups.

(2) Conflict is not always an unmitigated evil everywhere as it is generally assumed. It is a chief means of group contact, and it has played an important role in the development and spread of culture.

(3) Conflict may eventuate in peace through victory of one contestant over others.

(4) Conflict helps to define social issues and brings about a new equilibrium of contending forces. It may lead to the working out of non-violent techniques for resolving crises. The end result of conflict is that the issues are resolved atleast for a time.

(5) Conflict tends to stiffen the morale, promotes unity and cohesion within the group and may lead to expanding alliances with other groups.

(6) Conflict keeps groups alert to members' interests.

(7) Conflict generates new norms and new institutions. It happens mostly in economic and technological realms. Economic historians often have pointed out that much technological improvement has resulted from the conflict activity of trade unions. It leads to redefinition of value systems.

(8) Conflict within and between bureaucratic structures provides means of avoiding the ossification and ritualism which threatens their form of organisation.

(9) Conflict leads not only to ever-changing relations within the existing social structure, but the total system undergoes transformation through conflict (Marxian view).

(10) Conflict between vested interests and new strata and groups demanding share of power, wealth and status have proved to be productive of vitality.

(11) Conflict may lead to a new consensus.

(12) Conflict theorists believe that conflict is necessary for progress (Coser, 1956). They contend that societies progress to a higher order only if oppressed groups improve their lot.

Dysfunctions of conflict

Conflicts, as we know, disrupts social unity. It is highly disturbing way of settling issues. Conflict within a group makes it hard for members to agree on group goals or to co-operate in pursuit of them. It leads to group tension. It increases bitterness and leads to destruction and bloodshed. Conflict disrupts normal channels of co-operation. It diverts members' attention from group objectives.

Conflict of values

The conflict of values is a struggle of a different order and on a different plane from either the personal or the group conflict. It is an aspect of conflict that is purely objective and impersonal. In its simplest manifestations, conflict is merely a physical struggle between individuals or groups. But back of these physical facts is the social and psychological situation, i.e., the clash of interests and attitudes that leads the groups to physical struggles. The wars of nations may arise out of clash of attitudes and values. Value conflict between husband and wife sometimes results into mental stress which eventually may lead to divorce.

The values involved may be material or immaterial realities. Men and nations fight for food and lands and markets but they also fight for sentiments, beliefs and ideals. Some degree of actual or potential conflict between youngest and older generations is inevitable in a changing world.

But above and beyond the physical struggles of individuals and groups and apart from the interests and attitudes that motivate or accompany them is the conflict of values. Many of the ideas and ideals prevailing among human beings are opposed and mutually exclusive such as democracy v/s aristocracy, privatisation v/s state ownership, globalisation v/s nationalism etc. Evolution and fundamentalism are contradictory interpretation of reality. There is no resolution of conflict between such logically incompatible ideas and beliefs. The only resolution of such a conflict is the disappearance of one or the other from the realm of human values.

Co-operation and conflict

Society and civilisation are the product of human co-operative labour. But, by some strange act of the nature of the things themselves, co-operation and conflict reside side by side, affecting each other and often are placed in position of cause and effect. Both are universal and inescapable elements in social life and they often go together. They sometimes resemble in this respect—the equivalent of linked emotions of love and hate. According to Cooley, conflict and co-operation are not separable things but phases of one process which always involves something both. Even in the most intimate marital or friendly relations, there is some point where interests diverge or where attitudes are not in accord.

Co-operation is a condition of conflict. Conversely, there are examples of co-operative enterprises in society within which conflict in some form is not present. In this connection, MacIver aptly remarked *that co-operation crossed by conflict marks society wherever it is revealed.* In the co-operative culture of the Zuni tribe of

South-West America, in the collectivised economy of *Kibbutzim*, in the formal club etc. co-operation and conflict both were found side by side. It is difficult to eliminate conflict altogether from society. Though conflict threatens group solidarity, but despite it all conflict cannot be eliminated. Even if open conflict can somehow be eliminated, conflict in its partial form continues to exist.

Competition and conflict

Competition is a 'peaceful' conflict as argued by Max Weber (1968). He wrote: "A peaceful conflict is 'competition' in so far as it consists in a formally peaceful attempt to attain control over opportunities and advantages which are also desired by others." Competition describes a conflict over the control of resources or advantages desired by others where physical violence is not employed. Thus, regulated competition is a sort of peaceful conflict, which is resolved within the framework of agreed rules. A competitive process is 'regulated' competition to the extent that its ends and means are oriented to an order.

The difference between conflict and competition lies chiefly in the focus or attention and manner of achieving the goal. In competition, the primary focus is the goal, and interaction is according to culturally defined rules of behaviour and procedure. In conflict, the focus is on the competitor or opponent (not on the goal) themselves with an objective of annihilation or incapacitation of them, so that the way is cleared for achievement of the goal. This distinction can be diagrammatically represented as under:

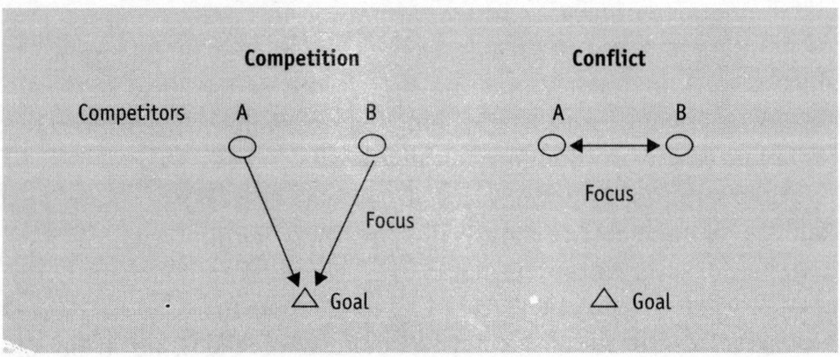

In competition the direct aim is the success of the actor in achieving the goal; indirectly, it may result in the failure of the competition but in conflict the direct result of the action of one person is to impede, prevent or destroy the act of another. For example, a running race is a competition, whereas a bull fight is a conflict. There are other distinctions also between competition and conflict, which may be presented as under:

Competition	*Conflict*
Unconscious process	Conscious process
Impersonal process	Personalised process
Continuous process	Intermittent process for a brief duration
Attention on the goal	Attention on the competitors (opponent) themselves
Non-violent	May involve violence or threat of violence
Regard for norms (rules and regulations of competition)	No regard for any norms

In the end, it may be stated that conflict and competition are sometimes difficult to distinguish, both being forms of rival behaviour. However, the difference in focus, as explained above, of the opposing parties serves as a generally useful guide. When the attention of the competitors is shifted from the goal to the competitors themselves, competition becomes conflict.

Chapter 14

Social Change

Key features

Everything changes, all the time. Everyday is a new day; every movement is a new instant in time. This is the why the Greek philosopher Heraclitus aptly commented that *a person cannot step into the same river twice*. What it means is that on the second occasion, the river will be different, since much water would have flown along it and the person has changed in subtle ways too. Thus, change is the law of nature. Human society is no exception as it is a part of the nature. There is no object in this world which is quite static and unchanging. Societies, what they are today, were not the same hundred years before. For instance, Indian society is not the same today what it was before independence. It has changed much in every field within just a space of about half a century.

No society can remain indefinitely static. Any change in the environing circumstances changes the character of the society. Even, the most stable society undergoes changes; some elements are added or replaced and others become modified or are lost. Contact with other cultures, invention or discovery brings new elements into the culture of a society.

The course of change may be gradual or rapid, peaceful or violent, continuous or spasmodic, orderly or erratic. For instance, changes in death rates when civil unrest is rampant or when diseases like cholera or bird's flu spread far and wide may be sudden, rapid, violent, spasmodic, erratic and deep-rooted. Long-term changes in the proportion of Scheduled Caste students or female students attending college, on the other hand, may be gradual, peaceful, continuous and orderly. The rate of change varies enormously from society to society and from time to time. It is generally continuous and irresistible, only its speed and direction vary. Change is always uneven and partial; only some parts change more than others. "The notion of total change is more akin to a myth than to a scientific social theory. Men dream of total changes; they almost never experience them" (Cohen, 1968).

What is Change?

Change simply means alterations in the underlying structure of an object or situation over a period of time. Change involves modification of the object or situation from its previous position. Defined by Joseph H. Fichter (1964), "change is a variation from a previous stage or mode of existence". All accounts of change involve showing what remains stable, as a baseline against which to measure alterations. Even, in the rapidly increasing world today, there are continuities with the distant past. 'Change' is a matter of inference. What we deduce is 'difference' within an object (it may be a society) from the analysis of a set of observations. And we interpret these 'differences' as change, as reference of an assumed point of departure. Thus, any change involves three things:

(1) Point of departure (baseline) of the object or situation under study.

(2) Time span.

(3) Difference observed (between, before and after situation) in respect of the point of departure.

The sense of time and perception of change are inextricably linked in human experience. One cannot think about change without including the concept of time, and without at least having sense of its passage. In other words, the sense of change really involves perceiving the difference between, before and after. Thus, without time, there is no change. Without change, however, there is no sense of time. Some evolution or devolution is essential for time to be regarded as moving and dynamic.

What is Social Change?

Any change that alters basically the established forms of social relationships, thus transforming in some measure the social structure, is social change. It is a change that reflects in all aspects of social life, i.e., family, neighbourhood, play group, work group (industry or hospital etc.), religion, economic and political spheres, leisure activities etc. Social change may be partial or total, though mostly it is partial. A change resulting from enacting a law prohibiting untouchability might be called a partial change in society. Total change hardly happens. We always find partial change in caste system, family or marriage systems. Societies do change, it is inevitable but total structure hardly ever changes. Changes are not necessarily good or bad. Sociologists do not necessarily consider social change *per se* to be good or bad.

According to Kingsley Davis (1949), "By social change is meant only such alterations that occur in social organisation, that is, structure and function of society." M.E. Jones (1962) states: "Social change is a term used to describe variations in, or modifications of, any aspect of social processes, social patterns, social interaction or social organisation." Horton and Hunt (1968) defined it as "changes in the social structure and social relationships of the society".

As sociologists we are not concerned with all types of changes that occur in society all the time. Our direct concern is with social relationships. It is the change which alone we shall regard as social change. Thus, any modification that occurs in the web of social relationships, which alters the long established pattern of social structure and social institutions, may be termed as social change. For sociologist, alterations in the properties of social structure (or social systems) through time constitute the focus of the subject of social change or social dynamics.

Nature of Social Change

Social change is not a uniquely modern phenomenon. Some kinds and degrees of change are universal in human experience. No society is static whether it is primitive or modern. The speed of change may differ from society to society. This speed may be so slow that it may appear that the society is static but it is not so. The so-called modern contemporary society is changing rapidly and constantly. These changes are neither temporally nor spatially isolated, that is, changes occur in sequential chains rather than as 'temporary' crises. Change takes place in chain-reaction sequence, i.e., change in one part of society brings changes in other parts also. But, the rate or speed and direction of change are not always uniform in all aspects of society. Some aspects change faster than the other. Material aspect of society (civilisation) changes faster than the non-material aspects (ideology, thinking pattern or social relationships). Causes and effects of change may also differ from society to society. The direction or patterns of social change may be linear, circular or fluctuating up and down. It is such a complex phenomenon that no prediction or measurement about its speed, direction and causes can be made in accurate and precise terms as we see in natural sciences. As an astronomer can predict the orderly relations among planets in a solar system, sociologist can not precisely predict about human relations. Whether a marital relation between a woman and a man will last for life long or will just end in divorce after sometime. The proportion of contemporary change (planned or unplanned—latent consequences of deliberate innovations such as information technology) is much higher than in former times. The range of material technology and social strategies is expanding rapidly and its net effect is additive or cumulative.

Contemporary change is probably everywhere and its consequences may also be everywhere. Besides, increasing the expectations of life, it has brought many social problems in its train to humanity. In the modern world social change has taken on some special qualities and magnitudes. The modes of life and social institutions characteristic of the modern world are radically different from those of even the recent past. During a period of only two or three centuries human social life has been wrenched away from the types of social order in which people lived for thousands of years. For more than any generation before us, we face an uncertain future. But though we are largely immune from the natural disasters such as flood, famine and diseases like plague in the technologically developed countries today, we have to deal now with the social forces we ourselves have created. These forces bring social change into our lives in a continuous way.

Social and Cultural Change

There is a great confusion about social and cultural change. Some early textbook writers have made distinction between social change and cultural change, while others have considered these two terms as one and the same thing. Such writers have used these two terms synonymously. For the writers like Gillin and Gillin (1954) and Dawson and Gettys (1948) there is no difference between social and cultural change. According to Dawson and Gettys, "cultural change is social change, since all culture is social in its origin, meaning and usage". Similarly, Gillin and Gillin wrote: "Social changes as variations from the accepted modes of life, whether due to alterations in geographic conditions, in cultural equipment, composition of population, or ideologies." For these writers, social change is a part of cultural change. Cultural change is more broader than social change which envelops social change also in its fold. For them, society is the product of culture. "Culture tends to give direction and momentum to social change and to set limits beyond which social change may not go" (Dawson and Gettys, 1048).

Really speaking, both types of changes have as much difference as it exists between society and culture. Sociologists use these terms (society and culture) to convey different meaning and sense. Clarifying the difference MacIver and Page (1959) writes: "Social change is a distinct thing from cultural or civilisational change.... cultural change includes change in ideology, administrative system, technology etc." Cultural change indicates changes in the accepted mode of life, habit patterns, and the life-style. These changes may include such things as the invention of the automobile, TV, changing concepts of property and morality, new forms of music, art, or dance or the trends of sex equality. For Davis (1949), "social change is only a part of a broader category of change called 'cultural change'. . . . . cultural change refers to all changes occurring in any branch of culture including art, science, technology, philosophy etc., as well as changes in the forms and rules of social organisations". In a nutshell, it may be said that social change refers specifically to alterations in social relationships among people in groups, whereas cultural change refers to change in material and non-material cultural elements both.

Social change refers to the changes in the social structure (status and role of persons), social institutions and overall social relationships that help in the making up a society. It involves modifications in the ways in which people make a living, rear a family, educate their children, govern themselves, and worship the deity. Some social changes may include changes in the age distribution, average educational level or birth rate of a population, family relationships (husband-wife, parents-child), caste and class structure, and neighbourhood relationships due to the shift of people from village to city, folkways and mores etc.

To conclude, it may be said that social change and cultural change are inextricably linked. It is very difficult to draw a line of demarcation between the two. At certain places both concepts overlap. The trend toward sex equality involves a changing set of cultural norms concerning male-female roles, and some changing relationships as well. Nearly all important changes involve both social and cultural aspects. As such, the two terms are often used interchangeably. The difference between social and cultural change is largely theoretical. Most sociologists use them interchangeably or combine the two under the head 'social change'.

Social Change and Progress

The term 'social change' is often confused with 'social progress'. In common parlance, both are used interchangeably. When society changes, it is assumed to be getting better. This notion is not correct. Change may lead to better side or it may lead to such a situation to which we call decay. The term 'change' itself is wholly neutral. It does not indicate good or bad. It only implies difference through time in the object or situation under study. It does not indicate any direction (upward or downward) in which the change takes place. On the other hand, the term 'progress' indicates the direction of change and generally it is goal directed and change in a desirable direction. 'Desirable' may be defined differently by different people and desirable for one may be undesirable for another.

'Progress' is not a scientific concept but a value judgement—change in an approved direction. "By progress, we imply not merely direction but direction towards some final goal" (MacIver and Page, 1959). It is an evaluative term while 'change' is a neutrally descriptive term. When we speak of social change, we simply mean that there is some alterations or modifications in social behaviour, social structure and social institutions. Since progress is an evaluative term, it is burdened with value judgement. This is why, most sociologists have abandoned the use of this term and prefer to use the neutrally descriptive term 'social change'. Social phenomena are relative and hence social progress has to be seen in its relative position. Thus, many of the variants of evolutionary theory which assume growth (say in levels of living, or size of social units or man's command over his environment) are progressive. Even cyclical theories may be interpreted in terms of progress. Such theories and many others which place emphasis on the evaluation of change in terms of progress or decay are now no more popular with the sociologists.

Factors and Mechanisms of Social Change

All societies are characterised both by continuity and change. Continuity is maintained by social controls, particularly through the process of socialisation and formal education, which transmits the accumulated social heritage (culture) to the new generation. In every society, there are also conditions which make for social change. Social change is a process responsive to many types of change, to changes in the man-made conditions of living, to changes in the attitudes and beliefs of men, and to changes that go back beyond human control to the biological and the physical nature of things. To understand how social change takes place, it is necessary to investigate its relation to the three great orders—the biophysical, the cultural and the technological.

Since the eighteenth century social theorists have tried to investigate the causes and sources of social change. They have distinguished many factors and mechanisms, which produce change. All their theories regarding factors of change can be grouped into two broad categories:

1. those explaining change in terms of endogamous factors or processes; and
2. those emphasising exogenous factors.

No 'single factor' theory can explain social change. In fact, social change is multifactoral. Ideas, new inventions, wars, the rise and fall of power groups, influential individuals (great men) and of course, globalisation and other factors all contribute to social change. The factors in social change are predominantly social and cultural, not biological or geographical. Some people have attributed the rise and fall of great civilisations to changes in the biological (racial) characteristics of nations. But most scientists have rejected this contention. It may be said that biological or geographical conditions play essential part in the life of human beings but these factors have lost their importance in the light of the modern advancement made in science. The development of science has made their effect less strong and deepening.

Some of the most important factors of social change are as under:

Physical environment

Certain geographic changes sometimes produce great social change. Climate, storms, social erosion, earthquakes, floods, droughts etc., definitely affect social life and induce social change. Human life is closely bound up with the geographical conditions of the earth. Human history is full of examples that flourishing civilisations fell prey to natural calamities. The distribution of population over various regions, the variations in the population densities, the agricultural production, flora and fauna, the joys and hardships—all indicate a change when a change in the physical environment occurs. What to talk of rise and fall of civilisations, even our day-to-day life—our clothes, eating material and habits, shelter design etc., all are influenced by the geographical conditions. Generally, changes in physical environment force migration of people in large numbers and this brings major changes in social life and cultural values also. Migration itself encourages change, for it brings a group into a new environment, subject to its new social contacts, and confronts it with new problems.

Though physical environment is an important factor which deeply affects social life, still it cannot be regarded as the only factor responsible for the growth of human society. This extreme approach was laid down by some geographical determinists (Buckle, Huntington, Miss Sample, J. Huxley etc.), who held that geographical setting ultimately governs the form of society (family, marriage, economy, religion, government) and explains social change. But this is not true today. Now man is in the position to affect change in his physical environment. Men adapt themselves to their environment but they have the capacity to transform their physical environment according to their needs and requirements. Bennett and Tumin (1949) aptly remarked: "It is perhaps as reasonable, if not more so to insist that man modifies his physical environment rather than the environment modifies man."

Demographic (biological) factor

Broadly speaking, demography is concerned with the size and structure of human population. The social structure of a society is closely related with the changes in the size, composition and distribution of population. The size of the population is based mainly upon three factors—birth rate, death rate and migration (immigration and emigration). The composition of population depends upon variables like age, sex, marital status, literacy etc. Changes in demographic structure, which may be caused by changes in mortality rates, will produce changes in the ratio of breadwinners to dependents. Such a change can have consequences for the structure of family, kinship, political and other institutions. The size of population affects each of us quite personally. Whether we are born into a growing or a shrinking population has a bearing on our education, the age at which we marry, our ability to get a job, the taxes we pay and many other factors.

Population analysis shows that there is a relationship between population changes and economic, social and cultural variables like poverty, illiteracy, ill-health, family structure, forms of marriage, work etc. Population growth is the most important factor in poverty. Poverty is related with health and the size of the family also. Nations with large population (e.g., China and India) are more poverty-stricken than the countries which have not much population. Sex imbalance affects the forms of marriage (monogamy or polygyny). It is seen that communities, which have more males than females, resorted to polyandry system. Polygyny was generally found in such communities where females were in more numbers than males.

The population of every society is always changing both in numbers as well as in composition. Population changes have occurred all through human history because of migration, war, pestilence, changing mores etc. In modern times, adoption of two artificial ways to population growth, viz., birth control and abortion are also affecting the number and composition of population structure. The decline of both the birth rate and the death rate bring social transformation. With changes in size go changes in composition. While the birth rate is falling, the proportion of younger people in the proportion of youths declines and that elders advances, significant social changes occurs.

Cultural factor

It is an established fact that there is an intimate connection between our beliefs and social institutions, our values and social relationships. Values, beliefs, ideas, institutions are the basic elements of a culture. Certainly, all cultural changes involve social change. Social and the cultural aspects are closely interwoven. Thus, any change in the culture (ideas, values, beliefs etc.) brings a corresponding change in the whole social order. Social institutions cannot live on life shells within which life is extinct. Social systems are directly or indirectly the creations of cultural values. The history of culture offers many evidences which confirm the role of culture. A religious doctrine, which persisted with variations throughout many centuries, has affected the course of society. For instance, a certain attitude toward sex formulated by the Church Fathers in the early Middle Ages still hold good in the Catholic sect.

"Culture gives speed and direction to social change and determines the limit beyond which social change cannot occur". (Dawson and Gettys, 1948). If we choose to travel by a ship, the direction in which we travel is not predestinated by the design of the ship but it is the culture that decides the direction and the destination both. The port we sail to remains a cultural choice. Cultural factor is not only responsive to technological change but also acts back on it so as to influence its direction and its character.

Cultural change in society has two major aspects: (a) cultural change by discovery and invention, and (b) cultural change by diffusion and borrowing. The first comes from within a society and culture, and the second from another culture outside of the society. A discovery or an invention adds to the fund of our verified knowledge which later on becomes a factor of social change. Knowledge of bacterial infection brought about many changes in the behaviour of people in the form of prevention and cure of disease. Socio-cultural changes are also brought about by people from other cultures all over the world. Diffusion is the spread of cultural traits or patterns from group to group. Borrowing refers to the adoption of a cultural trait by people whose culture did not have that cultural trait. We have borrowed many cultural traits (such as use of knife and fork in eating) from Western culture.

Culture operates not only directly as a source of change but also indirectly, by its impact on the utilitarian order. This idea was best exemplified by a German sociologist Max Weber in his study of sociology of religion. In his study 'The Protestant Ethic and the Spirit of Capitalism' (1930), he saw that there is a direct relationship between the practical ethics of a religion and the character of its economic system, but he refused to accept the position that the latter determines the former as argued by Karl Marx. (Marx believed that the nature of a society is determined by the manner in which economy is owned and organised.) Though Weber too appreciated the importance of economic factors, but he did not ascribe to them the importance that they have in Marxian theory. For Marx economic influences were paramount and determined all the rest, including religion, whereas for Weber economic phenomena themselves rest upon a broad ideological base and particularly upon religion.

In his above mentioned study, Weber asserted that the development of modern capitalism could be attributed to Protestant reformation, particularly Calvinism. Protestanism emphasised the autonomy and independence of the individual rather than dependence on the church, priesthood and ritual. Weber argued that Calvinist Protestanism motivated men to seek worldly success. It laid emphasis on rational calculation, the willingness to accumulate for long-term profit and success and the emphasis on entrepreneurial success as a virtue. Weber maintained that the ideas, ideals and attitudes towards work (work is virtue, time lost, money lost etc.,), savings and life played an important role in the economic development of Western Europe and USA Protestanism provided much of the cultural content of early capitalism—individualism, achievement motivation, hostility to inherited wealth and luxury, legitimation of entrepreneurial vocations, opposition to tradition and superstition, a commitment to organisation and calculation in personal and public life. In brief, Protestanism provided an element in the rationalisation (an important requirement of capitalism) of Western society. Weber did not simply explained capitalist development in terms of religious belief, but argued that the religious factor, if combined with others, of a political, economic and social nature, can produce a certain type of social change.

Ideational factor

Among the cultural factors affecting social change in modern times, the development of science and secularisation of thought have contributed a lot to the development of the critical and innovative character of the modern outlook. We no longer follow many customs or habits merely because they have the age-old authority of tradition. On the contrary, our ways of life have increasingly become on the basis of rationality.

Some writers have interpreted social change at ideational level and asserted that all social change is ideational. They argued that ideas could influence the course of social change. For them, ideational changes are important contributory factors to many or most types of social change. Ideas and ideologies together are powerful motivating forces in social change. For instance, after independence, the directive principles—equality, fraternity, liberty and justice laid down in our constitution—have not only revolutionised the Indian society but it has even affected greatly the relations between the members of the family. Social philosophers, who believed in the force of ideas, argued that no material or social factors can produce change unless there is also a change in ideas within society or ideas about society and nature.

In modern times, not only the way we think, but the contents of ideas have also changed. Ideals of self-betterment, freedom, equality and democratic participation are largely creations of the past two/three centuries. Such ideals have served to mobilise processes of social and political change, including reformation movements and revolutions.

Economic factor

Of economic influences, the most far-reaching is the impact of industrialisation. It has revolutionised the whole way of life, institutions, organisations and community life. In traditional production systems, levels of production were fairly static since they were geared to habitual, customary needs. Modern industrial capitalism promotes the constant revision of the technology of production, a process into which science is increasingly drawn. The impact of industrialisation (science and technology) we can easily see on Indian family system (joint family) and caste system. (For detailed analysis of the influence of economic factor, see Marx's views discussed in Economic Theory of Social Change).

Political factor

State is the most powerful organisation which regulates the social relationships. It has the power to legislate new laws, repeal old ones to bring social change in the society. Laws regarding child marriage, widow remarriage, divorce, inheritance and succession, untouchability are some of the examples which have brought many changes in the social structure of Indian society. The type of political leadership and individuals in power also influences the rate and direction of social change. In many societies the political leadership controls the economy also. Scientific-technological and non-technological change are also dependent on political development which indirectly affects social change.

There is a direct relationship between the type of political organisation and social change. In hunting and gathering societies, there were no political organisation capable of mobilising the community, as such, there were minimum changes in the societies. In all other types of society, however, the existence of distinct political agencies, such as chiefs, lords, kings and governments strongly affects the course of development of society takes. A ruler may choose to channel resources into building up his castle, for example, even when this impoverishes most of the population.

Political development in the last two or three centuries (in India especially after independence) has certainly influenced economic change as much as economic change has influenced politics. Governments now play a major role in stimulating (and sometimes retarding) rates of economic growth. In all industrial societies there is high level of state intervention in production.

Role of Great Men and Elites in Social Change

There is a controversy about the role of individuals and social forces in social change. At one extreme are those who hold that all important social and cultural changes are brought about by the men of genius like Gandhi, Lincoln, Lenin, Mandela and many others. At the other extreme are those who assert that men of genius owe their influence to the fact that they represent the dominant social forces of their times. They themselves are the product of the circumstances which helped them to induce change in the society. Here, we arrive at one of the most intriguing questions of all: Do men make history or does history make the man? This question has been debated endlessly. Ultimately, all social change occurs because of the actions of men and women. Culture is not self-creating and technology is not self-inventing. Somehow, somewhere, in a society, a man breaks, however, slightly from tradition. He does something in a different way. He has a new idea or makes a new discovery, whether he is a great man or not, he disturbs the stream of culture/society. It may affect all the aspects of society and the social change sets in motion.

It has been observed that social elites exercise great influence on society. Pareto held that the social elite of a society determines the course of social events. Similar ideas have been expressed by a prominent Indian sociologist Yogendra Singh who wrote: "Elites of a nation and their dominant personality character would determine the direction of change. All social change is essentially a process of communication which requires a symbolic medium and it is the elite and the intellectual who creates these symbols."

Elite, especially, the political elite play a very significant role in social change and modernisation of a country. Being the planners and decision-makers, they determine the nature and process of development in any society. Sometimes they also work as a barrier in the process of social change (modernisation). Their discriminatory attitude, feeling of casteism and communalism, blind conformity to tradition, indifference to development, their political rivalries, factionalism and corruption can affect the techno-social changes adversely as we see in India about the implementation of the polities of liberalisation and foreign investments.

Theories of Social Change

A variety of reasons have been offered throughout history to explain why social change occurs. The problem of explaining social change was central to nineteenth century sociology. Many earlier theories of society that claimed to be scientific were in fact theories of change. They sought to explain the present in terms of the past. Auguste Comte, the French sociologist, who coined the term 'sociology' described society as starting from the 'logical' stage, passing through a 'metaphysical' stage and finally reaching a 'positivistic' stage. Many different theories were propounded to define and explain social change. Broadly, theories of nineteenth century may be divided into theories of social evolution (Saint-Simon, Comte, Spencer, Durkheim etc.) and theories of social revolution (Marx).

Among the general theoretical explanations offered for understanding social change are geographical, biological, economic and cultural. All these we have discussed in the previous section. Theories of social change can be divided into two groups:

(1) *Theories relating to the direction of social change*: Various types of evolutionary theories, and cyclical theory.
(2) *Theories relating to causation of change*: (a) Those explaining change in terms of endogamous factors or processes; and (b) those emphasising exogamous factors such as economic, cultural or historical.

Evolutionary theory

Despite the wide variety in the possible directions change may take, various generalisations have been set forth. Because the lot of mankind generally has improved over the long term, by far the most numerous class of theories of the direction of change comprises various cumulative or evolutionary trends. Though varying in many ways, these theories share an important conclusion that the course of man's history is marked up 'upward' trend through time.

The notion of evolution came into social sciences from the theories of biological evolution. With the advent of Darwinian theory of biological evolution, society and culture began to be regarded as undergoing the same changes and demonstrating the same trends. It was conceived that society and culture were subject to the same general laws of biological and organismic growth. Some thinkers even identified evolution with progress and proceeded to project into the future more and more perfect and better-adapted social and cultural forms. Charles Darwin (1859), the British biologist, who propounded the theory of biological evolution, showed that species of organisms have evolved from simpler organisms to the more complicated organisms through the processes of variations and natural selection. After Darwin, 'evolution', in fact, became the buzz word in all intellectual inquiry and Darwin and Spencer were the key names of an era in the history of thought. Herbert Spencer (1890), who is known to be the forerunner of this evolutionary thought in sociology, took the position that sociology is "the study of evolution in its most complex form". For him, evolution is a process of differentiation and integration.

Basic assumptions and distinctive features of the evolutionary change

The basic assumption of this theory is that change is the characteristic feature of human society. The present observed condition of the society is presumed to be the result of change in the past. Another assumption is that change is inevitable or it is 'natural'. It was assumed that the change is basically the result of operation of forces within the society or culture. Underlying all theories of evolution, there exists a belief of infinite improvement in the next stage over the preceding one. All these assumptions can be summarised as under:

1. That change is inevitable and natural.
2. That change is gradual and continuous.
3. That change is sequential and in certain stages.
4. That all successive stages of change are higher over preceding stage, i.e., evolution is progressive.
5. That stages of change are non-reversible.
6. That forces of change are inherent in the object.
7. That the direction of change is from simple to complex, from homogeneity to heterogeneity, from undifferentiated to the differentiated in form and function.
8. That all societies pass through same stages of development.

All thinking of early sociologists was dominated by a conception of man and society as seen progressing up definite steps of evolution leading through every greater complexity to some final stage of perfection. The notion of evolutionary principles was extremely popular with British anthropologists and sociologists of nineteenth century, such as Morgan (1877), Tyler (1889), Spencer (1890) and Hobhouse (1906). Although evolutionary theory in sociology is attributed to Herbert Spencer, it is clear that it was taken for granted by writers as diverse as Emile Durkheim, Karl Marx, Friedrich Engels and V. Gordon Childe. The fact that it was used by both radical and conservative theorists is indicative of the profound cultural importance of evolutionism in the nineteenth century thought. The conception of evolution was applied not only to the development of societies but also to art, literature, music, philosophy, sciences, religion, economic and political life (state) and almost every other achievement of the mind of man. Both Spencer and Durkheim employed the concept of structural differentiation to indicate that as society develops more functions, it becomes structurally more complex. This perspective has been elaborated more recently by Talcott Parsons.

The general evolutionary model of society is represented by a large number of specific theories. C.H. Saint-Simon, one of the earliest founders of sociology, along with Auguste Comte, for example, put an evolutionary idea of social development, as a sequential progression of organic societies representing increasing levels of advancement. His three stages were later elaborated in Comte's evolutionary scheme. Comte linked developments in human knowledge, culture and society and delineated the following three great stages through which all societies must go—those of conquest, defense and industry. Societies passed through three stages—the primitive, the intermediary and the scientific, which corresponded to the forms of human knowledge (thought). He conceived these stages as progressing from the *theological* through the *metaphysical* to arrive ultimately at the perfection of *positive* reasoning. He argued all mankind inevitably passed through these stages as it developed, suggesting both unilinear direction and progress. Spencer also displayed a linear concept of evolutionary stages. He argued that the trend of human societies was from simple, undifferentiated wholes to complex and heterogeneous ones, where the parts of the whole become more specialised but remained integrated. William Graham Sumner (1934), who has been labelled as a 'Social Darwinist' also used the idea of evolution, as had Spencer, to block efforts at reform and social change, arguing that social evolution must follow its own course, dictated by nature. He said: "It is the greatest folly of which a man can be capable, to sit down with a slate and pencil to plan out a new social world."

The evolutionary approach to social development was also followed by radical thinkers, such as Marx and Engels, who were greatly influenced by the work of the anthropologist L.H. Morgan, who sought to prove that all societies went through fixed stages of development each succeeding the other, from *savagery* through *barbarism* to *civilisation*. Marx and Engels maintained that each stage of civilisation, such as feudalism, prepared the ground for the next. It contained within itself "the seeds of its own destruction", and would inevitably be succeeded by that stage next 'higher' on the scale of evolution. On this basis they concluded that the next stage in social evolution after the stage of capitalism could be attained only by violent revolution. All these theories are referred to as unilinear theories of social evolution.

Durkheim's view of the progressive division of labour in society and German sociologist Ferdinand Tonnies' view of *gemeinschaft* and *gesellschaft* types of society to some extent also represent the evolutionary perspective but their schemes of classifying societies are less sweeping and less explicit, and are, therefore referred to as *quasi-evolutionary theories*. For Durkheim the most important dimension of society was the degree of specialisation, as he called it, "the division of labour". He believed that there was a historical trend, or evolution, from a low to a high degree of specialisation. Durkheim distinguished two main types of society on the basis of this division of labour—the first based on *mechanical solidarity* and the second on *organic solidarity*. Durkheim believed that this second type always evolved from and succeeded the first as the degree of specialisation, the division of labour, increased. Tonnies' *gemeinschaft* type of society corresponded quite well to Durkheim's mechanical solidarity and the second *gesellschaft* to organic solidarity. Numerous other scholars put forth similar ideas. The scheme of the American anthropologist Robert Redfield, who elaborated on the contrast between 'folk' and 'urban' society, reiterates the same basic dichotomy of social types suggested by Durkheim and Tonnies. Modern theorist Talcott Parsons also viewed social change as a process of 'social evolution' from simple to more complex form of society. He regards changes in adaptation as a major driving force of social evolution. The history of human society from simple hunting and gathering band to the complex nation-state represents an increase in the 'general adaptive capacity' of society.

Types of evolutionary theory

There are three main types of evolutionary theory:

(1) *Theory of Unilinear Evolution:* It postulates the straight-line, ordered or progressive nature of social change. According to this theory, change always proceeds toward a predestined goal in a unilinear fashion. There is no place of repetition of the same stage in this theory. Followers of this pattern of change argue that society gradually moves to an even higher state of civilisation which advances in a linear fashion and in the direction of improvement. The pace of this change may be swift or slow. In brief, linear hypothesis states that all aspects of society change continually in a certain direction, never faltering, never repeating themselves.

Theories of Saint-Simon, Comte, Morgan, Marx and Engels, and many other anthropologists and sociologists come under the category of unilinear theories of social evolution because they are based on the assumption that each society does, indeed must, pass through a fixed and limited numbers of stages in a given sequence. Such theories long dominated the sociological scene.

(2) *Universal Theory of Evolution:* It is a little bit variant form of unilinear evolution which states that every society does not necessarily go through the same fixed stages of development. It argues, rather, that the culture of mankind, taken as a whole, has followed a definite line of evolution. Spencer's views can be categorised under this perspective who said that mankind had progressed from small groups to large and from simple to compound and in more general terms, from homogenous to the heterogeneous. The anthropologist Leslie White has been a leading exponent of this conception. Similar ideas were greatly elaborated by William Ogburn, who stressed the role of invention in social change. On this basis he gave birth to the famous concept of 'cultural lag' which states that change in our non-material culture, i.e., in our ideas and social arrangements, always lag behind changes in material culture, i.e., in our technology and invention.

(3) *Multilinear Theory of Evolution:* This brand of evolutionism has more recently developed and is more realistic than the unilinear and universal brand of evolutionary change. Multilinear evolution is a concept, which attempts to account for diversity. It essentially means identification of different sequential patterns for different culture or types of cultures. This theory holds that change can occur in several ways and that it does not inevitably lead in the same direction. Theorists of this persuasion recognise that human culture has evolved along a number of lines. Those who share this perspective, such as Julian Steward (1960), attempt to explain neither the straight-line evolution of each society, nor the progress of mankind as a whole, but rather concentrate on much more limited sequences of development. It does identify some social trends as merely universal: the progression from smaller to larger, simpler to more complex, rural to urban, and low technology to higher technology but it recognises that these can come about in various ways and with distinct consequences. This theory is related to what is known as *episodic approach*, which stresses the importance of accidents and unique historical, social and environmental circumstances that help to explain a particular course of social change. Later on, the views of Leslie White and Julian Steward were named as *neo-evolutionism*.

Criticism of evolutionary theory

Evolutionary scheme (gradual and continuous development in stages) of any kind fell under both theoretical and empirical attack in the last century. It was criticised heavily on many grounds but mainly for its sweeping or over-generalisation about historical sequences, uniform stages of development and evolutionary rate of change. The biological evolution, from which the main ideas of social evolution were borrowed, provided somewhat clumsy and unsatisfactory answers. Such explanations came under attack for lack of evidence. Evolutionary scales were also questioned from a somewhat different, but more empirical source. The easy assumption that societies evolved from simple to complex forms, was mainly based on a scale of predominant productive technology turned out to be unwarranted. The doctrine of 'cultural relativity' inhibited even static or cross-sectional generalisation, provided a new basis for satisfying the common features of societies. The evolutionary scheme also failed to specify the systematic characteristics of evolving societies or institutions and also the mechanisms and processes of change through which the transition from one stage to another was effected. Most of the classical evolutionary schools tended to point out general causes of change (economic, technological or spiritual etc.) or some general trend to complexity inherent in the development of societies. Very often they confused such general tendencies with the causes of change or assumed that the general tendencies explain concrete instances of change.

Because of the above shortcomings, the evolutionary theory is less popular today. A leading modern theorist Anthony Giddens (1979) has consistently attacked on evolutionism and functionalism of any brand. He rejects them as an appropriate approach to understanding society and social change. Spencer's optimistic theory is regarded with some skepticism. It is said that growth may create social problems rather than social progress. Modern sociology has tended to neglect or even to reject this theory, mainly because it was too uncritically applied by an earlier generation of sociologists. In spite of its all weaknesses, it has a very significant place in the interpretation of social change. The recent tentative revival in an evolutionary perspective is closely related to growing interest in historical and comparative studies.

Cyclical theory

Cyclical change is a variation on unilinear theory which was developed by Oswald Spengler (*Decline of the West*, 1918) and Arnold J. Toynbee (*A Study of History*, 1956). They argued that societies and civilisations change according to cycles of rise, decline and fall just as individual persons are born, mature, grow old, and die. According to German thinker Spengler, every society has a predetermined life cycle—birth, growth, maturity and decline. Society, after passing through all these stages of life cycle, returns to the original stage and thus the cycle begins again. On the basis of his analysis of Egyptian, Greek Roman and many other civilisations, he concluded that the Western civilisation is now on its decline. The world renowned British historian Toyanbee has also upheld this theory. He has studied the history of various civilisations and has found that every civilisation has its rise, development and fall such as the civilisation of Egypt. They have all come and gone, repeating a recurrent cycle of birth, growth, breakdown and decay. He propounded the theory of "challenge and response" which means that those who can cope with a changing environment survive and those who cannot die. Thus, a society can grow and survive if it can constructively respond to the challenges. Cyclical theory of change or sometimes called 'rise and fall' theory presumes that social phenomena of whatever sort recur again and again, exactly as they were before in a cyclical fashion.

A variant of cyclical process is the theory of a well-known American sociologist P.A. Sorokin (*Social and Cultural Dynamics*, 1941), which is known as 'pendular theory of social change'. He considers the course of history to be continuous, though irregular, fluctuating between two basic kinds of cultures: the 'sensate' and the 'ideational' through the 'idealistic'. According to him, culture oscillates like the pendulum of a clock between two points. The pendulum of a clock swings with the passage of time, but ultimately it comes to its original position and re-proceeds to its previous journey. Thus, it is just like a cyclical process but oscillating in character.

A sensate culture is one that appeals to the senses and sensual desires. It is hedonistic in its ethics and stresses science and empiricism. On the other hand, the ideational culture is one in which expressions of art, literature, religion and ethics do not appeal to the senses but to the mind or the spirit. It is more abstract and symbolic than the sensate culture. The pendulum of culture swings from sensate pole and leads towards the ideational pole through the middle pole called 'idealistic' culture, which is a mixed form of sensate and ideational cultures—a somewhat stable mixture of faith, reason, and senses as the source of truth. Sorokin places contemporary European and American cultures in the last stage of disintegration of sensate culture, and argues that only way out of our 'crisis' is a new synthesis of faith and sensation. There is no other possibility.

In Sorokin's analysis of cultures, we find the seeds of both the theories—cyclical and linear change. In his view, culture may proceed in a given direction for a time and thus appear to conform to a linear formula. But, eventually, as a result of forces that are inherent in the culture itself, there will be shift of direction and a new period of development will be ushered in. This new trend may be linear, perhaps it is oscillating or it may conform to some particular type of curve.

Vilfredo Pareto's (1963) theory of 'Circulation of Elites' is also essentially of this variety. According to this theory, major social change in society occurs when one elite replaces another, a process Pareto calls it 'circulation of elites'. All elites tend to become decadent in the course of time. They 'decay in quality' and lose their 'vigour'. According to Marx, history ultimately leads to and ends with the communist utopia, whereas history to Pareto is a never-ending circulation of elites. He said that societies pass through the periods of political vigour and decline which repeat themselves in a cyclical fashion.

Functionalism and social change

Functionalism, as a new approach of study of society, developed mainly as a reaction to evolutionism, in the early years of twentieth century. Critics of evolutionism advocated that there was no use to know the first appearance of any item of culture and social behaviour. They called it the "fruitless quest for origin". One of the most significant assumptions of functionalists is that society (or culture) is comprised of functionally interdependent parts or the system as a whole. These theorists believed that the society, like human body, is a balanced system of institutions, each of which serves a function in maintaining society. When events outside or inside the society disrupts the equilibrium, social institution makes adjustments to restore stability. This fundamental assumption became the main basis of the critics of functionalism to charge that if the system is in equilibrium with its various parts contributing towards order and stability, it is difficult to see how it changes. Critics (mostly conflict theorists) argued that functionists have no adequate explanation of change. They cannot account for change, in that there appears to be no mechanism which will disturb existing functional relationships. Thus, functionalists have nothing or very little to offer to the study of social change as this approach is concerned only about the maintenance of the system, i.e., how social order is maintained in the society. G. Homans, in one of his articles "Bringing men back" (1964) stressed that the dominant characteristic in the functionalist model is an inherent tendency towards stability. Society may change, but it remains stable through new forms of integration.

The functionalists responded to this charge by employing concepts such as equilibrium and differentiation. For instance, a leading proponent of functionalist approach, Talcott Parsons approaches this problem in the following way: He maintained, no system is in a perfect state of equilibrium although a certain degree of equilibrium is essential for the survival of societies. Changes occur in one part of society, there must be adjustments in other parts. If this does not occur, the society's equilibrium will be disturbed and strain will occur. The process of social change can therefore be thought of as a 'moving equilibrium'.

Parsons views social change as a process of 'social evolution' from simple to more complex form of society. Social evolution involves a process of social differentiation. The institutions and roles which form the social system become increasingly differentiated and specialised in terms of their function. As the parts of society become more and more specialised and distinct, it increases the problem of integration of parts which in turn set forth the process of social change and social equilibrium.

Some followers of functionalism argued that if it is a theory of social persistence (stability), then it must be also a theory of change. In the process of adaptation of social institutions in a society, change is a necessary condition or rather it is imminent in it. Thus, one can explain changes in the economy as adaptations to other economics or to the polity, or changes in the family structure in terms of adaptation to other institutions, and so on. In an article 'Dialectic and

Functionalism' (ASR, 1963), P. Van den Berghe states that according to functional theory change may come from three main sources:

1. Adjustment to external disturbances such as a recession in world trade.
2. Structural differentiation in response to problems within the system, e.g., electoral reforms in response to political unrest.
3. Creative innovations within the system, e.g., scientific discoveries or technological advances.

Economic (Marxian) theory of social change

Owing largely to the influence of Marx and Marxism, the economic theory of change is also known as the Marxian theory of change. Of course, economic interpretations of social change need not be always Marxist, but none of the other versions (such as Veblen who also stressed on material and economic factor) of the doctrine are quite as important as Marxism. The Marxian theory rests on this fundamental assumption that changes in the economic 'infra-structure' of society are the prime movers of social change. For Marx, society consists of two structures—'infra-structure' and 'super-structure'. The 'infra-structure' consists of the 'forces of production' and 'relations of production'. The 'super-structure' consists of those features of the social system, such as legal, ideological, political and religious institutions, which serve to maintain the 'infra-structure', and which are moulded by it. To be more clear, according to Marx, productive forces constitute 'means of production' (natural resources, land, labour, raw material, machines, tools and other instruments of production) and 'mode of production' (techniques of production, mental and moral habits of human beings) both and their level of development determines the social relation of production, i.e., *production relations*. These production relations (class relations) constitute the economic structure of society—the totality of production relations. Thus, the socio-economic structure of society is basically determined by the state of productive forces. For Marx, the contradiction between the constantly changing or developing 'productive forces' and the stable 'production relations' is the demiurage of all social development or social change.

Basic postulates

Change is the order of nature and society. It is inherent in the matter through the contradiction of forces. Marx wrote: "Matter is objective reality, existing outside and independent of the mind. The activity of the mind does not arise independent of the material. Everything mental or spiritual is the product of the material process." The world, by its very nature is material. Everything which exists comes into being on the basis of material course, arises and develops in accordance with the laws of motion of matter. Things come into being, exist and cease to exist, not each independent of all other things but each in its relationship with others. Things cannot be understood each separately and by itself but only in their relation and interconnections. The world does not consist of permanent stable things with definite properties but of unending processes of nature in which things go through a change of coming into being and passing away.

For Marx, production system is the lever of all social changes, and this system is dynamic. Need system determines production and the technological order, i.e., mode of production. *It is man's* material necessities that are at the root of his productive effort, which in its turn is the basics of all other forms of his life. Marx believed that change occurs through contradiction of forces and this is present throughout the history in some or the other form.

In the 'Preface' of his monumental work *Capital: A Critique of Political Economy* Marx's whole philosophy of social change is summarised: "At a certain stage of their development, the material forces of production in society come into conflict with the existing relations of production or . . . with the property relations within which they had been at work before. From forms of development of the forces of production these relations turn into their fetters. Then comes the period of social revolution with the change of the economic foundation, the entire immense superstructure is more or less rapidly transformed." Thus, the main thrust of the Preface is the emphasis on changes in the economic base (mode of production), and these in turn produce ideologies which induce people to fight out social struggles. As it stands, this materialist conception of history certainly encourages us to regard 'evolution' of the economic base as the key to social change—what Engels called 'the law of development of human history'.

Marx viewed the course of history (social change) in terms of the philosophy of 'dialectics'. (An idea borrowed from Hegel but Marx called it materialistic. According to Hegel, evolution proceeds according to a system of three stages—thesis, antithesis and synthesis). Accordingly, the change, development, and progress take place by way of contradiction and conflict and that the resulting change leads to a higher unity. In particular, Marx viewed the class struggle and the transition from one social system to another as a dialectical process in which the ruling class viewed as 'thesis' evoked its 'negation' ('antithesis') in the challenger class and thus to a 'synthesis' through revolutionary transformation resulting in a higher organisation of elements from the old order. In the dialectical point of view of change, sharp stages and forces are abstracted out of the continuity and gradations in the social process and then explanations are made of the process on the basis of these stages and forces in dialectical conflict.

Marx believed that the class struggle was the driving force of social change. For him it was the 'motor of history'. He states that "the history of all hitherto existing society is the history of class struggles" (*Communist Manifesto*, 1848).

Society evolves from one stage to another by means of struggle between two classes—one representing the obsolescent system of production and the other nascent (new) order. The emerging class is ultimately victorious in this struggle and establishes a new order of production; within this order, in turn, are contained the seeds of its own destruction—the dialectical process once more. Change will only occur as a victory of the exploited class.

Marx believed that the basic contradictions contained in a capitalist economic system would lead to class consciousness. Class consciousness involves a full awareness by members of the working class of the reality of exploitation, a recognition of common interests, the common identification of an opposing group with whom their interests are in conflict. This realisation will unite them for proletarian revolution. The proletariat would overthrow the bourgeoisie and seize the forces of production—the source of power. Property would be communally owned. Now, all members of society would share the same relationship to the forces of production. A classless society would result. Since the history is the history of the class struggle, history would now end.

Critique

Marx is often charged for his deterministic attitude toward society and its change. There is some controversy as to whether Marx really meant to assert that social and cultural phenomena are wholly or only determined by economic or 'material' conditions. His various statements are not fully reconciled and are susceptible of either interpretation. In his later writings he has objected to the interpretation of his ideas that makes other than economic factors purely derivative and non-causal (Selected correspondence). But he holds to the position that the economic situation is the foundation of the social order and this is the gist of Marxian theory.

Few deny that economic factor influences social conditions of life. Its influence is certainly powerful and penetrating. But, it cannot be regarded as a sole factor affecting social change. There are other causes also which are as important as the economic factor. To say that the super-structure of society is determined by its infra-structure, i.e., production system (economic system) of a society is going to far. The link between the social change and the economic process is far less direct and simple and sufficient than the Marxian psychology admits. Moreover, Marx oversimplified the class structure of society and its dynamics of social change in the form of class struggle. Dorthy S. Thomas (1925) commented that "it is not difficult to establish correlation between social changes and economic changes, though it is harder to interpret them". Thus, economic determinism does not solve the major problem of social causation.

Conflict theory

Social theorists in the nineteenth and early twentieth centuries were concerned with conflict in society. But, the label of conflict theorists is generally applied to those sociologists who opposed the dominance of structural-functionalism. These theorists contend that in functionalism there is no place of change and as such it cannot explain change. They have neglected conflict in favour of a unitary concept of society which emphasises social integration. By contrast to functionalist approach, conflict theorists contend that institutions and practices continue because powerful groups have the ability to maintain the status quo. Change has a crucial significance, since it is needed to correct social injustices and inequalities. Conflict theorists do not believe that societies smoothly evolve to higher level. Instead, they believe that conflicting groups struggle to ensure progress (Coser, 1956). Conflict theorists assert that conflict is a necessary condition for change. It must be the cause of change. There is no society, changing or unchanging, which does not have conflict of some kind or another. Thus, conflict is associated with all types of social change in some way or other.

The modern conflict theory is heavily influenced by the ideas of Karl Marx. It may be regarded as the offshoot of his economic theory of social change which states that economic change only occurs and produces other change through the mechanism of intensified conflict between social groups and between different parts of the social system. Conflict would ultimately transform society. While Marx emphasised economic conflict, Max Weber based his arguments on conflict about power. Ralf Dahrendorf (1959), although critical of Marxist notions of class, tried to reconcile the contrast between the functionalist and conflict approaches of society. He contends that these approaches are ultimately compatible despite their many areas of disagreement. He disagreed with Marx not only on the notions of class but on many other points also. Marx viewed social change as a resolution of conflict over scarce economic resources, whereas Dahrendorf viewed social change as a resolution of conflict over power. Marx believed a grand conflict would occur between those who had economic resources and those who did not, whereas Dahrendorf believed that there is constant simultaneous conflict among many segments of society.

Commenting on this theory, Percy S. Cohen (*Modern Social Theory*, 1968) writes: "This theory is plausible, but it is not necessarily true. The contention that group conflict is a sufficient condition for social change is obviously false. . . . . It is arguable that structured conflict, when it involves a fairly equal balance of forces, actually *obstructs* change which might otherwise occur. For example, in societies where there are deep divisions between regional, ethnic or racial groups, there may be little possibility of promoting economic development or welfare policies; such 'ameliorative' changes require some degree of consensus. *The simple point is that conflict may lead to impasse not to change.* . . . . . . It should be emphasised that social conflict is often as much the product of social change as the cause. And it is commonly a great obstacle to certain types of change."

Technological theory

When the average person speaks of the changes brought about by 'science', he is generally thinking of 'technology' and the manifold wonders wrought thereby. The 'technology' refers to the application of knowledge to the making of tools and the utilisation of natural resources (Schaefer and Lamm, 1992). It involves the creation of material instruments (such as machines) used in human interaction with nature. It is not synonymous with machinery as it is understood in common parlance. Machines are the result of the knowledge gained by science but they themselves are not technology.

Social change takes place due to the working of many factors. Technology is not only one of them but an important factor of social change. When it is said that almost whole of human civilisation is the product of technological development, it only means that any change in technology would initiate a corresponding change in the arrangement of social relationships. It is believed that Marx has attached great importance to technology in his scheme of mode of production, which forms the main basis for the change in society. For Marx, the stage of technological development determines the mode of production and the relationships and the institutions that constitute the economic system. This set of relationships is in turn the chief determinant of the whole social order.

Technological development creates new conditions of life which forces new conditions in adaptation. W.F. Ogburn, in his article, 'How Technology Changes Society' (1947), writes: "Technology changes by changing our environment to which we, in turn, adapt. This change is usually in the material environment, and the adjustment we make to the changes often modifies customs and social institutions." Anthropologist Leslie White (*Science and Culture*, 1949) held that "technology, particularly the amount of energy harnessed and the way in which it is used, determines the forms and content of culture and society". Technology affects directly and indirectly both. Certain social consequences are the direct result of mechanisation, such as new organisation of labour, destruction of domestic system of production, the expansion of the range of social contacts, the specialisation of function etc. Its indirect consequences are the increase of unemployment, the heightening of competition etc. Conflict between the states, as they strive for dominance, security or better prospects are the result of competition.

The invention of wheel, compass, gunpowder, steam engine, printing press, telephone (now mobile phone), radio, TV, internet, aeroplane, motor car and so many other inventions in medical and other fields have revolutionised the human life. Advances in agricultural technology, ranging from the iron-tipped plow to the tractor technology and the three-crop rotation system made possible the creation of a surplus. One of the earliest books on social change written by W.F. Ogburn (1922) has analysed such changes in detail. He has narrated about 150 such changes (both immediate and distant social effects) in social life brought about by the invention of radio alone. Ogburn gives many illustrations of this kind. He suggests, for example, that the invention of the self-starter on automobiles had something to do with the emancipation of women. The self-starter gave them freedom of a kind. Similarly, many labour saving devices in the home have also contributed to the emancipation of women. In this connection, Ogburn and Nimkoff (1958) argue: "An important invention need not be limited to only a single social effect. Sometimes it exerts many influences which spread out in different directions like the spokes of a wheel." Technological developments have affected a lot of changes in attitudes, beliefs and even in traditions. These influence almost all aspects of our life and culture. These include social customs and practical techniques for converting raw material to finished products. The production and use of food, shelter, clothing and commodities, physical structures, and fabrics all are also aspects of society's technology. The most important aspect of technology in that a man thinks rationally and objectively about things and events. Man has become more pragmatic in his outlook. He is more disciplined (time-oriented) in his working habits. New forms of transportation and communication, which have contributed to significant changes in social life, are all due to the change in technology. There is a greater mobility of population today than that was in the nineteenth or twentieth century because of the modern rapid means of transport. The life of the modern man is always on wheels. It is an important factor in the determination of spatial aspect of social relationships. Changes in communication devices (e-mail, internet, mobile phones etc.) have also influenced all aspects of social life (work, leisure, family, friendship, sports etc.) enormously. The basic function of all communication and transportation devices is the conquest of time and space. Shrinking space and time through the speed and low cost of electronic communication and air travel has developed a new phenomenon called 'globalisation'.

"Any technological change which is great enough will produce some other social change as a consequence" (Cohen, 1968). This is *summum bonum* (gist) of this theory. For example, new techniques of manufacture are found to affect social relations in the relevant industry. A single invention of geared wheel has produced thousands of inventions which in turn affected social relations enormously. The automobile has brought number of social changes which have altered individual lifestyles. Computers and the Internet are the latest of a long line of developments to prompt utopian and anti-utopian visions of a world transformed by technology. Computers have affected almost all aspects of our life from reservations at the railway ticket window or registration for hospitals or colleges to the maintenance of accounts in banks and large business corporations. The popularity of science fiction (Harry Potter) and the films like Jurrasic Park are other indicators of the mythical and abundant power which technology can have in the modern world. Modern technology has also revolutionised the concept and quality of the systems of production, communication, social organisation and various processes of acculturation and symbolisation in societies. Technology helps in realising of our goals with less effort, less cost and with greater efficiency. Technology creates desire for novelty and innovation. Novelty is sought everywhere and transient interests give a corresponding character to social relationships.

Technology has advanced in leaps and bounds over the last 25 years and the single invention that has had to greatest impact on our lives is the cell phone. It is now not only used as a means of communication but it has enabled us to operate home appliances and entertainment devices, monitor our home's safety, customise our internal home environment.

In the light of these technical advances the anthropologist Peter Worsly (1984) was actuated to comment, "until our day, human society has never existed", meaning that it is only in quite recent times that we can speak of forms of social association which span the earth. The world has become in important respects a single social system as a growing ties of interdependence which now affect virtually everyone. The idea of 'global village' developed by Marshall McLuban (1960) reflects that the world is becoming more integrated in economic, political and cultural terms.

Critique

The goals and consequences of technology and the production of material goods are being seriously questioned today. Does a high level of technology increase happiness and improve our family life? Do complex technologies bring us clean air, pure water and help us conserve natural resources? Do we not think that the rapidly changing technology is the cause of our all types of environmental degradation, pollution, health and social problems? People do not hesitate to say that modern technology (science) is responsible for moral degradation of our society. Medical advances that prolong life, for example, may surpass our ability for elderly or an honourable life for them. Technical advances have often been portrayed as routes to heaven or hell—a source of deliverance of damnation.

Every new factor, whether it be a creed or a machine, disturbs an old adjustment. The disturbance created by mechanism was so great that it seemed the enemy of culture. The wealth-bringing technology brought also ugliness, shoddiness, and haste standardisation. It brought new hazards, new diseases and fatigue. That was not the fault of the technology (machines). It was due to the ruthlessness and greed of those who controlled these great inventions. But human values started reasserting themselves against all types of exploitation (economic, ecological or social).

Though technology is an important factor of change, it does not mean that technological change alone can produce social changes of all types. Nor technological change always a necessary condition for other social changes. It may be that certain technological conditions are necessary before other factors can produce certain changes, but these need not precipitate social change. For instance, it required no change in technology to bring about a democratic society in India. Moreover, culture in turn seeks to direct technology to its own ends. Man may be master as well as the slave of the machine. Man is a critic as well as a creature of circumstances.

Cultural Lag and Social Change

The concept of 'cultural lag' was introduced by W.F. Ogburn in his book *Social Change* (1922). He distinguished between 'material' and 'non-material' culture and stressed that material culture changes rapidly than non-material culture. There is a tendency for non-material aspects of culture to persist longer than material aspects because of the strength and intensity of resistence to changes. When changes occur in 'material' culture, i.e., in our technology and invention, these in turn stimulate changes in the 'non-material' culture, i.e., in our ideas, values, norms, customs, beliefs, laws and social arrangements. In this process changes in our non-material culture always lag behind the changes in material culture. Moreover, the different parts of the culture do not change at the same rate and speed. The changes in technology and material culture come more rapidly than changes in non-material culture. The time interval between the appearance of a new trait (material culture) and the completion of the adaptation it forces (non-material culture) is known as 'cultural lag'. This concept of cultural lag indicates that various elements of culture change at different rates and shows how the technological aspects of culture affect and are affected by the non-material aspect of culture. He gave many illustrations to clarify his concept of cultural lag. We find a discrepancy between the number of policemen and the growth of population. With the growing cities The police force has not increased fast enough to keep pace with the growing population. People have changed their methods of cultivating their land, they are using new agricultural techniques and tools but the property rights of the land have not yet changed. People have changed their habitations, built gorgeous buildings fitted with all modern appliances of conveniences, but they have not yet changed their age-old habits accordingly. For instance, they have started using chinaware but for their washing, they are still using sand or ashes of the hearth. Similarly, a modern wife, while sitting on the back seat of her husband's motor-cycle, can be seen in any city, putting veil on her face.

Technology and material culture are cumulative, that is, when a more efficient method or tool is found, the old one is replaced. However, the new method or tool must be consistent with the values and beliefs of the culture in which it is used. For controlling population, for example, many effective contraceptive devices such as condoms, IUDs, diaphragms, foams, jellies and birth control pills have been developed, but these have not been adopted in some cultures because they are inconsistent with their societal or religious values and beliefs. These contraceptive devices were regarded as inappropriate and immoral in some communities. In rapidly changing societies, such situation (cultural lag) is inevitable. Rapidly changing societies retain old aspects of culture amid new technological and material developments.

This theory of cultural lag has been criticised on many grounds. Ogburn (1922) has been charged for giving the major role to material culture as the initiator of change. He has also been criticised for formulating a theory of change that in most essential respects resembles the Marxian generalisation which views the modes of production as deterministic of social forms. Sorokin (1941) has called Ogburn's theory as mild form of an economic interpretation of history. The main critics MacIver and Page (1956) put forth following arguments in against of cultural lag theory:

Firstly, the distinction between material and non-material culture, as made by Ogburn, is not clear and workable one. What lags behind what? Where no such standard is available, we cannot rightly speak of a lag. Secondly, material culture is nothing but civilisation and non-material is rightly called the culture proper. Thirdly, the term 'lag' is not properly applicable to relations between technological factors and the cultural pattern or between the various components of cultural pattern itself. Fourthly, the rate of change in the sphere of technology is always not uniform. Some technological articles advance too fast while the others remain behind. This situation is termed by MacIver and Page (1956) as 'technological lag'. Fifthly, for various types of disequilibrium or maladjustment different terms should have been used instead of lumping together indiscriminately in a single category. MacIver and Page (1956) have suggested four such terms: (1) technological lag; (2) technological restraint; (3) culture clash, and (4) cultural ambivalence.

Resistance to Social Change

Not all changes or innovations are accepted by the society. The attitudes and values of a group determine what kind of changes a group is likely to accept. A process of selective acceptance operates. Some innovations are accepted instantly and some are rejected entirely. We have accepted many material traits of Britishers such as dress pattern, china clay potteries etc., but not accepted the marriage system (courtship, premarital sex, frequent divorces etc.) because these would conflict with our values. An innovation is most quickly accepted when its usefulness can be easily demonstrated that it is cheap and helpful. Compatible innovations are more readily accepted than those which clash with important features of the existing culture. Innovations, which are substitutive and not additive, are less readily accepted.

A society's attitude and values greatly encourage or retard change. A people who revere the past, worship their ancestors, honour and obey their elders, and are preoccupied with traditions and rituals will change slowly and unwillingly. A changing society has a different attitude toward change, such attitudes powerfully stimulate the proposal and acceptance of changes. Attitudes and values also affect both the amount and direction of social change.

A society's rate and direction of changes are greatly affected by the needs its members perceive. The concept of cultural lag implies that changes in part of the culture create a need for adaptive changes in related parts of culture. "Necessity is the mother of invention", however, it is not guarantee that needed invention or discovery will be made. The structure of a society affects its rate of change in subtle ways. A highly conformist, authoritarian society or a highly integrated culture is less prone to change than the individualistic, permissive society or the less highly integrated culture. The structure of Indian society, which is traditional, rigid and tightly structured, does not permit changes easily. Such a system is strongly resistant to change.

The resistence to change by people in a culture is called *cultural inertia* and this resistence can be a liability of patterns of behaviour that have outlived their utility to persist. The attitude that retaining them is easier than discarding them. To change is a painful effort and to discard old ways and old values for new is not easy. Hence, all over the world, there is resistence to changes to new or improved practices. Resistence may be mild or may take the form of violent refusal depending on the nature and type of change. This inertia can constitute a major obstacle to improvement as we have observed in the matters of family planning and new methods of agriculture during early period of independence in India.

Since isolation retards change and cross-cultural contacts promote change, physically or socially isolated groups show fewer changes. Societies in closest contact with other societies are likely to change most rapidly. Conversely, isolated areas are centres of stability, conservatism and resistance to change.

Change is always costly. Not only does change disrupt the existing culture and destroying cherished sentiments and values, but it also involves some specific costs. Social and personal disorganisation are costs of social change. Discoveries and inventions, as well diffused new traits and complexes, are often set off a chain reaction of change disrupting to many aspects of the culture. The different parts of the culture, interrelated and interdependent though they are, do not change at the same rate of speed. This forces what is called the phenomenon of 'cultural lag'. All rapidly changing societies have many cultural lags. Changing societies are in constant process of disorganisation and reorganisation. Technical difficulties of fitting a change into the existing culture often cause great economic cost and personal inconvenience. Vested interests normally oppose change.

Planned Social Change

We may distinguish two types of social change. One is normal, routine and unconscious. It is inevitable and simply happens. It does not necessarily require concerted efforts on the part of the group. Change brought about by natural events like earthquakes, floods or famines etc., comes under this category. They forces migration of people, wars and disturb proportion of sexes. The other is deliberate or consciously planned social change. It requires concerted efforts to bring out change.

Planned change is to achieve some set of collective goals. Through planning, social changes can be controlled and its course can be ordered in the desired direction. This is possible to some degree through social planning or *social engineering* (the idea that governments can shape and manage key features of society, is much the same way as the economy is managed). Social planning is defined as "a conscious interactional process combining investigation, discussion, agreement and action in order to achieve those conditions, relationships, and values that are regarded as desirable" (Himes, 1958). Planning is a rational activity. It presupposes that an endeavour is made to bring about certain changes which are considered to be more efficient and more worthwhile. Planning for social change involves deliberate thinking, deliberate action and evaluation to determine the extent to which the planned programmes have been implemented in the society.

Social planning is increasingly being attempted in order to speed and simply the process and reduce the costs and wastes of social change. In the twentieth century there have been several attempts in many countries of the world (USSR, Germany, Japan etc.) to bring about social change by persistent and planned efforts. Since independence in 1947, the Indian government is also trying to bring about social changes through planned efforts. To this end, Five Year Plans and Community Development Projects and many other schemes and legislative changes have been formulated and launched.

Social Change and Social Problems

Social problem is a generic term applied to the range of conditions and aberrant behaviours which are held to be manifestations of social disorganisation. It is a condition which many people of a society consider undesirable and want to correct by changing through some means of social engineering or social planning. Many social problems result from the processes of social change. As such, a changing society inevitably develops problems. In perfectly integrated society, it is said, there would be no social problem because in such society all institutions and behaviour would be neatly harmonised and defined as acceptable by the values of society. Changing societies are in a constant process of disorganisation and reorganisation. Social problems are part of the price of social change. Periods of rapid change may bring about the disequilibrium and disorganisation of formal functioning of society. Social change considered generally desirable in society may precipitate and increase social problems. Equal rights and privileges given to women in developing countries, including India, may have been generally welcomed as a desirable change, for women can enjoy freedom and enter into economic, political and other spheres of social life. However, such action, particularly in urban industrial areas, especially in metropolitan cities, also has given rise to problems of the effective performance of women's role in the home as wife and mother, and sub-standard family life with inadequate nurture and care of children. These and many other circumstances associated with social change give rise to varied social problems. Thus, both are closely interwoven in their relationship.

Social and cultural change is related to social problems in two principal ways:

(1) change may be brought in by the existence of social problem; and

(2) social problem may be created by change.

These are merely two aspects of a dynamic and self-contained process, i.e., change brings in problems and problems bring change. Change is followed by problems and so on.

Founder sociologist, Durkheim, conceived society as primarily a *moral order* constituted by the institutionalised norms and values. But this moral order is disturbed by the *anomic* conditions—anomic division of labour, rapid social change, decline of moral authority (e.g., religion), increased complexity in social roles and rules, fragmentation of work, unfettered market system, unregulated competition and unequal opportunity for natural talents. These conditions lead to many types of social problems, which include many forms of deviant behaviour, such as suicide, crime, juvenile delinquency, prostitution, drug addition, unemployment, and the like. To remove or elevate the anomic conditions, Durkheim suggested some scientific remedies such as moral unity to be based on a sense of mutual social interdependence, a new non-religious civic moral order to be promoted through the state, laws and education, regulation of markets and working conditions, equality of opportunity and fair inequality or reward etc. In brief, Durkheim wished to apply sociological knowledge to social intervention by the state in order to recreate social harmony.

Social Change, Modernity and Development

Most modern sociologists, as said earlier, though have abandoned the use of the term 'progress' because of its evaluative overtones.

However, they prefer to use terms as development, undevelopment and underdevelopment to reflect their vision of social change and possible better society. Development implies some positive progress whereas undevelopment implies decline or stagnation (O'Donnell, 1997). On the other hand, the term 'underdevelopment' is used to describe the economic and social conditions of those Third World countries whose markets, labour and resources have been exploited by the development of western capitalism (Frank, 1971). Some scholars of Marxist leanings suggest that underdevelopment and poverty in these countries have been integral to the story of western development. The term 'underdevelopment' does not merely mean lack of development. At many times, the two terms—development and change are used interchangeably, but this is not correct. Development implies change, change does not imply development.

What is viewed as development varies somewhat from society to society. The goals of socialist societies are not the same as those of capitalist ones. The term 'development' tends to reflect a liberal-capitalist view that world 'progress' is likely, whereas that of undevelopment and underdevelopment have clearly negative overtones. There are some aspects of development on which in practice there is near universal agreement. These are mainly economic, educational and technological. Nearly all societies seek to improve their technology, increase their wealth and develop the skills (education) of their people. How this should be done and who should most benefit from development are, of course, matters of great disagreement. There is even less agreement about what constitutes a developed cultural life than about political development. This applies both to the level of popular culture, i.e., the quality of everyday life, and to 'high' culture—classical music, literature and rest of the arts.

The context of development/underdevelopment has been changed by a new recently developed phenomenon of 'globalisation' which is rooted in modernity—a term used to describe the particular attributes of modern societies. These attributes are industrial capitalism, rationalisation of all aspects of life, commodification, scientific thinking, and a speeding up of the pace of life, surveillance and so on. Modernity is associated with the onset of industrialisation, the growth of capitalism and the appearance of an increasing complex and differentiated culture. The dynamics of the modernity have made the world grow small, increasingly interlinked time and space, and so our sense of the local and the distant, the traditional and the strange have taken on new meaning in a context notable for its electronic and satellite communication, transnational corporations and international, even global, political authorities. The key term for this is the globalisation of modernity. Anthony Giddens (1990) has discussed the dynamics of modernity that produce a 'globalised modernity.' From his point of view, the globalisation of social life is unique to modernity and an expression of it. In his analysis, Giddens has suggested the following three unique processes that have made possible diffusion of modernity on a global scale:

(1) The separation of time and space.
(2) The disembedding of social systems.
(3) The reflexive ordering of social relations.

Each of these processes involves, in different ways, a going beyond of the here-and-now, beyond the physical and temporal constraints of immediate social relations. Globalisation has triggered forces of change, making people rethink about social relations encompassed between the institutions of caste, marriage, family and religion. It focuses on the emerging social realities especially those relating to changed gender equations, modified family ties etc.

Current Social Changes: Looking into the Future

We live in a time of turbulence. A shifting, unstable sense of transformation hangs in the air in all contemporary advanced societies (Indian society has not yet attained that advanced stage). Change that is so fast and so far-reaching must, it seems, take us a new phase, a new form of society. The founding sociologists (Durkheim, Weber and Marx) all saw profounding transformations in the shift to modernity but they differed greatly in their views on the potentials and the pitfalls of this new society.

What are the main trends of development likely to affect our lives as the twenty-first century proceeds? What sort of society we are moving towards? Some observers have suggested that what is occurring today is a transition to a new society no longer primarily based on industrialism—a characteristic feature of the society of 18th and 19th centuries based on the ethics of modernity. Social structures based on modernity have increasingly come into question. We are entering, they claim, a new phase of development to which a variety of terms have been labelled to describe this new social order such as 'post-industrial society'—a term first employed by Daniel Bell (1973) in the United States and Alain Touraine (1974) in France. For this new order, others have used terms like information society, service society, knowledge society, and post-modern society. All these terms, though having slightly different meanings and connotations, employed to analyse current social changes.

According to Bell, we entered into a post-industrial society—a new social order different from the old industrial order, based on knowledge and information. This new order, Bell argues, is distinguished by a growth of service occupation at the expense of jobs that produce material goods. It is a society where the more important jobs are those requiring technical and professional qualifications. The contemporary dynamics of globalisation have in some ways confirmed Bell's broad proposition of structural changes in the labour market.

Globalisation and Social Change

The profound social changes, including the economic and the political, that we are witnessing today, are to a great extent the result of the forces of globalisation. Globalisation is a term which refers to the process whereby political, social, economic and cultural relations increasingly take on a global scale. It operates beyond or above the national level and has profound consequences for individual's local experiences and everyday lives. Two most glaring examples are the media and the transfer of money.

Defining globalisation Malcom Waters (1993) writes: "A process in which the constraints of geography on social and cultural arrangements recede and in which people become increasingly aware that they are receding." in other words, physical distance and obstacle have become less important in communication and exchange in social, economic, political and cultural matters. Echoing more or less the same ideas, Anthony Giddens (1990) has used the phrase 'time-space distanciation'. In David Harvey's phrase it is time and space are compressed. Thus, a message that 200 years ago took several weeks and considerable physical effort to deliver, now only takes few seconds. Some scholars have argued that globalisation is primarily a cultural phenomenon and only secondarily an economic and political one. Here it is worth quoting the ideas expressed about globalisation in *Concise Oxford Dictionary of Sociology* (1994):

> Globalisation theory examines the emergence of a global system. It suggests that global culture is brought about a variety of social and cultural developments; the existence of a world satellite information system, the emergence of global patterns of consumption and consumerism; the cultivation of cosmopolitan lifestyles; the emergence of global sport such as the Olympics Games, world football competitions, and international tennis matches; the spread of tourism; the decline of the sovereignty of the nation-state; the growth of a global military system; recognition of a world-wide ecological crises; the development of world-wide health problems such as AIDS; the emergence of world political systems such as the League of Nations and the United Nations; the creation of global political movements such as Marxism; extension of the concept of human rights; and the complex interchange between world religions. More importantly, globalism involves a new consciousness of the world as a single place. Globalisation has been described, therefore, as "the concrete structuration of the world as a whole".

The above ideas reflect the broad sweep of theories of cultural globalisation which embrace political and social as well as cultural developments.

Forms of Globalisation

There are three main forms of globalisation, viz., economic, political and cultural. We will delimit our discussion only to cultural globalisation which has far-reaching effects on our social and cultural life and day-to-day activities.

Is there a common culture (global culture) developing across the globe? This is a huge and very complicated question. In general usage, the term 'culture' refers to a whole way of life, including patterns of consumption of media, dress style and leisure activities etc. Mike Featherstone in his book *Consumer Culture and Postmodernism* (1991) suggests a number of ways in which the globalisation of culture is occurring. One only has to see the global familiarity of Mickey Mouse, Levi jeans, Coca Cola, McDonald's hamburger, Kentucky chickens, or Madonna's latest hit single video to realise the globalisation of culture. When we buy a Coke in India, Pakistan, Singapore, Britain or Iran, we are all sharing in common transnational form of consumption. One of the first 'Western' stores in post-socialist states is the boutique selling Nike and Reebok sport/fashion shoes. A whole range of 'problems' such as Tsunami, earthquake, famine, bird's flu, environmental deterioration, global warming, pollution of all kinds and events like Rugby World Cup or publication of Prophet's cartoons routinely have a global dimension. Not only this, a kind of global humanism is also developing. All these examples suggest that the world has increasingly become a one place. Both the media and increased personal geographical mobility feed this perception.

It is not possible to understand the cultural globalisation without linking it to media. Exposure to and consumption of media products has become an integral part of the everyday lives of most members of contemporary society. The media occupies a considerable proportion of our leisure time, providing us to a considerable extent the picture of the wider world. Television, for example, represents the major and most pervasive mass medium of today. It is the principal leisure activity of most urban adults and children—the organiser of their entertainment and social life. By carrying advertisements and other images of 'desirable' consumer styles, the media helps to make global market.

Vast amounts of research have been done to try to assess the effects of media, especially television. Most such studies have concerned children given the sheer volume of their viewing and the possible implications for socialisation. Young people are socialised to pursue activities apart from the family. Because youngsters have learned to be active and competitive, they prefer movies that show action and competition, and movies in turn reinforce the aspect of socialisation. Violent horror films have been particularly popular over the last few years. Studies indicate the children can learn new techniques for being violent from watching a movie. Sociological studies done in America revealed that a substantial proportion of the population does not read newspapers. For them TV news has become a key source of information about what goes on in the world, especially about people, places and events. At school, work, university, in the home or the friends circle last night's 'tele news' makes for lively and easy conversation.

Given these high levels of exposure, the media (especially TV) constitute important agencies for socialisation. They represent an institutionalised channel for the distribution of social knowledge and hence a potentially powerful instrument of social change and social control sustaining or challenging the status quo. The globalised media allow us to travel virtually without moving from our chair to receive our home programmes on satellite TV or the internet. Although media products are no doubt entertaining, they also help construct and reproduce a broad range of social norms and values. As a result, traditional customs and patterns of family and overall lifestyle are undergoing a lot of change.

All above discussions apparently suggest that slowly but steadily we are heading towards a homogeneous, uniform 'global culture'. But, this is not so, we have failed to see the uneven and unequal impact of the globalised modernity on different societies. Global dynamics have at the same time created a countervailing localisation of culture. We are witnessing a dramatic global change, which only means that we have entered a period of transition to a new global context but whose character remains uncertain. Anthony Giddens has warned that the dynamics of globalisation are so complicated that it is very difficult to predict about the destination of the globe where it will reach.

Chapter 15

Social Control and Deviance

Key features

The study of social control begins with the study of the social order within which people interact. Order is a state in which social life—actions and interactions—can be conducted without major disruption. Social order means a system of people, relationships and customs operating smoothly to accomplish the work of a society. It depends upon the expectations of others and conformity to social norms or rules. A society must have some social order if it is to function smoothly and properly. Societies cannot function if massive members of people defied standards of appropriate conduct. The orderliness of a society rests upon a network of roles according to which each person accepts certain duties toward others and claims certain rights from others. An orderly society can operate only as long as most people will generally be observing most norms and fulfil most of their duties toward others.

What is Social Control?

In very simple terms, "the system or the organisation by which the social relations or behaviour is controlled is called social control". The word 'control' may refer to two types of acts:

(1) To an act of controlling; or

(2) To the process, technique, device by means of which changes in the behaviour is affected.

As applied to human relationships, the term may carry either of these meanings. Sociologists are generally interested in social controls (second meaning of control) rather than in the act of controlling. Not all control in human society is social; it is physical in so far as the relation between persons is purely external. It is social to the extent that it involves communication. The control becomes social only when it brings modifications in behaviour resulting from act of communications and not from arbitrary applications of physical force.

Definitions

According to Roucek (*Social Control*, 1947), "social control is a collective term for those processes, planned or unplanned, by which individuals are taught, persuaded, or compelled to conform to the usages, and life-values of groups".

MacIver (1946) observes, "social control is the way in which the entire social order coheres and maintains itself how it operates as a whole, as a changing equilibrium".

Parsons (1951) defined it as "the process by which, through the imposition of sanctions, deviant behaviour is counter acted and social stability is maintained".

Horton and Hunt (1964) state: "Sociologists use the term social control to describe all the means and processes whereby a group or a society secures its members' conformity to its expectations."

In the words of Peter L. Berger (*Invitation to Sociology*, 1963), "social control refers to the various means used by a society to bring its recalcitrant members back into line".

According to Roberts (1991), "the term social control refers to the'techniques and strategies for regulating human behaviour in society".

In *Oxford Dictionary of Sociology* (1994), "social control refers to the social processes by which the behaviour of individuals or groups is regulated".

For Bottomore (1962), "the term social control refers to the social regulation of human behaviour". In the end, we conclude this section with the definition of Gillin and Gillin (1948), which is quite exhaustive and easy to understand: "Social control is the system of measures, suggestions, persuation, restraint and the coercion by whatever means including physical force—by which a society brings into conformity to the approved pattern of behaviour of a sub-group or by which a group moulds into conformity its members." All above definitions of social control emphasise on three things: (1) it is a system of devices or processes or means and techniques through which (2) society brings its recalcitrant or deviant members back into the line, and (3) forces them to conform to the accepted standard behaviour.

Why Social Control?

What there is the need of social control? Many explanations have been given for this question. Generally, it is said that to satisfy peacefully the basic drives of humans—sex, shelter (security) and hunger—some kind of regulation is needed. This regulation put check on the individual desires of persons so that they cannot fulfil them they way they wish (as we see in animals). Human beings have to adhere to certain norms (folkways, mores, rules and regulations of the group) to satisfy their wants (needs and desires) without any clash. Thus, for the mutual welfare and well-being, some kind of control (inner as well as external, i.e., social control) is an almost necessity. Through social control, personal, cultural and social malarrangements are properly balanced and the struggle among the persons to satisfy their unlimited wants is eliminated or reduced to a manageable extent. According to Gillin and Gillin (1948) the main function of social control is to realise certain purposes of the group among which is the social equilibrium necessary for the continued existence of society.

Functionalists contend that people must respect social norms if any group or society is to survive. They stress that order is necessary for effective social life. In their view, societies literally could not function if massive numbers of people defied standards of appropriate conduct. To maintain unity, stability, continuity and the balance in the group or the society, some kind of social control is needed. By contrast, conflict theorists are concerned that the successful functioning of a society will consistently benefit the powerful and work to disadvantage of other groups. Marxists argue that not only does the law protect the powerful and perpetuate inequality but people have unequal access to the law.

Objectives

Kimball Young (1942) stated that the social control aims to "bring about conformity, solidarity, and continuity of a particular group or society". It is essential for the continued existence of the society. On the basis of above analysis, the main objectives of social control may be stated as under:

1. To regulate the individual behaviour and avoid clash in the society.
2. To maintain and re-establish the social order.
3. To establish unity and solidarity among the members.
4. To ensure the continuity of the group or the society.

5. To secure member's conformity to the group expectations.
6. To bring society's recalcitrant and deviant members back into the line.
7. To check cultural degeneration and social disintegration.

Functions

The major functions of social control are:

1. It forces persons to get obeyed social decisions.
2. It maintains the equilibrium and stability in the society.
3. It helps in choosing behaviour and fulfilling one's desire for social status.
4. It helps in proper socialisation of the individual.
5. It helps in performing social roles.
6. It helps in mitigating and tensions and conflict among members.
7. It breeds conformity in society.

Social control operates at three levels:

(1) Group over group.

(2) Group over its members.

(3) Individuals over their fellow members.

Thus, social control takes place when a person is induced or forced to act according to the wishes of others, whether or not in accordance with his own individual interests. It operates on the basis of the individual's desire for social status, induces him to conform to group standards of conduct whatever his personal inclinations or situational temptations. Social control occurs on all levels of society—in the family, in the peer groups, in bureaucratic organisations and in the government of every society.

Forms

Analyses of forms of social control differ. Different authors have used different terminology to refer different forms of social control as we see in the following table:

Authors	*Forms of Social Control*
E. A. Ross	Formal and Informal.
C. H. Cooley and Barnard	Conscious and Unconscious.
Karl Manheim	Direct and Indirect.
Kimball Young	Positive and Negative.
Gurvich and Moore	Organised, Unorganised, and Autonomous.
R. T. Lapiere	Authoritarian and Democratic.
Horton and Hunt	Planned and Unplanned.

The common distinction is between the formal (repressive or coercive) and the informal (persuasive or softer) forms of control. It has the universal sanction and liked by many sociologists. Social control may be positive or negative, i.e., consisting in rewards or punishment and repressive measures respectively. Similarly, social control may be planned (deliberate) or unplanned (incidental). If it is planned, it may be either formal (organised) or informal (unorganised).

Informal and unplanned (incidental) control

Informal social control, as the term implies, is used by people casually. Norms are enforced through the informal sanctions. These norms include folkways, customs, mores, values, conventions, fashions and public opinion etc. Ritual and ceremony also act as instruments of informal control. But ceremony plays a less important role in modern society than in the traditional societies. Informal control often takes the form of a look, nudge or frown which says "behave yourself " or "get into line".

Methods and techniques of informal control are numerous. They vary with the purpose and the character of the group in question. For example, in a homogeneous rural community, the gossip may be a potent means of enforcing conformity but would be of little importance in the personal life of a metropolis like Mumbai. They also vary greatly from one social situation to another. They are positive and negative both. Awards, prizes, wealth and power over others are examples of positive control through physical medium. Gossip, smiles, praise, persuasion, badges and titles are examples of positive control by symbolic means. Negative social control is represented by satire, laughter, raising of an eyebrow, opprobrium, name calling, negative gossip and ridicule, threats, physical torture and ostracism etc. Words and phrases (epithet, watchwords and slogans) are other means of informal control. They serve as collective representations symbolising the emotional attitudes of the group.

The above techniques of informal control are typically employed within primary groups such as families. Individuals learn such techniques early in their childhood socialisation to cultural norms—folkways, mores, values etc. Other than the family, these methods and techniques are also exercised by personal friends, colleagues and co-workers at the workplace.

Informal social control is based on this popular belief that "the all-seeing eyes of Gods are everywhere". It acts as mores (a controlling device). A belief in spiritual persons, who are omnipresent and omniscient, introduces an imagined presence which serves as a powerful controlling device.

Formal and planned (deliberate) control

Informal methods of social control are not adequate in enforcing and conforming of obedient behaviour in all cases and in every situations. It can serve as a last resort when socialisation and informal sanctions do not bring about desired result. In secondary groups and mass society where relations between individuals are impersonal, the primary group controls are not so effective. Control is then exercised through some agencies and formal institutions such as state, law, education, government, courts, police, military, administrators, corporate managers and bureaucrats etc. There are formal controls of licensing boards, professional organisations and trade unions also. As against the informal social controls, which grow out of necessities of the group or the society and which are the outcome of spontaneous growth, the formal social controls are created and imposed by man themselves. But, these are less powerful forms as they are not based on human instincts and basic necessities of life. Thus, they have not much importance in primary groups. Only one example will suffice to clarify this point. The law banning child marriage was passed as early as in 1929 in India but the thousands of child marriages are still performed on a single auspicious day of *Akshay Tritiya*. Thus, laws are not all-powerful. Laws which go against widespread customs are resisted and customs carry the day as it comes. Laws that are unpopular, such as prohibition of *gutka* (mixture of tobacco and flavoured betelnut), become difficult to enforce.

Distinction between informal and formal social control: A synoptic view

Informal Control	*Formal Control*
Operates mainly in primary groups and simple society.	Operates mainly in secondary groups and mass society.
Spontaneous growth or gradually emerge.	Consciously created or expressly enacted.
Mostly unwritten .	Written and codified.
More powerful.	Less powerful.
Punishment by society or the group concerned.	Punishment by the state or the institution concerned.
Important means—folkways, customs, mores, morality, religion, public opinion, leadership etc.	Important means—law, state and government.
Administration is impersonal.	Administered by persons.

Means of Social Control

There are many means of social control. They work either severally or simultaneously to maintain social order. Bottomore (1962) has enlisted them as the agencies of social control. On the basis of the above analysis of forms of social control, the means of social control may be grouped into two classes:

(i) institutional, and

(ii) non-institutional.

Institutional means

Following are the institutional means of social control:

(a) Political institutions—state, law and government.
(b) Religion
(c) Marriage, home and family
(d) Education
(e) Social classes

Non-institutional means

Following are the non-institutional means of social control:

(a) Ideologies, legends and myths
(b) Beliefs, ceremonies and rituals
(c) Art and literature
(d) Folkways, customs and mores
(e) Leadership
(f) Violence and terror
(g) Social suggestions—conventions, traditions, symbols, fashion, craze, public opinion.

Law and Society

Some norms are considered so important by a society that they are formalised into laws controlling people's behaviour. In a political sense, law is the "body of rules made by government for society, interpreted by courts, and backed by the power of the state" (Commings and Wise, 1989). Laws or legal rules have a sanction which cannot be evaded. Sanction means the penalty attached to the violation of rules.

Legal and political system is a potent means of social control under which one is obliged to live. This is the system that, quite against one's will, will tax one, make one obey its innumerable rules and regulations, and if need be put one in prison and in the last resort will kill one.

Social Control and Socialisation

Functionalists claim that order in a society is achieved partly through socialising members into the accepted values and norms. Socialisation is the means by which value consciousness (agreement) is brought about, and this is achieved through internalisation of norms. We learn expectations of others through socialisation and develop a desire to conform to them. The basic values members learn in a given society will generally lead them to conform and therefore behave in an orderly manner. Those who are not successfully socialised and become 'deviant' may be controlled by more coercive means such as police. Through socialisation social control becomes *ipso facto* effective.

The various agencies of socialisation like family, neighbourhood, community, school, working place, peer groups are also the agencies or means of socialisation. They exercise regulatory influence over the behaviour of the individuals.

Social Control and Social Change

With social changes the ideology, direction, methods and techniques of social control also change. Many a time and at several places, the negative controls instead of positive controls are given importance and free-will is crushed. Gillin and Gillin (1948) stated, "too rigid social control means repression of that dynamic person or minority group in any population supplying the ideas and actions on which social change depends". Excess regulation and rigidity often result into bad results as we have seen during the emergency clamped by the then Prime Minister of India, Indira Gandhi.

Deviance

Deviance is directly related to social order and control, i.e., how it is structured and how its moral, economic and political interests are protected. When a society functions in an orderly way, most people will generally be observing most norms. Deviance occurs when norms are broken or violated. Deviance connotes only those norm violations that make a person objectionable or at least significantly discredited. In its widest sense, it is a generic term referring to the activities described in such conventional expressions as ‘crime’, ‘alcoholism’, ‘immorality’, ‘cheating’, ‘sexual perversion’. Howerd Becker (1932), a leading proponent of the labelling theory asserted: “Deviant behaviour is behaviour that people so label.”

Deviance is universal and normal (Durkheim,). It exists in all societies (folk-urban or traditional-modern), wherever people interact and live in group. The notion of ‘deviance’ or ‘deviant’, as we shall see, is actually not an easy one to define. It meant different things to different people. Generally, it is defined as any “failure to conform to the customary norms of the society”. According to Wickman (1991), “deviance is behaviour that violates the standards of conduct or expectations of a group or society”. Being late for class is categorised as a deviant act; the same is true of dressings gorgeously for a funeral ceremony. Anthony Giddens (2000) defined it, “as non-conformity to a given set of norms that are accepted by a significant number of people in a community or society”. On the basis of these definitions, we are all deviant from time to time. Most of us on some occasions transgress generally accepted rules of behaviour. None of us are all rule breakers as well as conformists.

Main elements of deviance

There is no fixed agreement on the substance of deviance—even murder or incest is accepted at times. But there are a few interrelated elements which help characterise the phenomenon:

1. *Deviation is relative, not absolute:* In this sense, most people are deviant to some degree. When we say that deviance is relative, it only means that what is defined as deviant varies because different cultural groups have different norms. Thus, to consume alcohol would be a deviant act in an orthodox Muslim community, but not in Rajput community of Hindu society. Not only this, the relative nature of deviance also varies historically within a given culture.
2. *Deviance refers to norm violation:* There are wide range of norms—religious norms, legal norms, health norms, cultural

norms and so forth. Sometimes, there is a conflict between these different norms. In such situations, it becomes very difficult to decide about deviance or deviant behaviour. It should be noted that norm violation is somewhat broader conception than deviant behaviour since it connotes breaking any standard of expected conduct in a particular social setting.

3. *Deviance is also viewed as a 'stigma construct':* It is a label bestowed upon certain classes of behaviour at certain times. This characteristic can also be seen as very wide ranging. People may make friends deviant simply because they belch or talk too much. Terrorists at times may become political martyrs.

Because of its relative character, wide range of norms, and stigma construct, deviance is a shifting, ambiguous and volatile concept. This is why, Colin Sumner (1994) proclaimed that the concept of deviance is now dead and the focus should be on why some forms of difference are socially censured whereas others are not.

Forms of deviation

Deviation takes many forms. It can vary from political terrorism to failing to observe accepted eating habits. The juvenile delinquent, the hermit, the ascetic, the mentally ill, the hippie, the sinner, the homosexual, the saint and the miser gloating over his wealth all have deviated from the conventional social norms. But only those forms of deviation are considered deviant which are disapproved by the society or the culture. So, the scope of the concepts of deviant and deviance is very wide. More recently, sociologists have begun to advocate a relativistic view of deviance. This view suggests that like other behaviour, deviance can also be interpreted in the socio-cultural context in which it occurs. This view avoids the problems of the absolute, moral, medical and statistical models of deviance. According to this view, an act that is deviant in one context may not be deviant in another. A behaviour considered sick (mentally ill) in one society could be thought healthy in a different society.

Thus, deviance does not consist merely of acts or behaviours, but of group responses, definitions and the meanings attached to behaviours. Definitions of deviance vary with circumstances, time, place, situation, and even with social status. Sociologists almost always recognise socio-cultural relativity in deviance. An act considered deviant in one period may be considered non-deviant in another. Behaviours or social practice such as polygyny viewed as deviant in one society or culture may be considered non-deviant in others. Behaviour defined as deviant in one situation (wearing woman's clothes by a man to act in a play or consuming alcohol at public place) may not be deviant in another, even the same time period and place. Deviance also varies with social status. The status associated with person's sex, caste, age and income will influence which of his or her behaviours are considered deviant. To understand deviance, we must focus not only on people or acts but also on the conditions in which deviance occurs and how others react to it.

Individual and group deviation

Deviance does not refer only to individual behaviour; it concerns the activities of group as well. Deviation may be individual, in which a person deviates from the normal behaviour of his group or it may be group deviation, in which the entire group deviates from social norms. The individual deviates from the norms of his sub-culture. He is thus an individual deviant. In a complex society, however, there may be a number of deviant sub-cultures, whose norms are condemned by the conventional morality of the society.

Conformity, Deviance and Social Control

Conformity and deviance are two responses to real or imagined pressures from others. Conformity means going along one's peers—individuals of a person's own status. A recruit entering military service will typically conform to the habits and language of other recruits. Conformity is opposite to social deviance which imply obedience to the norms that make a person acceptable in a particular society, group, or social setting. The concept of conformity was also used by Robert Merton (1968) to refer to acceptance of cultural goals and the legitimate or approved means of achieving them. In his scheme of adaptations to the goals and means, only conformity to both indicates non-deviance.

Deviance is a behaviour that violates the standards of conduct or expectations or social norms of a group or society. Alcoholics, gamblers, sex deviants, drug addicts or late comers in the class are all classified as deviants or deviant acts. Deviance involves the violation of group norms. It is a very comprehensive concept that includes not only criminal behaviour but also many actions not subject to prosecution. Standards of deviance vary from group to group and also vary over time. Moreover, deviance can be understood within its social context.

A society must have social order if it is to function smoothly. But no society succeeds in getting all its members to behave as expected all the time. When a person fails to conform to the social norms of society, social deviation arises. If societies are to survive, they must have ways of making people conform to social norms. This situation gives rise to different types of controls—planned and unplanned or persuasive and coercive. Control works two levels: internal and external. Internal controls are those that exist inside individuals. It is sometimes referred to as self-control. It differs from social control. Self-control works from within while social control is from without. The working of internal controls can be explained through the process of socialisation that we have discussed earlier in this chapter and in the chapter on socialisation as well. External controls are those that come from outside the individual. They can be either formal or informal.

Chapter 16

Why Study Sociology?

Key features

> "Today, we are faced with pre-eminent fact that if civilisation is to survive, we must cultivate the science of human relationships."
>
> —Franklin Roosevelt

Sociology seeks to deepen our understanding of human relationships by uncovering new truths about them. It helps in removing ignorance about human relationships. It is relevant wherever human relations are at work. Whatever the field the emphasis will be on understanding human behaviour and relationships. "Sociology enables us to understand the world we live in but also to understand ourselves, for we are the products of that world. This understanding can help us to gain more control over our lives but it can also be put to more practical uses as well" (Fullchere and Scott, 2003).

"Sociology is not only an intellectual discipline; it is also a profession . . . . . when we speak of a profession, we refer mainly to themes as the uses or applications of a body of knowledge" (Inkeles, 1965). The student may sometimes confuse sociology with social reform. But sociology is not social reform.* The essential principles of sociology are a prerequisite in any study of human relationships and in any proposed solution of social problem. It is desirable, of course, that 'solutions' be found for the problems of society and that certain universal principles of social life be established.

The student may study sociology for its own sake, just to know more about society and culture. But mere knowledge does not satisfy him. He may probably seek sociological knowledge just to apply it to the social situations in which he finds himself. In general, it may be said that sociological knowledge lends itself to helping the individual and his society achieve results in terms of better social relations. But, a very few students take the subject of sociology to either seek knowledge for knowledge sake or applying it in the solution of their own day-to-day life problems. A person can be an expert in sociology but may not be able to solve his own family problems or may behave as a social deviant. Relatively few students become professional sociologists but everybody must be all times live in society, associate with people, and enact social roles. It is obvious that sociological knowledge is a basic help in choosing one's own career and vocation. Positions in teaching, salesmanship, business administration or local bodies administration, law, journalism and even in politics and other fields, where an essential occupational activity is "dealing with people", require more than ordinary knowledge of human relations in society. Reliable knowledge about social phenomena is an essential and basic prerequisite for better human relationships, for a better society.

In brief, the main uses of sociology may be listed as under:

1. It provides a basic understanding of human society, how social systems work, how people's behaviour is modified by their circumstances.

---

* The term 'social reform' has gone somewhat out of fashion because of its apparently moralistic overtones. Nowadays, its synonym term 'social engineering' is used, which involves the intelligent application of sociological knowledge.

2. It broadens the range of our perspective from which we try to understand the social world.
3. It gives us an insight into our daily life like a tourist guide.
4. It helps in removing ignorance about human relationships.
5. The world we live in is in trouble. It besets with many dilemmas. Sociology guides us in sorting out such dilemmas.
6. It provides us an orientation to the use of research techniques applicable in a wide variety of contexts.
7. It helps us understand ourselves and our positions in society. It is a source of self-enlightenment increased self-understanding.
8. It is a useful preparation for our careers.
9. It helps us in developing awareness of cultural differences. We adopt the views transmitted to us by our culture, but these views are often limited and superficial and do not constitute understanding. Quite often, if we properly understand how other live, we also require a better understanding of what their problems are.
10. There is educational value of sociology. Learning how other people arrange their societies and solve their problems. It may lead us to healthy scepticism, a tendency to ask intelligent questions, about our own. It has been said that the hallmark of a university trained mind is intelligent and unprejudiced scepticism.
11. Sociological research provides practical help in assessing the results of policy initiatives. A programme of practical reform may simply fail to achieve what its designers sought, or may produce unintended consequences of an unfortunate kind.
12. Knowledge gives humans the power to shake off the past and shape their destiny—and sociology brings this power into the social world.

All sciences are emancipatory including sociology. The prime objective of all sciences is to improve the human condition and liberate the man from all shackles of exploitation and deprivation. Anthony Giddens (2000) aptly remarked: "Studying sociology should be liberating experience: sociology enlarges our sympathies and imagination, opens up new perspectives on the sources of our own behaviour, and creates an awareness of cultural settings different from our own. . . . . sociological thinking is a vital help to self-understanding, which in turn can be focussed back on an improved understanding of the social world." Perhaps, the main contribution of sociology is that it makes more sense of our lives. It does so by explaining the relationships between personal experience and 'external events', between self and society. Charles Wright Mills (1959) described the links between self and society in terms of 'personal troubles'—such as losing one's job or being wounded in combat—and 'public issues'—such as rising unemployment or war phobia. It is befitting to conclude this section with the views of founder sociologist Max Weber who nearly a century ago argued in his lectures on 'Science as a Vocation' and 'Politics as a Vocation' (1970) that sociology could not tell members of society what values to hold, but it could demonstrate the possibilities and constraints facing them within their social structure.

Careers in Sociology

Sociology is not only an intellectual discipline, it is also a profession. When we speak of a profession, we refer mainly to such themes as the uses or applications of a body of knowledge. Sociologists play a rich and varied role in today's society. They serve in a variety of capacities such, as consultant, teacher, policy maker, researcher, administrator, clinical counsellor, social critic, interviewer, journalist, probation and parole worker, career counsellor, social worker, recreation worker, programme evaluator, urban planner, marketing administration coordinator and personnel manager etc. They work in areas as broad and diverse as the discipline they have chosen.

Knowledge of sociology can be used in the following areas of social life:

1. Teaching
2. Social research
3. Social work

4. Professions—medicine, law, engineering, business etc.
5. Industry
6. Rural and urban planning
7. Public administration—civil services
8. Policy making
9. Business consultancy
10. Politics
11. Architecture
12. Child welfare and health care
13. Gerontology (study of old age people)
14. Computer industry
15. Military intelligence and military
16. Entrepreneurship
17. International relations
18. Criminal justice
19. City management
20. New emerging careers: (a) action programme, and (b) development

Sociology and Social Policy

Sociology at its best is the study of the development and structure of society and social relationships. While not a precise science that can predict behaviour, it is nonetheless a valuable discipline assisting the search for more rational social arrangements and preparing social policy.

The term 'policy' commonly refers to clearly articulated set of ideas about what should be done in a particular sphere. It differs from a plan. Plans specify in detail the way in which objectives are to be achieved, whereas a policy is typically formulated at a more general level, indicating only objectives and the intended direction of change. A policy is begun in the hope that it will produce a desired effect.

What is social policy? To answer this question in few words is slightly problematic. Some people chose to answer this question by listing the areas of public (government) policy under this heading. The main areas are social security and social welfare, personal social services, health service, education, employment services and housing. This simple definition, i.e., listing the areas of welfare fields, is too narrow. It is argued that exclusive concentration on government policies is mistaken and that one should also include the policies of religious and charitable bodies as well as of private corporation which also aims to meet the social needs of the population. Some have gone to the extent of including even economic policies in the gamut of social policy. We shall use this term 'social policy' to mean all policies (carried out by government and private agencies) that are directed towards meeting the social needs (welfare needs) of the population including policies concerning social security, health, education, housing, child, women, sick and disabled and old age welfare. It also includes social division of welfare, or the management of public, fiscal and private allocation of wealth, the organisation of employment, the management of wage system and the creation of styles of living. In short, social policy is about the kind of society people want to create and what they do to create it.

There have been a range of approaches to the analysis of social policy. T.H. Marshall (1963), in his classic statement, stated that "the avowed objective of twentieth century social policy is welfare". Marxists and others argue that the objective of certain social policy measures is to control disaffected groups in the population rather than to act out of concern for their welfare. Peter Townsend (1981) argued that the main aim of social policy is the institutional control of services, agencies and organisations, which are engaged in maintaining of changing social structure and values. It is to be noted that much of the work has been done in departments of social administration outside the framework of sociology. Social administration refers to the means by which social policy is implemented.

Pure and Applied Sociology

All sciences contribute to the knowledge base and also to the solution and resolution of practical problems and issues. As such, all sciences have two faces:

(1) Pure Science/Pure Sociology

(2) Applied Science/Applied Sociology

Pure science/pure sociology

Pure science is a search for knowledge, without primary concern for its practical use. Knowledge for knowledge sake is the main aim of a pure scientist. Scientists, who seek knowledge for its own sake, no more moved by the question of its utility like the mother and the father who protect and nourish their children without expecting anything in return. Parents commonly love their children without calculating their usefulness. Many students/researchers of science feel much the same thing about their work. Pure sciences (Physics, Chemistry, Biology, Botany, Physiology, Economics, Political Science, Psychology, Anthropology and Sociology etc.) are concerned with the advancement of knowledge. Their main aim is to investigate the underlying principles of the natural and social world which sustain and change the natural and social order. They are not concerned with the practical application of their results or curing the immediate ills of our natural or social order. The goal of each natural science, including sociology, is the formulation of scientific laws.

Sociology is a pure science, not an applied one. The immediate goal of sociology is the acquisition of knowledge about human society, not the utilisation of that knowledge. According to Lester F. Ward (1841-1913), a pioneer sociologist of America, the main aim of pure sociology is "to investigate fundamental rules of social structure and social change". Bierstedt (1963) wrote: "Sociologists do not determine questions of public policy, do not tell legislators what laws should be passed or repealed and do not dispense relief to the ill, the lame, the blind, or the poor—except, of course, in their capacity as citizens—apply the knowledge that it is their duty and profession to acquire." This view was held by early sociologists between 1920-40 who believed sociology as a value-free science. But this view is now no more accepted in totality by all sociologists.

Applied science/applied sociology

Applied science is the search for ways of using scientific knowledge to solve practical problems. The sciences, which apply the principles of knowledge or use principles to manipulate something, gained from the basic or pure sciences, are known as applied sciences. All branches of engineering, science of medicine, architecture and social work come under the category of applied sciences. An applied science has quite opposite aim and intent than a pure science. It is not concerned with the theory or formulation of laws or development and systematisation of principles. For example, an average doctor is not primarily interested in the theory of disease or the principles that underlie diagnosis but he is primarily concerned with the treatment of the disease of his patient.

The social sciences (e.g., sociology) like all sciences have dual function. They serve to help the people to solve their problems and at the same time to explore and to understand the world around them. As such, there is an interest in application and an interest in understanding as well. When social scientific findings are applied to the solutions of social problems, it is called applied sociology. Sociology as an applied discipline, which uses the knowledge of the pure social scientist to improve social life. Immediately, sociology seeks to understand the fundamental mechanism of social reality, but the desire to understand is always motivated by the wish to control. The main aim of applied sociology is to bring social welfare in society through social scientific investigation. For example, a sociologist making a study of the social structure of a slum is working as a pure scientist but if he studies how to prevent or control delinquency in a slum or how to remove poverty, then he is working as an applied scientist. In the role of applied scientist, a sociologist tries to solve the social problems.

Though sociologists and social workers do share some common tasks, still it is a mistake to regard sociology as equivalent to social work or social welfare.

Types of applied sociology

Applied sociology may be divided into five main branches:

(1) *Clinical Sociology:* It refers to the use of sociological knowledge in providing assistance to individuals and organisations. This term, analogous to clinical psychology, was introduced in 1931 by Chicago sociologist Louis Wirth for the work of sociologists employed in clinical settings alongside social workers, psychologists, and psychiatrists. Clinical sociology involves the use of sociological knowledge to aid diagnosis, treatment, teaching and research. A clinical sociologist may study the ways of improving employee morale.

(2) *Social Engineering:* It attempts to use sociological knowledge to design social policies or institutions with a specific purpose. It refers to planned social change and social development. The planned improvement of society is practically impossible without the scientific knowledge provided by sociology. Social engineering involves the intelligent application of sociological knowledge. It is based on the idea that governments can shape and manage key features of society, in much the same way as the economy is managed. For example, the extent of women's employment is clearly determined in part by government policy to promote to impede women's paid work. For doing such works, applied sociologists use social indicators and social trend reports. Every family, school, club, business and local bodies recognises and pursues its goal. This is nothing more or less than social engineering.

(3) *Social Work:* Though it is a distinct discipline, it is considered as applied aspect of sociology. Social work is the field in which the principles of the social sciences, especially sociology, are applied to actual social problems in the same way the principles of physiology are applied in medicine or the principles of economics are applied in business management. A social worker might, for example, use information obtained from family research to try to place children in foster homes or to establish centres of spouse abuse.

The term 'social work' is applied to the various organised methods for promoting human welfare through the prevention and relief of suffering. In the late nineteenth century, social work was largely voluntary (notably as a charitable activity). Since the Second World War, social work practice has become increasingly professionalised. In India, many institutions of social work training and education were established, notable among them is the renowned Tata Institute of Social Work, Mumbai. Many state governments have also started such institutions on its pattern. These institutions have the aim to train people to step out into society and to assist in the solution of its immediate problems.

(4) *Applied Social Research:* It is similar in many respects to the basic/pure research conducted in universities and colleges. At one end of the continuum of social research would be the disciplines involved in research, not to solve a specific problem, but simply to increase our understanding of the social world. Such researches are known as pure/basic research. At the other end of the continuum would be the disciplines that use knowledge to solve actual problems, these researches are called applied social research. Social workers devise their own research methods and techniques to help people solve personal and group problems, and the resulting applications contribute to our existing body of knowledge. Applied social research may take the form of descriptive research, survey research, analytical or evaluation research such as systematic attempts to estimate the potential effects of a proposed social programme or effects of planned change or a new approach to management in a business firms.

(5) *Action Sociology:* Action sociology is also a form of applied sociology in which sociologist is asked to participate in the development process and tackle vital social problems actively. It is directly concerned with the solutions of the social problems. It requires the involvement of the sociologist in all stages of development or the solutions of the problem. This means not only to find out the roots of the social problem and suggest it remedy but to associate ourselves in the diagnosis of the problem,

planning, execution, monitoring and evaluation of the programme designed to solve the problem. In India, a fine example of this approach (action sociology) we find in the project of Sulabh International started by a sociologist Bindeshwar Pathak.

Action sociology/action research places emphasis on the sociologist not only to work as a researcher but to assume the role of a change agent also. Such change agents are often used in local communities, local bodies or in companies as consultants. They work as part of the change process itself. This view was supported by Herbert Gans (*Urban Poverty and Social Planning*, 1967). He wrote: "I believe that the sociologist ought to be more than a detached researcher and he should participate more directly in social action programmes. . . . . . The sociologist can help to develop the means necessary to achieve the goals, i.e., by participating in the development of programmes of action. It is here that he can perhaps make his most useful contribution."

Currently, there is a strong trend toward action sociology. Indeed, radical sociologists maintain that radical sociology is a sociology of engagement. Recently, French sociologist Alain Touraine (1960) developed a radical new theoretical framework known as *actionalism*. He claimed that the sociologist is an agent of change, not a neutral observer. He has a stake in the conflicts of his or her society. As such he or she should play the role of a 'sociological interventionist' in which he/she should study social change movements by participating in them directly. This actionalist sociology, Touraine believed, will "replace a sociology of society with a sociology of actors".

Bibliography

Text Books

Abel, T., *Sociology: Its Nature and Scope*, 1932.

Anderson, W.A. and Parker, F.B., *Society*, 1964.

Aron, R., *German Sociology*, 1957.

Balsara, F.N., *Sociology*, 1956.

Becker, H., *Systematic Sociology*, 1932.

Berger, P.L. and Berger, B., *Sociology: A Biographical Approach*, 1976.

Bierstedt, R., *The Social Order*, 1957.

Biesanz, F. and Biesanz, M., *Modern Society: An Introduction to Social Science*, 1964.

Bilton, T., Bomett, K., and Others, *Introductory Sociology*, 1996.

Bogardus, E.S., *Sociology*, 1954.

Bottomore, T.B., *Sociology: A Guide to Problems and Literature*, 1962.

Broom, L. and Selznick, P., *Sociology: A Text Book with Adopted Readings*, 1955.

Carr, L.J., *Analytical Sociology*, 1955.

Charon, J.M., *The Meaning of Sociology*, 1980.

Chinoy, E., *Sociological Perspective*, 1954.

Chinoy, E., *Society: An Introduction to Sociology* 1961.

Collins, R., *Theoretical Sociology*, 1977.

Cuber, J.F., *Sociology: A Synopsis of Principles* 1951.

Davis, K., *Human Society*, 1949.

Dawson, C.A. and Gettys, W.E., *An Introduction to Sociology*, 1948.

Donnell, Make O', *Introduction to Sociology*, 1997.

Douglas, J.D. (ed.), *Introduction to Sociology*, 1973.

Elias, N., *What is Sociology?*, 1970.

Eshleman, J.R., and Cashion, B.G., *Sociology: An Introduction,* 1983.

Eubank, E.E., *Concepts of Sociology,* 1932.

Fairbanks, A., *Introduction of Sociology,* 1964.

Fichter, J.H., *Sociology,* 1964.

Freedman et al. (eds.), *Principles of Sociology,* 1952.

Fullchere and Scott, *Sociology,* 2003.

Giddens, A., *Sociology,* 1997, 2000

Giddings, F.H., *Inductive Sociology,* 1901.

Giddings, F.H., *Principles of Sociology,* 1955.

Gillin, J.L. and Gillin, J.F., *Cultural Sociology,* 1948.

Ginsberg, M., *Essays in Sociology and Social Philosophy,* 1955.

Ginsberg, M., *Sociology,* 1934.

Gisbert, P., *Fundamentals of Sociology,* 1957.

Goldthrope, J.E., *An Introduction to Sociology,* 1969.

Gouldner, A.W. and Gouldner, H.P., *Modern Sociology: An Introduction to the Study of Human Interaction,* 1963.

Green, A.W., *Sociology: An Analysis of Life in Modern Society,* 1956.

Green, B.S.R. and Jolns, E.A., *An Introduction to Sociology,* 1966.

Hawkins, F.H., *An Introduction to the Study of Society,* 1928.

Haralambos and Holborn, *Sociology,* 2000.

Hiller, E.T., *Principles of Sociology,* 1956.

Himes, J.S. and Moore, W.E., *Study of Sociology,* 1960.

Horton, P.B. and Hunt, H.P., *Sociology,* 1964.

Hunt, E.A., *Social Science: An Introduction to the Study of Society,* 1955.

Inkebs, A., *What is Sociology,* 1963.

Johnson, H.M., *Sociology: A Systematic Introduction,* 1960.

Jones, M.E., *Basic Sociological Principles,* 1949.

Koeing, S., Hopper, R.D., et al. (eds.), *Sociology,* 1953.

Lapiere, R.J., *Sociology,* 1946.

Landis, P.H., *Introductory Sociology,* 1958.

Loomis, C.F., *Fundamental Concepts of Sociology,* 1940.

Lumley, F.E., *Principles of Sociology,* 1945.

Lundberg, G.A., *Foundations of Sociology,* 1956.

Lundberg, G.A., Schrag, C.C., and Larsen, O.N. *Sociology,* 1958.

MacIver, R.M. and Page, C.H., *Society: An Introductory Analysis,* 1956.

MacIver, R.M., *Society: A Text Book of Sociology,* 1937.

Mannheim, K., *Systematic Sociology,* 1959.

Martindale, D. and Monchesi, E.D., *Elements of Sociology* 1956.

Mazumdar, H.T., *The Grammar of Sociology,* 1966.

Merrill, F.E. and Eldrege, H.W., *Culture and Society: An Introduction to Sociology,* 1965.

Motwani, K., *Sociology* 1954.

Murry, R.W., *Introductory Sociology* 1946.

Odum, H.W., *Understanding Society: The Principles of Dynamic Sociology,* 1947.

Ogburn, W.F. and Nimkoff, M.F., *A Hand Book of Sociology,* 1958.

Park, R.E. and Burgess, E.W., *Introduction to the Science of Sociology,* 1921.

Quinn, J.A., *Sociology: A Systematic Analysis,* 1963.

Reuter, E.B. and Hart, C.W., *Introduction to Sociology,* 1933.

Reuter, E.B., *Hand Book of Sociology,* 1941.

Ross, A.M., *Sociology: The Study of Human Relations,* 1957.

Ross, E.J., *Basic Sociology,* 1953.

Sagarin, E. (ed.), *Sociology: The Basic Concepts,* 1978.

Schaefer, R.W. and Lamm, R.P., *Sociology,* 1992.

Small, A.W., *General Sociology.*

Smith, R.W. and Preston, F.W., *Sociology: An Introduction,* 1977.

Smelser, N.J. (ed.), *Sociology: An Introduction,* 1970.

Stewart and Glynn, *Introduction to Sociology,* 1971.

Sutherland, R.L., Woodward, J.L. and Maxwell, M.A., *Introductory Sociology,* 1961.

Ward, L.F., *Dynamic Sociology,* 1902.

Weignberg, M. and Shabat, D.E., *Society and Man,* 1956.

Woods, S.F.J., *Introductory Sociology,* 1956.

Worsley, P. (ed.) *Modern Sociology: Introductory Readings,* 1970.

Wright, F.J., *Elements of Sociology* 1965.

Young, K. and Mack, R.W., *Sociology and Social Life,* 1959.

Young, K., *An Introduction to Sociology,* 1942.

Suggested Readings for Detailed Study

Adorno, T.W. et al., *The Authoritarian Personality,* 1950.

Alexander, J.C. (ed.), *Theoretical Logic in Sociology (Vol. 1),* 1982.

Altheusser, L., *For Marx,* 1969.

Aron, R., *German Sociology,* 1957.

Aron, R., *The Industrial Society,* 1966.

Aron, R., *Main Currents in Sociological Thought (2 Vols.),* 1965, 1969.

Baudrillard, J., *Simulations,* 1983.

Beck, U., *Risk Society,* 1992.

Bell, D., *The End of Ideology,* 1960.

Bell, D., *The Coming of Post-Industrial Society,* 1974.

Bellah, R.N., *Beyond Belief,* 1970.

Bendix, R., *Max Weber: An Intellectual Portrait,* 1966.

Bendix, R., and Lipsit, S.M. (eds.), *Class, Status and Power,* 1967.

Berger, P.L., *Invitation to Sociology,* 1963.

Berger, P., and Luckmann, *The Social Construction of Reality,* 1967.

Blau, P.M., *The Dynamics of Bureaucracy,* 1963.

Bottomore, T.B. and Nisbet, R. (eds.), *A History of Sociological Analysis,* 1978.

Bottomore, T.B., *Marxist Sociology,* 1975.

Cohen, P.S., *Modern Social Theory,* 1968.

Cooley, C.H., *Human Nature and the Social Order,* 1902.

Cooley, C.H., *Social Organization,* 1909.

Coonor, S., *Postmodernist Culture,* 1989.

Coser, L.A., *Masters of Sociological Thought,* 1971.

Culf, E.L. and Payne, G.L.F. (eds.), *Perspectives in Sociology,* 1979.

Etzioni, A., and Etzioni, E., *Social Change: Sources, Patterns and Consequences,* 1964.

Faris, E.W. (ed.), *Hand Book of Sociology,* 1964.

Fletcher, R., *The Making of Sociology (Vols.2)*, 1971.
Freund, J., *The Sociology of Max Weber*, 1968.
Giddens, A. (ed.), *Positivism and Sociology*, 1974.
Giddens, A., *Politics and Sociology in the Thought of Max Weber*, 1972.
Giddens, A., *New Rules of Sociological Method*, 1976.
Giddens, A. (ed.), *Emile Durkheim*, 1978.
Giddens, A., *Central Problems in Social Theory*, 1979.
Giddens, A., *The Constitution of Society*, 1984.
Giddens, A., *Modernity and Self-Identity*, 1993.
Ginsberg, M., *Reason and Unreason in Society*, 1947.
Goffman, E., *The Presentation of Self in Everyday Life*, 1959.
Goffman, E., *Encounters*, 1961.
Gouldner, A.W., *The Coming Crisis of Western Sociology*, 1970.
Gurvich and Moore, *Twentieth Century Sociology*, 1945.
Habermas, J., *Towards a Rational Society*, 1970.
Habermas, J., *The Theory of Communicative Action*, 1981.
Harvey, D., *The Condition of Postmodernity* 1990.
Hobhouse, L.T., *Morals in Evolution*, 1907.
Hobhouse, L.T., *Social Development*, 1924.
Homans, G.C., *The Human Group*, 1950.
Homans, G.C., *Social Behaviour: Its Elementary Forms*, 1961.
Jameson, F., *Postmodernism*, 1991.
Lefebvre, H., *The Sociology of Marx*, 1968.
Levy, M.J., *The Structure of Society*, 1952.
Linton, R., *The Study of Man: An Introduction*, 1936.
Lipset, S.M. and Smelser, N., *Sociology: The Progress of a Decade.*
Lukes, S., *Emile Durkheim: His Life and Work*, 1972.
Lyotard, J.F., *The Postmodern Condition*, 1984.
Mannheim, K., *Essays on the Sociology of Knowledge*, 1952.
Mannheim, K., *Essays on the Sociology of Culture*, 1956.
Marcuse, H., *One-Dimensional Man*, 1964.
Marshall, T.H., *Sociology at the Crossroads*, 1963.
Merton, R.K. and Nisbet, R. (eds.), *Contemporary Social Problems*, 1961.

Merton, R.K., *Social Theory and Social Structure,* 1957.

Mills, C. Wright, *The Sociological Imagination,* 1959.

Moore, W., *Social Change,* 1963.

Nisbet, R.A., *The Sociological Tradition,* 1967.

Nisbet, R.A., *The Social Bond: An Introduction to the Study of Society,* 1970.

Nisbet, R.A., *The Sociology of Emile Durkheim,* 1974.

Ogburn, W.F., *Social Change,* 1922.

Pareto, V., *The Mind and Society,* 1963.

Parsons, T. and Smelser, N., *Economy and Society,* 1956.

Parsons, T., *The Structure of Social Action,* 1937.

Parsons, T., *Essays in Sociological Theory,* 1954.

Rex, J., *Key Problems of Sociological Theory,* 1961.

Rex, J., *Discovering Sociology,* 1973.

Robertson, R. and Lechner, F., *Modernization, Globalization and World-System Theory (3 Vols.),* 1985.

Ross, E.A., *Social Control,* 1901.

Roucek, J.S., *Social Control,* 1947.

Schutz, A., *The Phenomenology of the Social World,* 1972.

Schutz, A., and Luckmann, T., *The Structure of the Life-World,* 1074.

Simmel, G., *Conflict and the Web of Group Affiliations,* 1955.

Smelser, N.J., *The Theory of Collective Behaviour,* 1962.

Sorokin, P.A., *Social Mobility,* 1927.

Sorokin, P.A., *Contemporary Sociological Theories,* 1928.

Sorokin, P.A., *Social and Cultural Dynamics,* 1941.

Sorokin, P.A., *Sociological Theories of Today,* 1966.

Spencer, H., *Principles of Sociology,* 1886.

Sumner, W.G., *Folkways,* 1906.

Timasheff, N.S., *Sociological Theory,* 1967.

Tonnies, F., *Community and Association,* 1957.

Touraine, A., *The Postindustrial Society,* 1971.

Tumin, M., *Social Stratification,* 1967.

Turner, J.H., *The Structure of Sociological Theory,* 1978.

Turner, R. and Lewis, M.K., *Collective Behaviour,* 1972.

Veblen, T., *The Theory of the Leisure Class,* 1953.

Wallace, W.L., *Sociological Theory: An Introduction,* 1969.

Wallerstein, I., *The Modern World-System,* 1974.

Weber, Marrianne, *Max Weber: A Biography,* 1975.

Important Works of Some Classical Sociologists

Comte, A., *The Course of Positive Philosophy,* 1838.

Durkheim, E., *The Division of Labour in Society,* 1893.

Durkheim, E., *The Rules of Sociological Method,* 1895.

Durkheim, E., *The Suicide,* 1897.

Durkheim, E., *The Elementary Forms of the Religious Life,* 1912.

Marx, K., *The Communist Manifesto,* 1848.

Marx, K., *Capital, 3 Vols.* 1867, 1885, 1893.

Weber, M., *The Religion of India,* 1916-17.

Weber, M., *The Protestant Ethic and the Spirit of Capitalism,* 1930.

Weber, M., *Economy and Society,* 1922.

Weber, M., *The Methodology of the Social Sciences,* 1949.

Dictionaries

Abercrombie, N., Hill, S. and Turner, B.S., *The Penguin Dictionary of Sociology,* 1994.

Fairchild, H.P., *Dictionary of Sociology,* 1944.

Gould and Kolb, *Dictionary of Social Sciences,* 1964.

Johnson, G.A., *The Blackwell Dictionary of Sociology,* 1995.

Marshall, G., *The Concise Oxford Dictionary of Sociology,* 1994.

Mitchell, D., *Dictionary of Sociology,* 1968.

Theodorson, G.A. and Theodorson, A.G., *A Modern Dictionary of Sociology.*

Index